'Education is not the fillin
but the lighting of a fire.'

W.B. Yeats

HELP YOUR CHILD THROUGH SCHOOL

Dr David Lewis

VERMILION
LONDON

This book is dedicated to Jane Booth-Clibborne, an inspiring teacher and friend, with grateful thanks for all her help in its preparation.

Published in 1992 by Vermilion
an imprint of Ebury Press
Random Century House
20 Vauxhall Bridge Road
London SW1V 2SA

Catalogue record for this book is available from the British Library.

ISBN 0 09 175443 5

Edited by: Sophie Figgis
Designed by: Bob Vickers

Typeset in Century Old Style by
Hope Services (Abingdon) Ltd.
Printed in Great Britain by
Mackays of Chatham Plc, Kent

CONTENTS

INTRODUCTION

As a caring parent, I am sure you are already doing all you can to help your child through school. Even so, there are bound to be occasions, perhaps following a disappointing end of term report, when you wonder whether you are *both* achieving all you could.

If so the questionnaires below could provide part of the answer. All you have to do is rate the statements below on a scale of 0 to 3 where 1 means not true at all, 2 means true to some extent, and 3 means completely true.

My child . . .   *Score*

Is happy at school.

Succeeds in his/her studies.

Has little difficulty learning new subjects.

Reads fluently for his/her age.

Writes and spells well for his/her age.

Has an excellent memory.

Has great powers of concentration.

Enjoys mental challenges.

Is creative.

Is rarely made anxious by his/her studies.

                                                Total _____

Your check list

I know how to ...

Score

Boost his/her confidence over difficult lessons.

Improve his/her handwriting and spelling.

Teach him/her to learn and study more efficiently.

Enhance his/her memory for facts and figures.

Resolve homework difficulties.

Show him/her how to develop thinking skills.

Increase motivation for school work.

Overcome anxieties about learning.

Enhance creativity and imagination.

Encourage a positive attitude towards school.

Total _____

How did you do? Full marks – 30 out of 30 – on both lists? If so congratulations. Both you and your child are clearly exceptional and the practical guidance offered by this book will be of little or no relevance. But if, like most of the parents who have completed these questionnaires, your scores fell somewhat short of perfection, don't worry. Virtually every child has some problems in learning and every parent has difficulties in helping them realize their true potential in class. What a painful experience that can be!

You may know your child is falling behind and the misery this failure is causing. You may long to offer practical help but not know how best to set about it. One father told me he felt like a poor swimmer seeing his daughter drowning at sea yet was unable to do anything about it. 'I desperately want to mount a rescue but just don't know where to start or what to do.' When *your* child is floundering in schoolwork or drowning during homework wouldn't it be wonderful to *know* exactly how best to save them? My purpose in writing his book is to help you do just that. After reading it you should be able to show your child ways of improving their:

1. Number skills.
2. Spelling and handwriting.

3. Reading.
4. Ability to remember and recall new information more easily and accurately.

In addition to these basic classroom skills you will also know how to produce your child with:

5. Increased motivation.
6. A stronger, more positive, self-image as a learner.
7. Greater confidence and self-assurance.

Giving your child the chance to choose

In a world where examination passes and school achievement are an essential passport for success, achieving children have a far better chance of choosing their path through life. We can never know how many opportunities are lost in childhood or how many adults look back with regret on what they might have achieved in life had their intellectual potential been realized while still at school. Never has the challenge been so great, the rewards of attainment more exciting or the penalties for intellectual inadequacy so terrifying.

Experts agree that mankind has embarked on the most mentally challenging era in human history. As American futurologist John Naisbitt has remarked, 'We now mass-produce knowledge and this knowledge is the driving force of our economy.' By using the methods I describe, you will be able to influence your child's development in a positive and constructive manner. By helping your child through school you will also be helping him, or her, to confront the challenges this future poses and immeasurably increase his, or her, chance of enjoying a happy and fulfilling adult life.

CONQUERING THE HIDDEN FEARS OF LEARNING

Learning is a risky business. Every time you attempt anything new there is a danger of making mistakes and being made to look, and feel, foolish. In a school, not long ago, I watched a timid 13-year-old being sarcastically informed he was 'pig stupid' for giving an incorrect answer in a history lesson. Needless to say his fellow pupils greatly enjoyed this marvellous joke, sniggering and honking like pigs in appreciation of the teacher's wit.

Even without such a public humiliation, children can still be left feeling bad about getting things wrong. The frown of disappointment on the face of a favourite teacher, a parent's unspoken but unmistakable dismay over low marks, the child's sense of failure at having let themselves down by doing poorly in a test or exam. These less obvious, but no less hurtful responses, reinforce in their minds the dangers of taking risks when learning. Often the difference between setting off along the road to school success or down the path to scholastic failure, turns on a single event. An incident so apparently trivial, it may pass virtually unnoticed by the adult concerned.

A few years ago, while visiting an American school, I sat in on a class of 12-year-olds struggling with algebra. The teacher posed a problem and, as so often happens, a few hands instantly shot up, their owners' faces glowing with confidence and eager to answer and hoping she would single them out for the honour of showing everybody else how clever they were. Other children looked uncertain, hands half rose, wavered, then descended. The faces of these youngsters registered conflicting emotions: a desire to put their understanding to the test combined with apprehension over getting the answer wrong. The remainder, especially those seated furthest from the front, crouched lower over their desks, studiously avoiding the teacher's eyes, clearly terrified she would ask them.

In the event she called on one of the waverers, a fair-haired girl whose hand raise had been among the most tentative, to provide an answer. Uncertainly she did so. 'That's right,' the teacher said. 'That's correct!' 'It is?' for a moment the girl seemed stunned. Then her face broke into a joyous smile. 'I got it right.' What she learned here, of course, was far more than how to solve an algebraic equation. The girl had taken a vitally important learning step that morning. Although she would probably never realize just how significant it was, or appreciate the difference it might make to her life. Chatting to her after class, she told me: 'I always believed I would never understand. Now I think perhaps I can.' This made it much more likely that the next time that 12-year-old was faced with an unfamiliar problem she would see herself as sufficiently capable of rising to the challenge to take a chance.

The difference between an achieving child and one falling behind in class often comes down to just this: a greater readiness to take risks. For her the outcome was positive. But what of the remaining youngsters in that class? Those confident that they knew the answer were, perhaps, disappointed at not being able to demonstrate their superior ability. Those who did not have a clue merely confirmed their pessimistic belief that algebra – like so many other subjects – must forever remain an impenetrable mystery. Others, the majority, remained in learning limbo. Knowing when they didn't understand but not convinced they would ever understand.

Some might get a lucky break and prosper. They would discover, perhaps through their own efforts or maybe as a result of meeting an inspirational teacher, that learning and understanding were well within their grasp. Others, less fortunate, would fall behind further and further until they joined the ranks of the unqualified, and uncomprehending.

This transition from being a 'can't know' to a 'don't know' or a 'don't know' to a 'can't know' can be one of the shortest and most crucial intellectual journeys a child ever makes. For the 'don't knower' the world remains open to learning and filled with possibilities. For the 'can't knower' it is a closed book. A world filled with impossibilities. 'I don't know how to do this,' says the confident, risk-taking, youngster. 'But I can learn.' 'I can't know how to do this,' says the child who has learned to fear taking risks, 'so I will never learn.' We all start life as a 'don't knower', never as 'can't knowers.'

No baby is ever a can't knower

All babies are natural scientists performing countless experiments in their attempts to bring sense to what American psychologist William

James described as the 'booming, buzzing confusion' of the world around them. 'What happens if I drop this rattle once, twice, twenty times?' 'What happens if I splash my spoon on the food?' 'What happens if I try to stand up?' 'What happens if I tear this paper?'

Gradually, through a process of almost endless trial and error, their surroundings start making more sense, becoming more ordered and more predictable. Unfortunately, as children get older, they learn an additional and most unhelpful lesson. They learn to regard failure not as an inevitable but trivial consequence of learning, but as something more important than learning itself. As something so frightening that it is best avoided, even at the cost of remaining ignorant. They come to appreciate the implications of such remarks as: 'John is so clever. He picks everything up very quickly,' or 'Martin is slow. He tries his best, but his younger sister runs rings around him intellectually.'

Before long children confuse *what* they know with *who* they really are. That is:

A bright child.
An average child.
A stupid child.

They also learn this damning equation:

Success = Good, but Failure = Bad.

Success is obviously 'good' because it means praise, admiration, respect, being applauded and talked to in a warm, encouraging way. It means feeling confident and pleased with yourself. Failure is just as clearly 'bad' because it brings humiliation, embarrassment, indignity, scolding, accusations of laziness or not trying hard enough. It means being pitied, patronized or cast onto the educational scrap heap. It means feeling so bad about yourself that your only defence may be to stop caring what parents or teachers think, and seek out friends who share your contempt for learning and confirm your view that school is a waste of time.

Children who come mid-way between confidence and uncertainty are trapped in what psychologists term an approach-avoidance conflict. The desire to learn and demonstrate that knowledge is counter-balanced by a fear of failure. As a consequence they are reluctant to take risks while learning.

There's nothing strange or unusual about this. It's our normal reaction when running scared. We play safe, keep our heads down, stick with what we know. Such children fail in school not through stupidity but because they are smart enough to realize that it's safer to avoid mistakes than to take the risk of making them. Who teaches them this fatal lesson? We all do. Parents, teachers, friends, relatives, even casual acquaintances.

I was in a shop recently when a boy, aged five or six, came in to buy a magazine for his mother who stood waiting by the door. He strode in looking pleased and proud to have been trusted with such an important mission. Striding up to the counter he asked for the magazine. The shop keeper handed it to him and held out his hand for payment. The boy opened his purse, which was one of those with a tray for loose change, and started picking out the coins. He was doing very well, and I was impressed by his grasp of money and counting. Unfortunately the shop keeper was impatient. 'Oh, for heaven's give it here . . .' he commanded and snatched the purse. He took his money and gave the purse back. The boy who had entered the shop so confidently left on the verge of tears. 'Kids!' said the shop keeper and gave an awkward laugh, the way people do when inviting you to become a fellow conspirator in some act of ill manners.

What had the boy learned from that brief encounter? That he was too little to deal with responsible things like buying and paying for goods? Probably. But there was another lesson taught in that shop as well. That learning to get things right is not enough. You have to get them right fast.

After accuracy, speed of response is what we most admire. Nowhere is the cult of the fast fact more dramatically illustrated than in quiz programmes such as *Mastermind*. Here the contestant has to answer obscure questions on arcane subjects against the steadily beating clock, and in circumstances calculated to produce the maximum anxiety.

Fast, correct answers. It's the same in most schools. Research suggests that having asked a child a question, most teachers wait, on average, no more than 5 seconds for the answer, before either turning to another child or providing it themselves. Five seconds for the child to gather his, or her, thoughts, summon their courage and venture an answer with all the risk that entails, or else stay silent and branded as ignorant by default.

Examinations, of course, are the ultimate expression of timed recall. Two hours, three hours, or whatever to come up with solutions to problems, write essays, gather your wits and generally show how smart you can be. What a change from babyhood to childhood. A shift from:

Learning = Taking Risks = Making Mistakes = Understanding.

to:

Learning = Avoiding Risks = Fast Answers = Being admired, respected, perhaps even loved and wanted.

No wonder so many children quickly come to regard school learning as more painful than pleasurable. You may not be able to change all that. But you can make a difference. A difference sufficiently great to transform not only your child's opportunities for successful understanding, but the amount of enjoyment and fulfilment he or she finds in their 15,000 hours of compulsory education. This book is a practical guide to help you to make that difference.

The title *Help Your Child Through School* seeks to convey two slightly different, but equally important and ultimately convergent, messages. The first meaning is, of course, how to encourage your child to do well in school. Not because exams, grades and marks are the only things that matter, and certainly not to make your child smarter than other children. But mainly because realizing his or her true intellectual potential significantly enhances your child's confidence, self-image and self-esteem. That is not to say exams are unimportant. Perhaps they ought not to matter as much as they do. But make no mistake, they really do matter.

Exams are, increasingly, becoming an essential passport to almost all worthwhile work. Our industrialized world is already cruel to the unskilled and unqualified. In the years ahead it is set to become even harsher. The second meaning in my title is to help your child by becoming an active partner in his, or her, education. Working not in competition but in collaboration with their teachers.

How you can do it

If you have unhappy memories of your own school days, then the prospect of helping your child with lessons and exams may appear daunting. But there's no reason to feel that way. For a start providing the necessary help does not depend on having a Mensa level IQ or on completing higher education. Having worked with parents over many years, it is my experience that adults who have striven hard to understand often make the best teachers.

If you understand something quickly and easily it is usually far harder to appreciate why others find it such a struggle. An experienced motorist finds changing gears, manoeuvring through traffic, judging distances, even that bane of the learner driver's life, the hill start, present little or no difficulty. In this confident state it can be very hard to recall how much of a problem all these once seemed. How many mistakes were made, and how hard the skills were to perfect. A problem, once solved, seldom poses much of a challenge.

The same applies to school work problems. Adults who instantly see how to answer a question are likely to become impatient with a child struggling for insight. Even when able to suppress irritable comments, your body language will still betray you. Your child will know you feel annoyed, puzzled and perhaps disappointed by their inability to come up with the right answer. And such knowledge will inevitably erect yet another emotional barrier along the road to learning. If you have a job making sense of something, you will have far greater understanding and sympathy for children going through the same painful process of learning and discovery.

The second reason not to be daunted by the task, is that none of the methods described in the following chapters are like formal lessons at all. In fact they are unlike any either you, or your child, will have ever seen before. One of the key ideas behind this book is to encourage children to learn for themselves and by themselves. Because we all learn fastest and most efficiently when relaxed, entertained and motivated, the powerful skills described here can be mastered easily and enjoyably.

Later in this book I shall be explaining how to exploit 'learning opportunities', moments when your child's brain is primed and eager for knowledge, most effectively. By providing facts and figures at these psychologically sensitive moments, you can not only *double* the amount of information remembered and the accuracy with which it is recalled, but greatly increase your child's desire for further learning.

Questions and answers that enhance your child's mind

Another key to successful learning and teaching is the asking and answering of questions – something you almost certainly do many times each week. Yet this commonplace family activity is rarely used to maximum effect.

Did you realize, for example, that by asking 'How?' or 'Why?' rather than the more usual 'What?' questions you will enhance thinking and reasoning skills without investing a single extra minute of your time?

Games and puzzles make learning fun

I shall be offering many games and puzzles which enhance your child's mind naturally and enjoyably. These can be played alone, or shared with the rest of the family. You will find many of them ideal for making constructive use of time which would otherwise be squandered, such as during journeys or on wet Saturday afternoons. Fantasy Films, the game described on page 164 for instance, takes only a few moments to master and is fun to play, yet it can boost the speed and accuracy of your child's memory by up to 100 per cent.

Those crucial three Rs

With the emphasis in education increasingly focusing on regular testing throughout your child's school career, it is more vital than ever that he or she becomes proficient in the basic skills of reading, writing and arithmetic. These are important not so much in themselves, but as essential learning tools without which little knowledge can ever be acquired.

Some 75 per cent of formal learning, for instance, takes place via reading. Here parents can play a major role in developing fluency. Research suggests the progress of children helped to read at home often exceeds that of youngsters receiving guidance from specialist teachers at school.[*]

Developing your whole child

Classroom attainment is not just about intellectual success. It is also, crucially, about your child's feelings. The motivation, self-image and anxieties aroused by learning challenges. Perceptively the Chinese use a symbol for intelligence incorporating both heart and head. For centuries they have appreciated the powerful role which the emotions

---

[*] Report to House of Commons Select Committee by National Association for the Teaching of English, March 1986.

play in successful learning. Yet we, in the West, have tended to ignore the way a child *feels* about their studies.

Given two children of equal intelligence, one motivated and self-assured, the other apathetic and anxious, there will be no contest between them. The confident, anxiety-free child's work will far outpace that of the no less clever but much less confident youngster. So unless your child feels emotionally positive about school studies, wants to learn, to reason, to think and to create, the years invested in full-time education will be largely wasted. He or she will either fail to realize their true potential or achieve success only at a high emotional cost.

This was brought home to me some years ago when a mother sought advice about her teenage daughter who was hopeless at arithmetic. She was headed for exam failure in a subject vital to her future happiness. Without a good grade this otherwise achieving girl was never going to fulfil her ambition of becoming a doctor. 'We've given her endless coaching, but she get's worse, not better,' the mother explained despairingly. 'Why can't she learn?' Why indeed? She was certainly intelligent enough to understand the concepts. But, like millions of children and adults, she had a block. A block which the endless hours of extra tuition had actually made worse.

Because number problems made her so anxious (I shall explain the key role anxiety plays) learning was essential to reduce her intense fear of figures, increase her confidence and provide the motivation to tackle these challenges before any progress could be made. Which is why I will be showing you not only how to help your child with the essential classroom skills, but also offering practical advice on ways of improving motivation, creating a strong, positive self-image and reducing handicapping anxieties.

Which children most need help through school?

My research has identified four types of child who can most benefit from parental help.

1. The Fear of Failure Child, who often makes a bright start when starting school but fails to realize early promise.
2. The Could Do Better Child, who gets only average marks and examination grades although teachers and parents are convinced he or she has the ability to enjoy considerable classroom success.

3. The Needs Stretching Child, who has too much ability for his or her own good, and as a result gets quickly bored and may behave badly in class.

4. The Overly Anxious Child, who frequently gets off on the wrong foot from almost their first day in school and then has great difficulty making up lost ground.

Despite clear evidence that positive involvement in learning makes a vital difference to their child's success in school, some parents are still reluctant to offer that help. Not because they are uncaring, too busy or lack confidence, but from their firm belief that how well, or badly, a child does in class has little to do with upbringing and everything to do with their genes.

Do children inherit their brains?

Glance around a play group and you will immediately see the extent to which children of a similar age differ. There will be tall ones and short ones, some with blue and others with brown eyes, plump youngsters and skinny ones. You will also notice considerable differences in the way they relate to others. Some are bold and confident, taking the lead in inventing new games. Others are timid and tearful, only joining in reluctantly. Finally they will differ in mental agility. Given a problem to solve, some are quick witted while others struggle to make sense of it.

The question is, to what extent do these obvious differences depend on inherited characteristics? Most physical differences are controlled by the genetic blueprint. This determines whether a child has his father's chin or her mother's eyes.

Genes in action

Forty-six thread-like structures, chromosomes, in the nucleus of every cell, contain thousands of genes. Genes carry information 'written' in deoxyribonucleic acid or DNA. This blueprint tells the cell what kind of proteins to manufacture. Genes come in pairs, one from you and the other from your spouse. Identical twins, from the same egg, have exactly the same genetic make-up.

Even with physical characteristics, however, upbringing does have a role to play. A baby given insufficient food during the first few years of life may remain small and underweight throughout life, even though the genetic blueprint should have produced a tall, well-developed child. Emotionally deprived children may also be stunted, even when given enough to eat. The condition, termed *deprivation dwarfism* is believed to result from abnormal sleep patterns inhibiting the production of growth hormones. The terrible pictures of Romania's cruelly neglected orphans are a tragic illustration of what happens to youngsters deprived of both food and love. But while everybody agrees that genes determine skin, eye and hair colour, the extent to which personality and intelligence are inherited is a far more controversial issue.

This debate between the *naturists* who believe intelligence to be largely inherited and *nurturists*, who consider upbringing more significant, has been long and bitter. The man credited with sparking the 'is intelligence inherited?' controversy was Francis Galton, a cousin of Charles Darwin. In his book *Hereditary Genius*, published in 1869, Galton made three crucial distinctions.

The first was between intellectual abilities and temperamental and moral qualities. The second, between the inborn or inherited tendencies which underlay each of these. The third between special abilities, or 'faculties', and a super faculty which ensured maximum efficiency in everything a person says or does. 'Without a special gift for mathematics,' he explained, 'no man can become a mathematician; but without a high degree of general ability he can never make a great mathematician.' From this distinction was born the notion of an innate, general, intellectual factor.

Three years later, in his *Principles of Psychology*, a book he claimed to have dreamed up while 'reclining in a boat on the Serpentine,' Herbert Spencer replaced 'intellectual factor' with 'intelligence' and the word quickly caught on. Although Francis Galton suggested methods for measuring intelligence it was a French educationalist, Alfred Binet, an ardent admirer of Galton, who created the first widely used intelligence test. Later, William Stern, a German psychologist, hit on the idea of dividing a child's mental age (measured using the test) by his chronological age to provide a measure of his ability. Four years later, an American psychologist, Lewis Terman, removed the fraction produced by Stern's method by multiplying the result by 100. This gives us the Intelligence Quotient or IQ.

Here's how it might work. A child aged ten who solves test problems at the level of a 12-year-old, is said to have an IQ of $12/10 \times 100 = 120$. On the other hand a 12-year-old only able to solve problems at the ten-year-old level will have an IQ of $10/12 \times 100 = 83$. Clearly a 12-year-old who completes tests designed for his age group, but fails at the higher level, will have an IQ of 100. This is the average IQ. Children with a score above 100 are of greater than average intelligence, those scoring below 100 are said to be of less than average intelligence.

Until the late sixties most British psychologists believed IQ was largely innate. They partly supported this view by the result of studies using identical twins who had been separated from their natural parents, and from one another, at birth and raised in different families.

One of the most energetic researchers in this field was Cyril Burt, a highly influential educational psychologist. He claimed to have studied scores of such twins, and found that despite being raised in very different homes their level of intelligence was very similar. This is, of course, exactly what one would expect if intelligence were inherited. I say 'claimed' since, after his death, evidence came to light which suggested he had 'fudged', and perhaps even faked, some of his results. Although, for many psychologists, the case against him remains far from proven. But evidence from identical twins was only one of the pillars Burt used to support a naturist view. He also pointed out, for instance, that intelligence 'runs in families'. 'For children with fathers in one of the higher professions the IQ mean is well over 120,' he commented. 'For children of skilled manual workers approximately the mean is 100; for children of unskilled labourers it is just below 90.'

Nurturists countered the naturist arguments by pointing out that when identical twins are adopted, they are likely to be placed with families socially and economically similar to their natural parents. Furthermore a child born to a professor is more likely to be raised in a home which sharpens and stimulates the intellect. The child has access to books, exposure to interesting ideas and is encouraged to study. The child of a labourer, by contrast, is liable to have much less opportunity and encouragement for study. These differences alone, they insist, would explain the IQ differences between various classes.

In America, maybe because the culture assumes all men are 'born equal', nurturists have been rather more influential than naturists. One result of this belief was *Project Head Start*. A national programme, started in 1965, it was intended to close the gap between poor and middle-class children by providing socially deprived under-fives with 'an educational environment calculated to encourage social competence and motivation.' Despite early criticism, it is now accepted that Head Start makes a significant difference to school achievement. With the experts in such disarray, what ought parents to believe? Should you do everything possible to give your under-five a stimulating, mind enhancing upbringing, or just sit back and let nature take its course? Before we consider these vital questions, let's consider the third way children differ, in terms of their personality.

Several years ago, New York psychiatrists Drs Alexander Thomas and Stella Chess, along with clinical psychologist Dr Herbert Birch, set out to find answers by studying 141 children from birth to adolescence. They discovered a child not only responds to the world in a characteristic way at birth, but that these reactions persist into adolescence. Their study showed, for example, that a passive, withdrawn baby is most likely to grow into a quiet child who fears unfamiliar situations. An active, responsive baby, on the other hand, is more likely to develop into an energetic, and enquiring child. The researchers identified three general groups of infants which they labelled 'easy', 'difficult' and 'slow to warm up'. Easy babies have regular habits, adapt quickly to changes and approach unfamiliar situations without fear. Children in the 'difficult' category are the exact opposites. They have irregular eating and sleeping habits, cry a lot and take time to adapt to new surroundings. The final category of 'slow to warm up' children were, in some ways, similar to the difficult ones.

This suggests that a child's personality is largely inherited, although upbringing obviously plays an important role in determining how those innate traits develop. What's more, difference in temperament will influence the way a child uses their intelligence.

A timid youngster, for example, may be reluctant to tackle anything new, and become fearful when confronted by an unfamiliar problem. A confident child, on the other hand, may only have to be shown or told something once to master the lesson successfully. The slow to warm up youngster requires patient explanation and encouragement to arrive at the same level of competence. While there can never be a cookbook approach to this difficult and demanding task, these suggestions should help you realize your child's full intellectual potential.

1. Never jump to negative conclusions about your child's mental abilities, since this creates a self-fulfilling prophecy of failure.

In many families one child is looked on as being 'less bright' than his brothers or sisters. This belief may be due to the fact he or she doesn't seem able to grasp things quite so quickly or is less willing to tackle novel tasks. Such early judgements can significantly influence the way adults respond to the child.

In one study, a number of teachers gave one-to-one tuition to the same 11-year-old boy. They were variously told he was 'very bright', 'average' or 'a bit slow'. When they believed him bright, the teachers gave more eye-contact, smiled more and showed other non verbal signs of interest and encouragement, than they did when told he was 'dull'. They also allowed him longer to answer questions and were more tolerant of mistakes.

2. Never adversely compare one child with another. For instance by saying, 'Why can't you be clever like your sister?' Such remarks undermine self-esteem by creating a 'can't do' attitude in the child's mind. A youngster who feels unable to compete successfully with a brother or sister will quickly stop trying.

3. Instead of striving to make your child fit into his or her surroundings, change those surroundings, as far as possible, to meet their unique needs. A 'slow to warm up' youngster, for example, requires much more encouragement than an 'easy' child. Be guided by how your child responds to different situations. If he or she seems eager for greater variety and stimulation in life, then provide a wide range of toys and games. But if your child is timid and requires longer to adapt to a new plaything, be patient and allow them that time.

4. Never make your child fear learning by adopting an overly perfectionist attitude. Many children strive for success not because they have a need for achievement but from a fear of failure. They are frightened of letting their parents down.

Such children look upon even nursery school as a place where their abilities will be judged. So rather than take a chance by learning something new, they stick with what they know how to do. This means, of course, they miss out on vital learning experiences.

Harvard psychologist Dr Carol Dweck believes this leads to 'intellectual helplessness'. A child stops trying because he or she has come to believe that nothing they do will ever be good enough. They consider the FQ, or 'fatalism quotient' this creates to be a far more important factor in school achievement than IQ.

Never punish mistakes, especially by threatening to withdraw love or affection if your child fails to achieve expected goals. A child who believes 'Mummy only loves me when I get things right . . .' may grow up emotionally as well as intellectually impoverished.

Help your child to see learning as a way of *improving* rather than *proving* themselves.

5. Let your child learn and discover at their own pace by creating a schedule which matches their ability to deal with time pressure. An 'easy' child may not mind being hurried along to get dressed or finish a painting. The 'slow to warm up' infant may become discouraged or distressed if forced to work at the same rate.

6. Because none of us ever uses more than a small proportion of our intellectual potential, the arguments between naturists and nurturists strike me as like a row between two farmers over who has the larger farm. While one indeed owns 1000 acres and another only 800, since each farms only 400 acres the dispute seems pointless. Far better for them to stop squabbling and concentrate on bringing more land into productive use. Adopt a similarly optimistic outlook when providing your child with the richest and most stimulating possible environment in which to let his or her mind grow and flourish.

2

BEGINNING AT THE VERY BEGINNING

Unless you are expecting a child, or have an infant under 12 months, you may like to skip this chapter. However, I wanted to include some comments about the earliest months of life because, although no formal learning takes place during this period, it remains of great significance to the way your child responds when structured lessons start. If you have the opportunity to enrich your child's mind from the very beginning, even before birth, then it is well worth doing so. For the brain's development is crucially dependent on the amount, and type, of stimulation provided.

Lessons in the womb

Seven months before he was born, Mary's baby started school. Her lessons were informal but intensive. Every day, 24-year-old Mary would provide her unborn infant with information about the world beyond the womb. While preparing food, for instance, she would explain 'I am rolling pastry. Now I am whisking egg whites. That's the sound of a whisk you can hear.'

Mary believes that, thanks to these prebirth lessons, 18-month-old John is brighter, happier and more sociable than other infants of the same age. 'From the moment of birth he was extremely responsive, alert and aware of everything going on around him,' she says. While lessons in the womb strikes many as bizarre, the belief that this really can enhance mental ability finds support in a number of research studies. San Francisco paediatricians have even set up the world's first Prenatal University to teach mothers-to-be how to give birth to brighter babies.

Until recently doctors believed the baby developed passively within the comforting safety of the mother's body. Today the womb is regarded more as classroom than waiting room. At the University of North Carolina, psychologist Dr Anthony DeCasper and his colleagues have been exploring the abilities of the unborn, and coming up with some remarkable findings. They have discovered, for example, that months before birth a baby is capable of recognizing and remembering speech. To do this, pregnant women were asked to read the same story aloud three times a day for four weeks. Then a new story was introduced and the heart rate of their unborn baby monitored. When the familiar story was read the rate increased, showing recognition and interest. The unfamiliar tale, by contrast, produced a slowed heart rate. Classes before birth can begin at any time, but are probably most worthwhile from the third month of pregnancy onwards. Here are six simple, but effective, lessons you can teach:

1. Pat your stomach three times, then rub it three times. While doing so, say loudly: 'Pat, pat, pat . . . rub, rub, rub.'

   Developed at San Francisco's Prenatal University, this teaches your baby to associate sounds with movements while, at the same time, making him or her more attentive to the outside world. Persuade your partner to take part in this exercise, patting and rubbing your stomach while talking aloud to the baby.

2. Pat and rub as before, only this time first introduce yourself then hold a conversation along these lines: 'This is Mummy. How are you today baby?' At first you'll feel rather foolish and self-conscious. But any embarrassment soon passes and the action comes to be seen as natural as it would be to address the same remarks to an actual infant.

3. While working provide your baby with a running commentary about what's going on. Explain what various sounds and actions mean.

4. When talking to your baby, speak three times louder than normal and direct your voice towards the baby. Some mothers find it helpful to construct a simple megaphone using a cone of folded paper and direct this towards their abdomens.

5. Sit down, relax and listen to some music. Experiment with different types of music, ranging from classical to pop music. While doing so pay attention to your baby's reactions. He, or she, will often let you know, by moving and kicking, when any sounds are disliked. Favourites with many babies are anything by the 17th-century Italian composer Antonio Vivaldi. This is probably because the structure of his music is mentally and physically soothing.

6. Relax, close your eyes and escape to a quiet, peaceful place, such as the sunny beach of a lovely tropical island. Picture yourself lying on the sand, listening to the ocean gently lapping the golden shore. Feel the sun warming your body. Smell the rich perfume of the flowers. See the blue sky and clear, blue waters. When deeply relaxed, describe these feelings aloud to your baby. Your tranquil mood and soothing words should help the baby to feel relaxed and secure as well.

It is important not to overdo any stimulation. Brief but frequent lessons are better than infrequent and much longer sessions. If your baby starts becoming agitated by what's happening, stop immediately. These prebirth lessons could help you produce a livelier, brighter and more responsive infant. And the lessons are great fun for both of you.

The Dos and Don'ts of prebirth lessons

DO – talk to your baby each day.
DON'T – make the sessions too long.
DO – talk loudly and address your baby directly.
DON'T – give lessons when tired or stressed.
DO – start around the third month.
DON'T – feel embarrassed or silly. It's a natural way to respond to your baby.
DO – link words to actions, massaging your tummy while talking to your baby.

After birth there is much you can do to stimulate the mind of even the smallest baby.

Six games to build your baby's brain

By playing the right kind of games you can develop your baby's brain naturally and enjoyably. And the earlier you start the better. Recent research has shown that regular play can delight and benefit babies at just *three days* old. Here are six amusing ways of helping your baby to perfect key intellectual skills:

Funny Faces. Can be played only a few days after birth. Holding your baby so she can see your face, make a series of exaggerated expressions, happy, surprised, sad. Become a clown, monkey or gargoyle. Hold each expression until your baby looks away.

When this happens, make your baby do a couple of deep knee-bends, clicking your tongue to recapture his or her attention. The moment he or she looks back at you, repeat the same face or make a new one. After a time, infants vary in how long it takes them to respond, babies will attempt, often with remarkable accuracy, to copy your expression. This helps your baby to discriminate between various surrounding features, enhances powers of recognition and provides practice in responding to others.

Tell-me-a-story. May be played long before your baby can speak. Turn gurgles, burps, coos and chuckles into the words needed to create a story. This game teaches your baby that his or her responses are capable of evoking interesting and exciting responses from others. They learn that it is possible to control events at a distance by means of sounds. At the same time those areas of the brain responsible for understanding speech are stimulated.

The body game. Is played from about six months onwards. Moving an arm in a gentle, playful way you say: 'This is (your baby's name) arm.' Continue touching, moving and naming the different parts of your baby's body. Tap the nose lightly and say 'This is (his or her name) nose'. Tug gently at the ear lobes and repeat the comments. The purpose is not to try and teach words, although the game does help language to develop, but to enhance bodily awareness. It helps the baby to understand the way different parts of the body are related to one another, in addition to stimulating the brain and improving co-ordination.

I'm After You. Make your eyes wide and bob towards your baby saying: 'I'm after you . . . ' or 'I'm going to get you.' This produces great excitement and laughter, while making your baby work hard at understanding what is happening. As with our muscles your baby's brain needs regular exercise to grow strong.

Big as This. Lift your baby's hands upwards and say 'It's as big as this . . .' Allow them to drop back then ask: 'How big is it?' Lift their arms again while repeating. 'It's as big as this.' Playing this game regularly stimulates your baby's vision, hearing and sense of touch.

Exploring. Collect a wide variety of materials to stimulate sight, touch and, perhaps, taste. Dry things like flour and rice which can be mixed up with water or used to conceal things. Soft materials such a silk, or coarse fabrics like hessian. Cotton wool and modelling clay provide experience with soft materials, while wooden bricks and pots help babies to learn about hard things. Find as many different shapes and colours as possible. Use cloth to wrap up, hide, disguise or transform other objects.

Between six and eight months babies will start to crawl around and investigate the world. Infants have a tremendous curiosity about everything in their surroundings, and it's essential to their development that you encourage this inborn need to experiment and explore. If possible make an entire room into a safe play area. This means removing everything which could be pulled over or down, covering electric sockets, closing and locking, or sealing with sticky tape, the doors of cupboards containing anything valuable or dangerous. Especially, of course, bottles of drink, medicines or household cleaners. Within this area, place plenty of toys and harmless household objects, such as pots and pans, plastic utensils and so on. Now your exploring games can be more elaborate, but with the same purpose of exposing your baby to as many new, different and stimulating experiences as possible. The more ingenious you are, the more enjoyable – and beneficial – your baby's fun and games will be.

Six ways to make the most of playing

- Spontaneous play is best. Do it when you are both in the mood.
- Never miss an opportunity to play, for example while changing, dressing or bathing him.
- Choose times in the day when your baby seems most alert and active. Never force play if your baby is unwilling.
- Never be afraid of repeating a game over and over again. Repetition is essential if your baby's brain is to grasp the game. Far from making it boring, familiarity is reassuring and pleasurable for young children.
- Always come down to the baby's level so that you can look directly into one anothers' faces.
- The more enjoyable a game is to play the better it teaches.

In addition to games, you can do a tremendous amount to stimulate your baby's mind simply by chatting.

How to talk to your baby

Children want and need to talk long before they are able to speak. These conversations take place using not spoken words but movements of the body and facial expressions. Unfortunately many parents either never see, or ignore early attempts at conversation. Because of this they not only miss enjoyable chats but opportunities to stimulate their baby's brain. To talk successfully to your baby follow these five simple rules:

1. Place him, or her, in a comfortable chair which is secure while still permitting complete freedom of movement. This is important as the arms and legs have a lot to say during baby talk. If your baby is less than eight weeks old, make certain that the seat supports the head, neck and back firmly. Babies under two months have a tendency to curl up, not because their spines are weak, but in search of warmth and comfort.

2. Your baby should be sitting as vertical as possible. Because infants under eight weeks find this posture rather uncomfortable you'll have to angle their seat sufficiently to ensure they remain relaxed.

3. When talking, your face should be at approximately the same height as your baby's. Usually this means placing the seat on an armchair and then kneeling down.

4. Make sure your baby can clearly see your hands, arms, and upper body. Position yourself at a distance of between two and three feet.

5. All your movements must be deliberate and slightly exaggerated. Talk slowly and clearly, emphasizing each syllable. Smile a great deal, keep your expression animated and use expansive and frequent gestures.

To discover what happens during active baby talk, let's eavesdrop on a conversation between Susan and her ten-week-old daughter Katie which I video-taped during the course of my research into infant body language. The conversation begins as Susan touches her daughter's left foot. Up to then Katie was staring inquisitively around the room. Now she gazes directly into her mother's eyes. After studying her with a rather serious expression for several seconds, Katie smiles delightedly. This is her way of saying, 'Hello. Nice to see you. Let's chat . . .'

These initial stages, termed *Initiation* and *Mutual Orientation* by psychologists, are the equivalent of two friends greeting one another with an affable 'Hello'. Do not be put off if, during *Mutual Orientation*, your baby looks perplexed or even glum. He, or she, is simply deciding whether or not to chat. If babies wants to talk, they'll smile and often wriggle with excitement. When unwilling to join in, perhaps because they are feeling sleepy, eye contact will be discontinued. Never feel discouraged by this rebuff. It's not that your baby is anti-social, only reluctant to start a conversation at that moment, perhaps because of feeling sleepy or a bit irritable. Allow a little time to pass, then try again. Keep a note of the time of day when he, or she, is especially alert and interested in conversing.

After the *Greetings* comes the longest and most interesting part of baby talk, the *Play Dialogue*. This usually lasts between 20 and 30 seconds, but can last longer as your baby grows older. Susan and Katie enjoy a lengthy and mutually exciting conversation. The baby watches her mother intently, mimicking arm and leg movements. Her lips and tongue also attempt to copy her mother's mouth movements.

During the *Play Dialogue* watch carefully for these. You will notice your baby's mouth deliberately attempting to mimic the vocal sounds you are producing. These pre-speech movements of lips and tongue are a first, tentative step towards mastering the spoken word.

Notice also that her hand gestures, leg wags and body wriggles are synchronized with the rhythm of your words. Although this is sometimes hard to detect with the unaided eye, slow motion films reveal these rhythmic movements to be in perfect harmony with the rise and fall of speech. By making such movements your baby is acquiring an understanding of the unique rhythms of her native language. Without mastery of this rhythm the spoken word will sound unnatural, even though words and grammar are perfectly correct. This is why the speech of a person born deaf never sounds the same as one who can hear the language of others.

Your baby will talk about things of special interest by wriggling or waggling arms and legs more vigorously. But if distressed or distracted, perhaps because you glance away to talk to another adult, notice how abruptly the body language changes. He or she will become either more animated or suddenly subdued. Your baby's face may wrinkle in irritation or look sad, and arms may waggle frantically in an effort to recapture your attention, or hang dispiritedly. When your baby feels there has been enough chat then he or she brings the conversation to an end by glancing away. That is what happens to Susan and Katie after some sixty seconds of active exchanges. This

Disengagement phase marks the end of that particular dialogue. Notice that babies may now slow down their body movements for a while and stare straight ahead as if thinking deeply. In fact that is probably just what they are doing, reflecting on all the information gained during your conversation and trying to make sense of it. When your baby is ready for further conversation he or she will look back at you, establish eye contact again and start the enchanting, mind enriching, dialogue all over again.

How well do you know your child?

In order to help your child learn before school starts, it's important to match the play lessons you provide to his or her individual needs. For this, you have to gain insight into his or her strengths and weaknesses. This is not always as easy as it appears. Often being so physically and emotionally close to a child makes it harder to produce an objective assessment.

When a nursery teacher said her four-year-old was unsociable, Molly's immediate reaction was utter disbelief: 'I felt certain Lucy was friendly and outgoing,' Molly recalls. But after watching her child at play, she came to agree with the judgment. 'I found Lucy did have difficulty making friends,' she says. Molly's blindness over her daughter's shyness is far from unusual. Many parents can provide only a vague and woolly description of their child's personality. Usually an adult's assessment reveals more about them than about the youngster. There is a natural tendency to see what we expect, or hope, to see instead of what is actually there. If we have decided a boy is aggressive, for instance, we pay more attention to bullying behaviour than occasions when he plays peacefully with his friends.

Research by psychologists David C. Rowe and Robert Plomin, of the University of Colorado, has shown that a child's temperament can be assessed by exploring six vital factors.

These are given below with questions adapted from their test. Score each statement as follows: Very true = 5; True to some extent = 4; Only occasionally true = 3; Seldom true = 2; Not true at all = 1.

1. **Attention**
- Plays happily with the same toy for a long time.
- Perseveres despite set-backs.
- Enjoys playing with complicated or difficult toys.

● Persists with a task rather than jumping from one activity to the next.

2. Feeding
● Refuses to eat many sorts of food.
● Is reluctant to try an unfamiliar dish.
● Has strong likes and dislikes in food.
● Having decided a food is disagreeable will not be persuaded to try it.
● Makes a face when given new food to try.

3. Soothability
● Can be easily distracted from crying.
● Calms down quickly after being startled or upset.
● Quickly stops crying if talked to.
● Does not become too upset when things go wrong.
● When fussing, quickly calms down if held or spoken to.

4. Activity
● Always rushing about.
● Is lively from the moment of waking.
● Moves briskly.
● Prefers playing active games.
● Has lots of energy.

5. Emotions
● Gets upset very easily.
● Has a tendency to be over emotional.
● Is easily moved to tears.
● Frequently cries and makes a fuss.
● Shows intense feelings when distressed.

6. Sociability
● Has little fear of strangers.
● Makes friends easily.
● Likes joining in games.
● Enjoys the company of others.
● Gets on well with most people.

What the score reveals
These scores are averages, they do *not* represent some normal or ideal value: Attention – 17; Feeding – 13; Soothability – 17; Activity – 20; Emotions – 15; Sociability – 17.

Using this knowledge to help your child

As with any simple psychological test, this provides only a thumbnail sketch of your child's personality, not a detailed picture. But comparing your results with average scores allows you to pin-point any significant aspects of your child's personality. Even when your child has scored above or below average, this does not imply that he or she is abnormal. Healthy, well adjusted children may have different totals from those given above. They should help you understand why your child responds in a certain way under particular circumstances. If the assessment appears to have identified a minor problem, such as difficulty in concentrating or making friends, find practical ways of helping.

A child who gives up too easily, for example, can be taught the importance of persevering through encouragement and demonstration. While carrying out a skill with which he or she has difficulty, for instance tying shoes laces, never allow the task to seem easy. Make deliberate errors and then notice, or encourage your child to point out those mistakes and ask their assistance in putting them right. Talk out loud while doing such tasks, saying for example, 'That doesn't look right . . . how can I make this loop bigger . . .' and so on. Once your child realizes even grown-ups have difficulties they will feel less embarrassed over making and correcting mistakes themselves. Do not expect to make too many changes in your child's basic temperament. Inborn differences mean that some youngsters will always be harder to sooth or have higher energy levels than others. Be patient with the naturally emotional child and channel the energies of a very active youngster along constructive lines instead of attempting to curb their boundless enthusiasm.

3

THE NURSERY SLOPES

Not long ago I visited the nursery class of a privately run infants' school. When I arrived, soon after 9.30 am, the children were already busy creating clown faces from paper plates, using strands of coloured wool for hair, and plastic bottle tops for noses. The room was buzzing with activity as the whole class laboured industriously and enjoyably. That task completed, and everything tidied neatly away, it was time for a game of 'Naming the Numbers'. The children, all wearing the school's uniform of dark blue jumpers with grey skirt or trousers, sat in a circle and called out answers to simple sums.

Later some played another numbers game. Brightly-coloured paper fish, with a metal clip glued to one side, were fished from a large jar using a magnet attached to a piece of string. Each was counted by the children, who worked in pairs, writing the numbers down and adding them up. Another popular numbers game was the hard boiled egg rolling contest. Each child had to try and roll the egg as far as possible, while one measured the distance with a tape and a third wrote the figures down on a record form. The whole class co-operated to produce large scale projects, such as the mural, covering almost an entire wall, of characters from a book by the author Roald Dahl. The morning ended with them quietly listening as the teacher read a story, and following the action in colourfully illustrated books.

I was told the class make regular trips to places of local interest and recently, when building work was taking place on a nearby site, the teacher arranged a weekly visit. The children were shown what was involved with each stage of the construction. As with every trip they made notes and drawings on returning to the classroom. This nursery school has a structured timetable and high educational expectations. By the age of three every child knows his or her alphabet. At four most can do simple sums and recognize geometric shapes. Many are competent readers before moving up to primary school. Yet despite these intellectual demands, every child appeared genuinely interested in the activities which were tackled with enthusiasm and confidence.

Structured learning versus free play

A few weeks later, my morning began in another preschool class, staffed by equally dedicated teachers and with no less happy and enthusiastic children. But the educational philosophy here was clearly very different.

There were no uniforms or structured activities. Each child was able to wander around the cheerfully decorated room selecting any task which appealed. Some were rolling out play dough at a long table while others played with big, brightly painted, wooden building blocks. A third group was constructing robots out of old egg boxes while others enjoyed a boisterous rough-and-tumble game on well padded mats around the Wendy House. Children wanting to draw and paint simply collected materials needed from a store cupboard and then created whatever they wished. A large wicker basket was filled with fancy dress costumes for fantasy play. There was a climbing frame, wooden slide, tricycles, plastic push cars and a rather ragged tailed rocking horse for active play. A cupboard filled with painting and craft materials was for creative activities. The teachers mingled with the children offering help and advice where needed and acting as peace makers in occasional squabbles over toys.

The only signs of organized play was group discussion about some topic of interest (on the day of my visit it was Spring) followed by an arts and crafts session based on that conversation. The children fashioned weird and wonderful flowers, of any shape, size or design which appealed to them, from crepe paper and pipe cleaners. This preschool made no attempt to offer even informal teaching in sums or reading. By the age of four very few children knew their alphabet and an even smaller minority could do basic arithmetic.

Each school was filled with happy, energetic and involved children. Each was turning out youngsters with quite different levels of skills, knowledge and, perhaps even aspirations. So which school would have served *your* child the better?

A hundred-year-old debate

If you are unsure of the answer, don't worry. You are not alone. The debate has been raging among educationalists for more than a century and, even today, experts are far from certain which approach better meets the needs of developing minds.

'Everyone demands certainty,' comments Professor Lilian Katz, from the University of Illinois, one of America's foremost early education specialists. 'But they are probably not going to get it. Both systematic instruction and child-orientated activities, if done properly, can benefit preschool-age children.'*

As competition in the classroom intensifies, and the emphasis on academic success increases, more and more parents are opting for 'back to basics' preschool teaching. They are more comfortable with the thought that their child will learn to read and do sums rather than 'waste time' in unstructured play. Many believe that 'messing around' with crayons or dressing up for fantasy games contributes nothing to subsequent classroom performance. As one father told me: 'If my son can read and do numbers when he starts primary school, he'll be way ahead of most other children. Play is fun but teaches nothing. It's in every sense infantile.' Other parents, and most early learning experts, disagree. Far from an optional extra during the first five years, they consider free-play essential for intellectual, emotional and social growth.

'Young children have a number of developmental tasks,' says Marian Blum, educational director of the Child Study Centre at Wellesly College in Massachusetts,' 'the most important of which is to come to understand themselves in relation to peers and parents . . . learning to read or add in a formal manner is not an appropriate activity for preschoolers.' In the company of specialists, on both sides of the Atlantic, Marian Blum regards the preschool's role as providing a smorgasbord of stimulating activities. Tasks should enable the under-fives to learn from experience instead of attempting to deal with abstract concepts, such as letters and numbers. I too believe children should be allowed to decide *which* activities they would like to follow, *when* they want to do them and *how* long they wish to continue.

For some youngsters the freedom of choice offered by unstructured play can be overwhelming. Lacking clear guide lines on what to do and how to do it, they become anxious and confused. Timid children, especially, can be pushed aside by more assertive youngsters. They might well make better progress and develop strong self-confidence, in a class offering structured activities and more formal teaching. Other children, of course, flourish in a free and easy atmosphere. Far from feeling apprehensive when faced with a wide variety of activities,

* Psychology Today, December 1989. pp. 52—57

having plenty of choice unlocks creativity while enabling them to satisfy their intense curiosity. Which of these approaches is more likely to inspire than intimidate your own child? The answer may come easily from your knowledge of their outlook and personality.

You should also find that the assessment and suggestions below offer useful insights. If you are undecided but able to choose between either approach, start with the one you intuitively feel most likely to prove effective. Monitor the situation carefully for around three weeks. If your child is obviously happy and flourishing, well and good. There is clearly no need to make further changes. But if he or she shows signs of uncertainty or unhappiness, quickly change to a different regime. Do this even if you personally favour the methods used by that preschool.

For instance, where you prefer structured teaching while your child feels happier when allowed free play. Or, if you endorse free play but your child enjoys more formal lessons. In the first instance do not feel concerned that playing wastes time. The self-assured and motivated child quickly catches up when schooling starts. Equally, if your child likes formal learning do not worry that they are missing out on opportunities for play. For children whatever they find fun *is* playing, no matter how much like schoolwork it seems to adults. Trust your child to know what is right for him or her.

Is preschool education really necessary?

Before considering how to select the best preschool for your child, it's useful to ask whether such an experience is even necessary. On the plus side a well run class or group will help your child learn to socialize and become more independent by cooperating with others in a secure and friendly environment. This can be especially valuable for an only child or for those with fewer opportunities for playing with other children. But before deciding to send your child to preschool classes or groups ask yourself what you both want to get out of it.

If you are able to offer plenty of stimulating activities at home (*see below*) and enjoy one another's company, a few half days at a playgroup, to help your child to get used to being away from you, could be all that's needed. If, however, you have difficulty keeping your child constructively occupied all day, a longer spell in a nursery class could satisfy the desire for stimulation from a wide variety of learning experiences.

Where no suitable preschool facilities exist in your area, and you are not in a position to help start up a group (*see The ABC of Learning*) work at home to provide sufficient stimulation. You might also enquire about starting primary education early (*see The ABC of Learning*). Going to school slightly ahead of the legal age allows a child who has spent most of the first four years at home to become familiar with the routine before formal teaching starts.

Choosing the best preschool for your child

Having decided preschool will be beneficial, the next step is to locate one which is suitable. Start looking early, since the best schools usually have a waiting list. You must find a school with which *both* you and your child feel happy. One which you regard as excellent may have little appeal to your child. Sources of information include the grapevine, social services and your Local Education Authority. If you know which primary school your child will attend, ask the head teacher for her recommendations. How much choice you have depends on where you live and what is affordable. Some areas are well served while others offer limited options.

Make a call – pay a visit

Having prepared a short-list, phone and ask the head teacher about her child-care philosophy. If your question is met with confusion or incomprehension, cross that school off your list. When satisfied, ask whether you might pay a brief, unannounced, visit. Suggest a time, such as mid-morning or mid-afternoon, when this will cause the least disruption. Early in the day teachers are busy settling the children, while late afternoon sees the bustle associated with preparing them for home. Good teachers welcome parental interest and will readily agree. So if this request is met with a refusal or prevarication, cross that group off your list.

What to look for during your visit

When visiting the school, check these key points:

The surroundings. While it's important for the room to be clean, neat and well organized, efforts to impress prospective parents rather than their children should be viewed with suspicion. Adult tastes may run to pastel decor, colour co-ordinated fabrics and subdued lighting, but most youngsters feel far more at home with crayon scribbles on the walls and paint splashes on the tables. As well as an area set aside for active play, the premises should offer a quiet place for children to look at books, take a nap or simply day dream. Each child should be given a secure place in which to leave such personal belongings as a blanket, sleep toy and extra clothes.

The equipment. Should include bikes, tunnels and climbing frames, for active games; modelling clay, paper and paint for creative play; and sand, flour and water for 'messy' play, as well as construction toys, books, games and puzzles, plus dressing-up costumes for fantasy play. While all toys receive pretty hard wear at the hands of active under-fives, they should never be allowed to get too scruffy or have parts missing. Check for sharp corners on furnishings, unprotected floor around the climbing frame, or any other hazards which might lead to injury.

The teachers. Notice the ratio of adults to children. The preschool ideal is no more than eight per teacher, with a maximum of sixteen in the whole class. How involved are teachers and children? If the adults huddle together drinking coffee and gossiping it's unlikely they have much interest in their charges. Notice too whether, when listening or talking to a child, they pay close attention or appear impatient. Do they take the time and trouble to answer questions sensibly or is there a tendency to try and fob the youngsters off with silly or patronizing answers? If a child tumbles and bursts into tears does the adult provide genuine sympathy or deal rather unsympathetically with the upset? Do the teachers spontaneously hold a child while talking, or do they keep their distance. Ideally they should always come down to the child's level when chatting so as to converse face-to-face. This is the most reassuring and effective way in which adults can communicate with small children.

Are they able and willing to take advantage of learning opportunities? Those precious moments when a child is poised to make a great discovery if given just that little bit of extra help and encouragement. Is a child who wants to follow some independent activity, such as drawing or looking at a picture book, allowed to do so during group activities, or compelled to join in?

Is discipline imposed in a friendly and reassuring manner? Distrust teachers using ridicule or ritualized punishment, such as forcing a naughty child to sit in a 'bad chair', to keep order. Are teachers guilty of sexual stereotyping? Encouraging boys to use the climbing frame and girls to play with what used to be called the Wendy House, but is now often termed the Home Corner for that very reason. Girls have a hard enough time attracting attention in class without the handicap of a prejudiced teacher. Be cautious of adults who endlessly read stories, put on puppet shows or provide similar diversions. Preschool is where children come to learn for themselves, not to be entertained by grown-ups.

The other children. Is there a rowdy free-for-all, which might intimidate a nervous youngster, or discreet but vigilant supervision on the part of teachers? Do the children seem happy, relaxed and confident, or watchful and wary? Does bullying occur and seemingly go undetected? Because bullying is usually sporadic, it may be hard to detect during your brief visit. But you can often tell from the way children respond to one another. What matters is not whether a disruptive child is present in the class, they exist in all schools, but how teachers deal with his – and it usually is a boy – outbursts.

In one playgroup, where I did research, there was a little boy known to the adults as 'Oh God Harry'. This referred to the fact that every time he turned up at the playgroup, all the grown-ups murmured: 'Oh God, Harry!' Harry was an aggressive four-year-old who had no idea how to co-operate with others. If Harry wanted something he simply took it and his play consisted mainly of pushing, pulling, snatching, grabbing, or in some other way intimidating the younger, smaller or more timid youngsters. It was apparent to me during my very first visit that Harry was a problem child for whom none of the adults had an answer. As a result many of the youngsters attending that playgroup were fearful and miserable. It wasn't Harry's fault that he was so aggressive, nor was it the adults' fault he had behavioural problems, but they should have taken positive steps both to help him learn better social skills and to protect vulnerable children from his aggression.

Sum up all your impressions and observations by asking this single, most important question: 'Would I enjoy spending my time here?'

Use a trial period

The only person who knows whether the preschool is right for your child is – your child. If everything checks out, bring them along for a trial visit. Should the reaction be favourable, stay for a few hours during the first week to help your child get used to the new surroundings.

Do not worry too much over a few tears on parting. These are perfectly natural since a fear of separation is part of the developmental process. The tears should, however, stop after a couple of weeks. If crying and clinging continue longer than this then something is not quite right. Talk over any possible problem with teachers and review your choice in the light of your child's unhappiness. It's far better to move a child rapidly than to allow misery and apprehension to continue. I shall be talking about this further later in the chapter, where we look at helping the timid child.

Your child's personality

Whether your child will thrive in a large class or do better in a smaller group depends to a great extent on his or her personality.

As all parents know, from the very first moments after birth, every baby is different. Some are very active while others more passive. Some adore novelty, they wriggle and gurgle with delight when a new mobile is suspended above their cot. Others dislike even minor changes in routine, becoming wary and fretful when faced with anything unfamiliar. The extent to which such personality differences are inborn or result from upbringing is part of the *nature versus nurture* controversy which I discussed in the previous chapter.

During the early seventies, the role of *nature* was emphasized in a study by New York psychiatrists, Drs Alexander Thomas and Stella Chess and by psychologist Dr Herbert Birch. After following more than 140 children, from birth through to adolescence, they concluded that while child rearing methods can obviously encourage or repress inborn characteristics, a child's basic personality is primarily inborn. A passive, apprehensive baby appears destined to grow into a timid, rather lethargic teenager. An active, confident infant is likely to develop into a lively, self-assured adolescent. To illustrate this point, they quote the case of a ten-year-old girl who was working well and happily in a small school. On transferring to a larger one, however, she abruptly changed into an anxious underachiever. When the researchers examined their records of her infant years they found that, even as a baby, she disliked new situations and took a long time adapting to change.

While not all psychologists accept that personality is as unalterable as Drs Thomas, Chess and Birch believe, most agree biology plays a significant part in deciding how people react to life. Some are born with a nervous system which responds swiftly and powerfully to even moderate stimulation. Others require considerable stimulation to achieve the same level of mental and physical arousal. Most of us come between these extremes, enjoying both periods of tranquillity as well as a fast paced lifestyle. While many traits go to make up a complete personality, four are especially significant in determining your child's behaviour. The first is Active versus Passive; the second Confidence versus Apprehension. These are called bi-polar traits, since each can be seen as one pole on a continuum.

ACTIVE ——————— PASSIVE

CONFIDENT ——————— APPREHENSIVE

What do these differences make in terms of behaviour? To find out let's consider each of the four poles in turn. Although, of course, few children are located at either end of the continuum, with a majority being found somewhere between these extremes. The assessment below, together with your knowledge, will help you place your child somewhere along each line.

Four personality types

Active children are full of energy. They are animated, active and seemingly tireless. Even if you are wilting from fatigue they'll still be eager for more games, more stimulation, more activities. They tend to be quick, alert, impulsive, but readily distracted.

Passive children respond slowly to demands. They seem to tire easily and show little enthusiasm for active play. It takes them quite a while to warm to anything new, although once their attention has been caught they'll play happily for hours. Unlike active children, who are easily distracted, passive children show great persistence once they have become involved in a task.

Confident children quickly adapt to change and enjoy meeting new people, playing with unfamiliar toys and tackling novel challenges.

Apprehensive children are a reverse image of the confident youngsters. They are fearful of change and dislike being challenged by anything new. They need time to adapt to unfamiliar surroundings, may be tearful when first left in preschool classes and are reluctant to join in games.

Whether your child responds confidently or apprehensively, energetically or slothfully to challenges largely depends, of course, on their individual genetic make-up. To criticize your child for being fearful or passive is, in some ways, as unjustifiable as blaming him or her for having blue eyes or blonde hair. Yet such criticisms are frequently made and can, all too easily, create a self-fulfilling prophecy of success or failure. The power of prophecies is illustrated by two examples from my files.

Margaret – an active/confident baby. Energetic and self-assured as a baby, grew up into a bright, confident and affectionate child. The praise and encouragement she received for what adults regarded as her 'positive' personality led to strong self-esteem. This, in turn, made her feel even more self-confident and eager to tackle unfamiliar challenges.

Tom – a passive/apprehensive baby. Tom, by contrast, had been easily distressed as an infant with irregular patterns of eating and sleeping. By the age of five he had grown into a timid boy who found difficulty in making friends, was very tearful when first left at nursery school and took a long time to settle into new surroundings. Although this was not his 'fault', he was often blamed, especially by his father, for being fearful and 'unmanly'. Such criticism only made him more nervous and less self-assured. Tom grew up with a negative self-image and low esteem. He required constant encouragement to persevere with any new challenges, encouragement which was not always forthcoming. Parents and teachers were often irritated by his timidity, and blamed him for not trying. Privately his teachers regarded him as being of below average intelligence. Yet once something caught his interest and he overcame his anxiety Tom was both capable and persistent.

Assessing your child's personality

Read the statements below and note those which best describe your child's response to the situation described:

1. *During meals my child . . .*
   Wriggles and fidgets.
   Sits quietly.

2. *While playing alone my child . . .*
   Always wants to play actively.
   Can amuse him/herself with a quiet game.

3. *In unfamiliar surroundings my child . . .*
   Explores confidently.
   Remains close to me much of the time.

4. *If offered unfamiliar food, my child . . .*
   Is eager to try it.
   Refuses to even taste it.

5. *When faced with a novel challenge my child . . .*
   Tackles it with little or no hesitation.
   Becomes nervous and/or confused.

6. *While being read a story, my child . . .*
   Fidgets and wants to play a more active game.
   Enjoys sitting quietly and listening.

7. *When dressing, or being dressed, my child . . .*
   Pulls on clothes without much care.
   Dresses carefully.

8. *Given a difficult task, my child . . .*
   Quickly grows bored and distracted.
   Persists until a solution is found.

9. *When faced with a major change of routine, my child . . .*
   Shows little or no apprehension.
   Becomes very apprehensive.

10. *My child . . .*
    Finds it hard to settle at night.
    Sleeps easily.

11. *When meeting new children, my child . . .*
    Makes friends with little or no difficulty.
    Is timid and unwilling to make friends.

12. *My child* . . .
> Seldom cries without good cause.
> Becomes tearful for no apparent reason.

How to score
This questionnaire explored:

Activity – Passivity with questions: 1, 2, 6, 7, 8, 10.
Confidence – Apprehension with questions 3, 4, 5, 9, 11, 12.

Score each group of six questions separately. Award +1 for every top
statement ticked and –1 for any of the lower statements. The higher
the positive score on either set of questions the more active or
confident is your child's approach to life. The higher the negative
score the more passive and/or apprehensive.

In the example below, I have plotted the positions of Margaret and
Tom, the two youngsters whose very different personalities I briefly
described above. The little boy scored –4 on the Passivity/Activity
scale and –3 on the Apprehension/Confident scale. Locating these two
scores on the appropriate scale, we can drawn a line from each. The
point at which they meet identifies his position on the chart. Margaret
scored +5 for Activity/Passivity and +4 for Confidence/Apprehension.
Her position has also been plotted. The advantage of this slightly complicated way of recording scores is that it allows you instantly to compare the relative positions of different children.

See first chart.

You may find it helpful to plot your child's position on the second
chart.

Use this diagram to chart the position of your child on these two
personality factors. My comments below explain how best to help children whose scores place them in each one of these four quadrants. The
further out from the centre of the grid your child lies, on either or both
scales, the more important it becomes to provide the appropriate reassurance, guidance and practical help.

Helping the active/apprehensive child – zone A

Strengths. The impulsivity found in active/apprehensive children is
tempered by a natural caution. Instead of leaping headlong into unfamiliar challenges, these children take more time to reflect on the situation and only act if certain of what is expected. This helps avoid

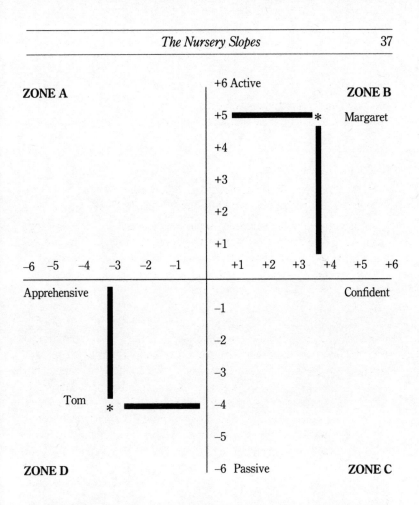

foolish, perhaps hazardous, mistakes. At the same time they have plenty of energy to invest in any task they feel comfortable with.

Possible problems. Where apprehension runs high, for instance if your child is confronted by an anxiety-arousing task, they may expend their energy in unhelpful ways. For instance, given a set of blocks for constructing a complicated-looking building, the active/apprehensive child might refuse even to attempt the task. Instead the child may loose his or her temper and hurl the bricks away in frustrated fury.

How you can help
Channel this energy into the most constructive direction by planning activities which build on what is familiar. Introduce unfamiliar tasks

```
ZONE A                           +6 Active                    ZONE B

                                 +5

                                 +4

                                 +3

                                 +2

                                 +1

-6   -5   -4   -3   -2   -1         +1   +2   +3   +4   +5   +6

Apprehensive                                              Confident
                                 -1

                                 -2

                                 -3

                                 -4

                                 -5

ZONE D                           -6 Passive                   ZONE C
```

only slowly so that the transition from the known to the new is as gradual as possible. If your child seems overly apprehensive or reluctant to attempt an unusual challenge, do not try and force him to do so. Instead, redesign that activity to remove some of the novelty. Develop knowledge and confidence progressively, with each task building on the one before it like stepping stones across a river. These children often do best in a preschool environment offering more formal instruction with close supervision of activities.

Helping the active/confident child – zone B

Strengths. Approaches life with tremendous enthusiasm. Has a great deal of energy to invest in any projects which capture his or her interest. Always willing to attempt new challenges and enjoys learning by experimenting. Self-assurance makes it easier to tackle unfamiliar activities with a confidence which enhances their chances of success.

Possible problems. May not always be sufficiently cautious for his or her own good. Sometimes lands in difficulties and dangers by being too bold, especially in the early years where there is insufficient understanding of risks. High levels of confidence may make them reluctant to admit mistakes or follow instructions. Tends to be impulsive and too easily distracted. May do poorly in class because they find it difficult to sit still or concentrate for very long.

How you can help

Recognize your child's need for energetic play. Long periods of inactivity lead to boredom, resentment and misbehaviour. Allow plenty of opportunities for exercise to burn up excess energy. Whenever possible teach by allowing your child to learn through experience, for instance by making things or carrying out simple experiments.

With the confident child you tread a narrow line between allowing your child enough freedom to grow and protecting him or her from danger. So far as discipline is concerned, the best advice is to have as few rules as are necessary to protect both your child and their surroundings. These rules should, however, be consistently and firmly enforced. Never undermine your child's confidence in order to control their behaviour. For instance by saying: 'You're much too little to do that.' It is more constructive to transform an overly complex or demanding activity into a task within your child's capability. These children often do well in a preschool which emphasizes freeplay and independence.

Helping the passive/confident child – zone C

Strengths. Because they are reflective these children often do better at abstract tasks than those involving the physical manipulation of objects. When we explore different ways of thinking, in Chapter Four, you will notice similarities between this combination of personality traits and the 'Intellectual' learning style.

Possible problems. These children dislike being hurried and may be especially reluctant to exert themselves at any task which fails to capture their interest. They are sometimes, unfairly, accused of being lazy or not trying hard enough. They may also get overlooked in class, because they take time thinking out answers to questions. This is not due to a lack of confidence in their answers, a reason why (as we shall see later in the book) some children seldom put up their hands. Unfortunately by the time they have got around to finding the solution a more active child will have answered. You will recall the very short amount of time, some 5 seconds on average, that teachers allow for a child to respond before either providing an answer themselves or moving on to another child.

How you can help

Passive children risk losing their confidence if they are constantly being criticized as slow or lazy. Never compare the passive child adversely with a more energetic and active sibling or companion. The trouble is that parents and teachers often find it easier to relate to energetic youngsters whose enthusiasm is infectious and inspiring.

The structured approach is often better for these children than the free to play atmosphere. But make sure the teacher to child ratio is low enough to ensure individual attention. It is also very important for your child to feel secure with the teacher who should show great patience and allow them sufficient time to find answers.

Helping the passive/apprehensive child – zone D

Strengths. Although this is the least favourable combination of traits these children do have some things going for them. They can usually concentrate for longer periods than active children and are less likely to be impulsive. Careful and reflective, they consider all aspects of a situation before attempting it.

Possible problems. Life can be especially difficult for these children who are usually described as timid. Not only must they cope with high levels of anxiety but often endure teasing and ridicule from children and sometimes teachers. They need time to warm to a task and may not show much enthusiasm, especially at first. They easily become dependent and unwilling to stand on their own feet. Reluctance to tackle unfamiliar activities slows down learning, while social anxiety handicaps them in making friends. In class excessively timid children rarely put up their hand even if they know the answer. When solving problems they can be rigidly stereotyped in their thinking.

How you can help

1. Avoid labelling. Describing a child as 'timid' creates a self-fulfilling prophecy.

2. Notice those occasions when your child is especially timid, as well as those he or she deal with confidently. You may find that apprehension only arises in certain specific situations (*see box*) while other challenges arouse little or no apprehension.

3. Try to find out whether there is any common factor in the various displays of timidity. A child who desperately wants to be thought well of by grown-ups, for instance, may be so afraid of failing that they become excessively fearful in unfamiliar situations. Being unsure how to behave for the best, they then avoid that activity entirely.

   Take off any pressure to succeed. Never let your child believe love and affection depend on their achieving some type of goal. The dangers of creating an overly striving, overly perfectionist child are, of course, far greater in primary and secondary education so I shall be dealing with the problem, and offering practical advice, in later chapters.

4. A major difficulty is knowing how hard to push a timid child. The 'sink or swim' approach, where the youngster is thrown in at the emotional deep end can occasionally prove effective. A youngster may protest loudly and tearfully when first left in a nursery class. Yet within minutes of you leaving, their fears are forgotten and they play happily with the other children. Unfortunately this approach can go badly wrong, leading to further loss of confidence and even greater timidity. If you are uncertain whether your child will be able to cope with the challenge, build self-assurance slowly.

   A youngster whose timidity makes them refuse all invitations to play with other children at their houses, for example, might be encouraged to have one or two friends around to play at your home. Familiar surroundings reduce anxiety as your child learns important social skills.

5. Avoid making adverse comparisons with other children, especially brothers or sisters. It's all too easy for an exasperated parent to say: 'Why can't you be like . . . ' but this makes the timid child feel even more ashamed and inadequate.

6. Build on your child's strengths instead of focusing on weaknesses. A youngster who is timid in a large group for example, may greatly enjoy playing with one or two close friends.

7. Never try and shame a timid child into being bolder, by suggesting that you will no longer respect or admire them. Such threats lead to great insecurity and make them even less self-assured.

8. Both structured and free play preschool environments can be suitable for these children. What matters most is the atmosphere of the class. They need a great deal of encouragement and reassurance with a fairly quiet group. Avoid classes with lots of rough-and-tumble play, or adults who seem insufficiently attentive to the children's needs.

Six worst fears of the timid child

- Separation from parents. Usually outgrown by eight to nine.
- Being away from familiar surroundings. Likely if a child seldom spends time away from home.
- Meeting strangers. Provide opportunities to meet as many people as possible.
- Being the centre of attention, for example when asked a question in class. Practice increases confidence. For older children, joining a drama class, choir or debating society often helps.
- Unfamiliar challenges. Coach in the special skills needed.
- Team games. Encourage more individual pursuits.

Dealing with temper tantrums

Another common problem in the preschool years are temper tantrums. Although these peak at around 24 months, during the so called 'terrible twos' they can continue for some time afterwards. A child who has learned to get their own way by throwing a tantrum whenever thwarted will have difficulty adjusting to preschool life. They run the risk, too, of being branded as a 'difficult' child and gaining a reputation which, like a branding mark, remains throughout school life.

The child nicknamed 'Oh God Harry,' I described earlier, was difficult and disliked. His behaviour stemmed from being the only child of overly protective, spoiling parents. At the age of three, his mother became pregnant again and Harry found himself no longer the centre of attention. This frustration, combined with his lack of play skills and the fact that he was a big boy for his age, caused him to turn to bullying. That reputation stuck. The label of bully followed him through primary and into secondary education. It was how he came to be seen by other children and teachers. Ultimately it was how he came to see himself.

So it is important, during the preschool years, to help your child cope with the intense feelings of anger and frustration which underlie the tantrums. Temper tantrums, which can start as early as 18 months and last until the start of primary school, leave many parents feeling utterly inadequate. Here's the way Liz described her son Tony's first tantrum. 'It happened at a supermarket checkout! I refused to buy him some sweets and suddenly all hell broke loose. One moment he was his usual angelic self, the next I had a screaming demon on my hands. His piercing screams and wildly kicking heels made us both an instant centre of attention. I was completely demoralized and felt sure I must be a dreadful Mum to have such a horrible son!'

Although understandable, self-blame is misplaced. Tantrums are a sign that your child is growing up and developing a greater need for independence. They arise when a desire for autonomy is frustrated. Maybe because small fingers lack sufficient dexterity to fasten buttons or after you've refused a request for extra playtime. At this point rage builds so swiftly your child is overwhelmed by emotions. While you'll never entirely prevent tantrums there are practical ways to reduce their frequency and make them slightly more bearable.

1. Watching for situations or activities likely to trigger a tantrum will help you avoid many outbursts. For example, if your child is deeply absorbed in a game and you want to go shopping, it may be possible to wait until they've grown bored with playing and would welcome an outing.

2. Resist the temptation to give in 'just this once' to stop a tantrum. If you do so your child quickly learns to throw a tantrum just to get his or her own way. When you've always given in before, your child's immediate reaction to a firm refusal will probably be an even worse tantrum. If this happens take a deep breath, grit your

teeth and stand your ground. This is the only way to convince them that losing their temper is not going to win the argument.

3. However angry or embarrassed you become, never smack or hit your child. This not only makes things worse but it's unjust. A child throwing a tantrum is incapable of exercising even modest self-control.

4. Children often hold their breath during a temper tantrum, sometimes long enough to turn blue and even pass out. If this happens do not panic. The moment they pass out their breathing automatically resumes without any harm being done. Try gently blowing on their face, or splashing it with a little cold water, to help them catch their breath. If this happens on more than one occasion, however, consult your doctors.

5. Once the tantrum is over you may want to cuddle and comfort them, or just go on as if nothing has happened. Either response is satisfactory.

6. Distracting their attention, or making them laugh can help speed the tantrum on its way. One mother, after her three-year-old had been yelling her head off, appeared with their pet cat dressed in a dolls overcoat. 'You're making such a din puss can't stand it any more,' she announced, 'so he's taking me out for a walk.' The little girl stopped bawling in amazement then burst into delighted laughter.

7. Talk about the tantrum when your child has calmed down. You might say something like: 'You really were angry with me today . . . ' Discussing these powerful, and often frightening, feelings calmly helps your child to cope with them more effectively.

8. Tantrums tend to increase at times of family changes or upheavals, such as the birth of a new baby or a home move. These are signs that your child is feeling a bit unloved or neglected and wants more attention. Provide this, but not immediately after a tantrum to avoid turning it into an attention seeking habit.

   While tantrums usually end with the start of school, you may not have seen the last of them. They can reappear around the early teens, when you have a repeat performance of shouting, yelling, and slamming doors. As with infants, teenage tantrums result from conflicts between a desire for independence and family rules or restrictions. Remember that the emotional energy which fuels a tantrum is also a powerful force for growth. Once your child learns how to tame and manage those emotional tempests the same energy will help him or her become an assertive, confident and self-possessed adult.

Helping the 'difficult' child

Tantrums apart, some children can be fairly described as 'difficult'. These youngsters are usually gravely disadvantaged in preschool. Not just because of the negative labelling I mentioned above, but because being so busy 'being difficult' they have insufficient time for learning. The sooner such problems can be resolved, the less damage they will cause to educational prospects.

Difficult children are hard to handle. Some may be disobedient and disruptive, others prone to prolonged sulks. All try your patience to the limits. 'I usually end up slapping my badly behaved four-year-old', one mother admitted, while agreeing physical punishment did nothing to improve his behaviour. Nor is it likely to! Difficult children are showing signs of inner conflicts and the only way of helping them is by getting to the root of such problems. There are six main reasons why children behave badly:

To gain attention. As an only child Judy, aged four, was quiet, affectionate and obedient. All that changed after her baby brother was born. The little girl's anger at no longer being her parent's centre of attention led to disobedience and even spiteful attacks on the baby.

From frustration. This arises when a child's wishes are thwarted, perhaps because adults forbid a desired activity or out of a lack of skill. Frustrated at not being able to read as well as his eight-year-old sister, Alex, aged five, tore her books to shreds.

Out of anger. A preschooler who feels angry towards adults or older children may express this powerful emotion by aggressing against those smaller or weaker than themselves. Such youngsters are often condemned as bullies but there is nothing personal in such attacks. Other angry youngsters will attack property rather than people, often causing expensive damage through vandalism.

Due to depression. Often caused by emotional stress. Once a child's capacity for coping with painful feelings has been exhausted they may withdraw into themselves. After his parents' marriage had failed, Mark, aged five, changed from a cheerful extrovert to a sulky young-ster who rebuffed any attempts at friendship.

Because of anxiety. Which can be a cause of bad behaviour in class. Being expelled from the class allows an anxious child to avoid the fear that lessons arouse.

Due to a negative self-image. Resulting from the child being told he is lazy, stupid, naughty or wicked. In time those hurtful descrip-tions are internalized, and they begin to see themselves as others apparently see them. In order to help, you should first try and identify which of these causes is most likely to be responsible. It is useful to keep a diary in which you carefully note down everything that hap-pens before, during and after your child's outburst. This is sometimes called the ABC method of recording behaviour. It stands for *Antecedent*: what happened immediately before the bad behaviour? Did any particular situation or circumstance trigger the conduct? Is this a pattern which gets repeated under similar circumstances? *Behaviour*: exactly what the child said or did, observed as carefully and objectively as possible. How long did the outburst last? *Consequence*: what was the outcome of their bad behaviour? Did the child in some way gain from their misconduct? A youngster who feels neglected, for instance, may look on even a scolding as more desirable than inattention. Monitor your child's actions for two weeks without trying to change it. This provides a baseline of difficult behaviour which you can work gradually to reduce.

If, for instance, there were ten incidents of misbehaviour during the observation period, a realistic starting goal might be to reduce these to five over the next 14 days. The following fortnight bring them down to three, eliminating most or all within six weeks. If you can remove the cause of their emotional difficulties the bad behaviour will often disappear almost immediately. Start rewarding your child more when they do things of which you approve. Many parents tend to take good conduct for granted while only noticing bad behaviour. Notice and praise any conduct you wish to encourage. Never try talking to your child when you are both very het up. It is impossible to have a worth-while discussion when angry or upset. Allow time for you both to cool down before trying to discuss as rationally and non-judgementally as possible the reasons for their behaviour. Having identified likely causes you can then make practical suggestions about ways in which their conduct could be improved.

Judy became her former, affectionate self after being given more attention and greater responsibility. 'I realized how much we had been shutting her out in our excitement over the new baby,' said her mother. 'Once she was reassured and, as she saw it, restored in our love, the disobedience and spitefulness disappeared.' Similarly Alex's hatred for books ceased after his mother gave him extra reading practice so he no longer felt humiliated by his relative lack of skill.

Always make certain your child has really listened to and understood your orders or instructions. Very active youngsters are sometimes seen to be disobedient because they never really heard what was said. Come down to their level, hold his or her head gently but firmly between your palms and make your requirements known clearly and slowly. Ask him or her to repeat them back to ensure they have properly understood just what is expected. Only once this is done to your satisfaction should they be allowed to leave. It is easy and natural to blame the difficult child for the upsets they cause. But very often such children believe they are behaving reasonably in what they regard as impossibly difficult situations.

Stimulating your child's mind

So far we have concentrated mainly on emotional enrichment during your child's first five years. I have done this because the way they feel about learning and about themselves as somebody capable or incapable of mastering new skills is fundamental to educational fulfilment. The confident child who has a strong, positive, self-image will persist in the face of set-backs and will be willing to take the risks on which, as I explained at the start of this book, all successful learning demands. But this is not to say that intellectual stimulation should take a back seat in the preschool years. Far from it.

There is ample evidence, from neurological studies, that the more stimulation (and the wider the variety of that stimulation) the developing brain receives, the greater the number of neural pathways and interconnections created. As Glenn Doman, founder of The Institutes For The Achievement of Human Potential, has commented, 'The brain is the only container which gets bigger the more you put into it.'

During these early years your child's brain is capable of greater intellectual development, of the most fundamental kind, than at any other time during their entire life. Let's take one example. The auditory nerves, by which sounds travel to the brain, are 'fine tuned' to the language, or languages, to which a child is exposed. Pathways receiving the greatest stimulation are enhanced while those receiving little or none, decline.

This means that a child whose native tongue is Spanish has their auditory pathways differentially tuned to sounds of between 300 and 500 cycles per second (known as Hertz, abbreviated to Hz) since these are the dominant frequencies of the Spanish language. English, however, has a higher average frequency of around 1000Hz. This means a child hearing only English during their first years will never hear Spanish in exactly the same way as a native speaker. When, later in life, they attempt to learn Spanish no amount of fluency is likely to overcome those subtle discrepancies of accent which betray the non-native speaker to one brought up with that language. Interestingly Slavic languages have a very wide frequency range, making it easier for a child who masters one of them to become proficient in another even in adulthood. The bottom line of this message is simple: don't waste the first five years, and constantly provide your child with stimulation of every type.

Games should include the chance to experiment with as wide as possible a range of materials: paint, paper, cardboard, plasticine, Lego, play dough, fabrics such as silk and cotton, pebbles, twigs, leaves, grass, the list is virtually endless. Expose them to music of all kind, not only pop or solely the classics. Use outings to the park, shops, country and seaside as opportunities to teach, not in a formal, structured way, but informally and, wherever possible, practically. Remember that during this period of development your child may find it impossible to grasp abstractions. So keep your teaching firmly rooted in hands-on experience.

Watch out for the kind of 'learning opportunities' I mentioned earlier in connection with the good preschool environment. Encourage questions by providing thoughtful and interesting answers. If possible those answers should be of the 'let's find out', practical type. For example when four-year-old Ben visited the seaside he was intrigued by the yachts in a marina. 'Wood floats,' he said, 'but metal doesn't. How do metal boats float?' A theoretical explanation would clearly have been little use. But his question gave rise to a fascinating beachside lesson as he and his father scavenged around for different objects, such as plastic bottles, cans, pieces of drift wood, pebbles and so on, some of which floated and some of which sank without trace.

Fantasy play

Most parents expect their children to indulge in occasional fantasy games, to spend some time in a land of make-believe. Many, however, become concerned or even irritated if they slip away into fantasy too frequently. Experts too have, in the past, voiced alarm over make-believe. Freud regarded fantasy as a sign of unfulfilled needs and desires, while even Marie Montessori condemned make-believe as a 'pathological tendency of early childhood.'

Other parents resist fantasy from the belief that it's somehow unhealthy for a child to develop too strong an imagination. 'I don't want any nonsense being drummed into my son's head,' the father of a five-year-old insisted after finding his child playing a game of make-believe. Such views significantly underestimate the vital importance of fantasy in intellectual, emotional and even social development. After the age of three, children not only enjoy games of pretence but need them to nourish the mind just as much as they need food and drink to build the body. Later they draw on these experiences when writing imaginatively and teachers report they make far more interesting and stimulating students.

Dr L Singer, a clinical psychologist at Yale University, has shown that make-believe helps a child become more creative as well as a better, more flexible, problem solver. Other studies suggest it helps increase attention span, improve self-control and enhance the ability to interact and communicate with other children. High fantisizers, who are more likely to be only or older children than middle or younger ones, are less aggressive and express themselves more fluently than children whose make-believe skills are poorly developed.

Dr Sophie Lovinger of Central Michigan University, for example, found that children encouraged to enjoy free play fantasizing, pretending for instance they were cooking, shopping or looking after a baby, used significantly more words and achieved a higher score on a standard test, the Verbal Expression Scale.

To encourage fantasy play, follow these simple rules:

1. Provide a quiet, private place in which to play. A child can't get involved with make-believe if the television is blaring away in one

corner. Plenty of props are needed around which to create the fantasy, dressing-up clothes, pots and pans, construction toys, and dolls as well as simpler things such as cartons to be turned into pirate ships, paper rolls that become telescopes, a sheet-draped table to transform into Aladdin's cave. Do not insist on meticulous order, what seems like a mess to you is a rich environment for the child.

2. Be careful about sending out subtle, non-verbal, signals of disapproval, such as the slight frown of irritation when your child describes some elaborate fantasy. Instead join in and elaborate that fantasy. Ask questions about what they saw, did and said in that world of make-believe. When Susan was playing a make-believe game of mixing up a magic fizzy drink potion which turned her into all kinds of animals, her mother encouraged the four-year-old with questions like, 'Is it fizzing on your tongue now?'

3. If your child has difficulty fantasizing, provide suitable props and prompts. Take an everyday object, and play a game to see how many different uses your child can come up with for it. For example, a wooden pole could be a fishing rod, the mast of a pirate ship, the bar for invisible weights, part of a banner, a sword, pogo stick or a musical instrument.

Reading and story telling is another excellent way to develop the imagination. Use different voices for the characters and provide sound effects. Encourage your child to do the same. Meal and bath times provide valuable opportunities for the busiest parent to initiate a fantasy, such as going on a voyage or keeping shop.

Always show a positive attitude towards pretending, and seize any opportunities which offer themselves for make-believe play. 'The job of early education is to excite children about learning not cram it down their throat,' says Professor Lilian Katz. My sentiments entirely.

The most important goal for your child to attain during this preschool period is to begin a love affair with learning. To be thrilled and inspired by the prospect of acquiring and using new knowledge. To become what I described in Chapter One as a 'Don't knower' who *can* know rather than a 'Can't knower' who can never know.

Light the fires of interest during the first six months of life and you will be able to help fan those flames into a burning desire for achievement and fulfilment in the years of formal education that follow.

4

RIGHT FROM THE START

After the play orientated atmosphere of a nursery school, the start of full-time primary education can come as a disagreeable surprise to many children. From being among the older children in a group of tinies, they find themselves at the bottom of the learning ladder.

To make matters worse the high teacher to child ratio of one to seven or better present in nursery education, abruptly changes to around one teacher for thirty children. Which means that from having every need instantly attended to, your child may find him- or herself struggling hard to catch the teacher's eye. This means that even with project-based teaching (*see page 54*) it is not possible for a teacher to provide every child with undivided attention. This makes your active participation in providing guidance, encouragement, and practice, more important than ever if your child is to make good progress with the basic skills of reading, writing and arithmetic. In this part of the book, I shall explain how best to provide that practical help so that your child is given the very best start in their school career.

Choosing your child's first school

Today's primary schools may be so different from the one you attended, many teaching methods and terms, like 'emergent writing', 'project-based teaching' or 'vertical grouping' are likely to be unfamiliar. This can make it hard to judge just how good a particular school is and whether its style would suit your child.

Since the National Curriculum was introduced, all *State* schools are obliged to follow a core curriculum of English, mathematics, and science and technology, with additional subjects such as history and geography also included. Although the teaching emphasis varies from school to school, every child has to be tested in the core subjects at the age of seven. When making your choice keep these four issues in mind. They will help you to ask the right questions during visits to schools and, just as important, make sense of the answers!

Subjects taught

Narrow curriculum. A more traditional approach to teaching with an emphasis on the 'three Rs' of reading, writing and arithmetic.

In favour. Your child will receive a thorough grounding in basic literacy and numeracy skills.

Against. Some children find this approach dull and become demotivated to learning. If your child has other talents, such as creativity, these may not be sufficiently developed.

Broad curriculum. Similar to that found in the majority of infant schools, a broad curriculum covers not only basic literacy and numeracy, but also significant amounts of other subjects such as art, music, science, social and environmental studies, games, drama and religious education.

In favour. Your child's talents will be more broadly developed.

Against. Your child is likely to make slower initial progress with the 'three Rs'.

Class size

The Government's recommendation is for a maximum of 35 children, and although most reception classes aim for less than 25 a recent study showed over a quarter of primary school children in England were being taught in classes of more than 30.

Small classes. With 20 pupils or less these allow your child greater individual attention, leading to greater security and confidence. Recent research has shown a link between lifelong educational attainment and a high teacher to pupil ratio in primary schools.

Larger classes. Offer your child greater opportunities for making friends.

Against. Some children, especially rather underconfident or timid ones, find the numbers and noise of a large class overwhelming and have difficulty in concentrating.

How the classes are organized

This depends on several factors, including the amount of space available, staffing levels, number of pupils and the preference of the head teacher. Two main systems exist.

Horizontal grouping. Children of the same age work together in class divided by year groups. In larger schools expect to find two or three year groups running in parallel.

In favour. Teachers find it easier to keep track of each child's progress since they stay with the same group from one year to the next.

Against. Classes can be large.

Vertical or family grouping. These classes contain a mix of five-, six- and seven-year-olds. Sometimes children of the same ability are grouped together, sometimes children of different abilities are mixed.

In favour. When the numbers of children in a particular age group are unequal, for instance 50 five-year-olds, 14 six-year-olds and 20 seven-year-olds, this method allows class sizes to be balanced. Older children gain more confidence by helping smaller ones while younger children may learn faster through working alongside older pupils.

Against. It is more difficult to ensure every child covers all aspects of the curriculum. If the teacher is inefficient some may fall behind undetected.

How lessons are taught

A large number of factors influence teaching methods, including the school's culture, whether traditional or more modern, teacher preferences, and class size and structure. In most schools you will find a mixture of group work, directed activities, children working in pairs and individual projects. However the emphasis given to each varies greatly.

Whole class work. The whole class is set a task by the teacher, who then helps children complete it one-on-one.

In favour. All aspects of the curriculum will be covered methodically. Progress is easier to monitor and children having difficulties can be identified and given special help.

Against. There will be a wide range of abilities and maturity levels even in a single age class. This can leave brighter children feeling bored as the slower ones catch up, or slower learners falling behind as others race ahead.

Group work. The class is divided into groups, some working independently, others under supervision, others playing games. The groups are moved around so that each child gets the same amount of personal attention from teachers.

In favour. The teacher can set your child tasks most appropriate to their particular abilities. Those in need of help with a particular subject can receive it promptly. Children working in a group also learn valuable social lessons about sharing and co-operating. They are also encouraged to solve problems unaided and find things out for themselves.

Against. A disruptive child can do a lot of damage, while industrious ones may find themselves doing most of the work on a project. Finally, if the teacher is not up to their job, children with difficulties may slip through the net.

Project-based teaching. Several aspects of the curriculum are brought together as the whole class works to find out as much as they can about a particular topic. The time set aside for projects varies greatly between schools, depending largely on teacher preference. Some favour a traditional 'chalk and talk' approach while others stress the value of projects in learning.

In favour. Children enjoy taking part in a project which captures their imaginations. The variety of tasks involved is usually stimulating and satisfies the young child's need to find out about the world around them. Projects help develop a range of individual and social skills, such as observing and recording information, asking questions, group discussions, perseverance and taking notes.

Against. If a child loses interest half-way through a project it becomes a disincentive to learning. Other areas where you may want to question teachers are in their approach to reading, writing and arithmetic. There are several different ways of teaching these basic skills, some of which may prove more effective with your child than others. I will be discussing these later in this part of the book, when describing the best ways of helping your child develop literacy and numeracy skills.

If your child says – 'I don't want to go!'

It's the first morning of your child's first day at school. In a few moments you'll be watching them walk away to start more than 15,000 hours of full-time education. If there are tears in their eyes and a lump in your throat don't worry. Research has shown that four out of five primary school children have difficulty settling down in class. Even if they have visited the school before, know some of the teachers, have a friend or older brother or sister at the same school and are warmly welcomed by friendly staff, there will still be tears, reluctance and anxiety. Less expected, and for most parents more worrying, are the emotional upsets which occur a few weeks into the first term. Just when you thought your child had settled down to the new routine, they can suddenly show signs of distress (*see box*).

This is what happened to five-year-old Billy soon after he started school. 'We didn't anticipate any difficulties because he'd longed to begin school so as to be like his big brother James,' his mother Julia told me. 'The night before term began was like Christmas Eve he was so excited. When I said goodbye at the school gate, he ran eagerly into the playground with hardly a backward glance.' Sadly, within a fortnight, Billy's enthusiasm had vanished along with most of his self-confidence. 'We noticed the change after just a few days,' Julia remembers. 'He became moody and tearful, pleading with me to let him stay at home.'

While not every child looks forward to starting school as much as Billy, the little boy's reaction is far from unusual. There are a number of reasons why children suffer from the new school blues, and several practical steps you can take to ease the process of settling into learning.

Six warning signs of new school blues

- Lack of enthusiasm and energy.
- Becoming irritable and edgy.
- Loss of appetite.
- Disturbed sleep.
- Grows tearful for no apparent reason.
- Increase in minor illnesses such as tummy upsets.

Possible problem 1 – separation anxiety

The first source of difficulty is unhappiness over being parted from you. This is most likely with an only child who lacks playgroup or nursery school experience. The trauma of suddenly being away from home for a large part of the day can create considerable distress.

Ask whether your child would go to school more happily if you were able to stay? Is he or she equally miserable before going out to a party or to play with friends? If the answer is 'yes', it is likely your child is afraid of parting from you rather than going to school. This is an extremely common problem, especially among children who find it hard to form a close relationship with their mothers during the first two years. If your child resists changes, has difficulty in making friends or is very timid, choose a school which allows you maximum involvement.

How you can help

Never become irritated. Sometimes parents get cross, dismissing the protests as nonsense and scolding, threatening, bribing or even smacking the reluctant child. Anger is the worst possible reaction, as it only leaves your child even more distressed and confused. Talk to your child calmly and patiently. Try to find out whether there is any special reason for their panic. This is especially important when relucance follows a period of cheerful acceptance. Is your child being bullied (*see page 62*) or has there been an upset with a new teacher? Have they fallen out with a friend, is a favourite teacher away from class, has he or she had an accident and wet themselves the previous day?

Be patient. Some children express their distress through tantrums rather than tears, and you could find yourself going through a rerun of the terrible twos. Remain calm and refuse to rise to the bait. Turning a a blind eye to minor naughtiness speeds emotional adjustment.

Explain the purpose of school. Make certain your child knows *why* they are going to school in the first place. This is less likely to be necessary for a child with brothers or sisters already in full-time education. But a first or only child, especially those without nursery experience, can be baffled by the whole process. My own mother tells me, that I loved my first day in class. But on day two, when she came to take me to school, my response was utter bewilderment. 'But I've done that!' I insisted.

Children who don't properly understand what lessons and learning are all about, may regard being sent to school as a punishment for some act of naughtiness they can no longer recall. As a result they feel guilty, resentful and rejected.

Never tease over tears. Never tease or scold a tearful child, or allow an older brother or sister to do so. Some parents do this on the mistaken assumption that sarcastic comments will make the child feel ashamed of their unhappiness. This is most likely to happen with boys whose fathers have rather 'macho' notions of the male role, and look on tears, even at the age of five, as unacceptable 'weakness'.

Make goodbyes brisk and brief. At the school gate, part affectionately but briefly. The longer it takes the more emotional you are both liable to become. And seeing you distressed will only make your child even more upset. A quick kiss and a cuddle, then having made sure your child is safely inside the school gates, walk away without looking back.

Describe your own day. An especially apprehensive child can be reassured by being told what you will be doing during the day. Some children are fearful of going to school because they worry about something dreadful happening to you in their absence. But avoid attempting to cheer your child up by describing the exciting things you'll be doing together after school. This makes lessons seem like a disagreeable intrusion into their lives, instead of an essential and potentially rewarding experience.

Talk about their day. Encourage a discussion of what your child will be doing in school. Chatting about lessons makes them seem more familiar and less intimidating.

Discuss the problem with your partner. While separation anxiety usually stems from the mother-child relationship, it is important for both parents to be involved.

Consult your child's teacher. Don't be afraid to share your concerns with the school. See the class or head teacher, with your partner, whenever possible, and discuss possible solutions, such as getting a family friend or neighbour to take them to school or having them home for lunch. But resist the temptation of immediately changing schools. Unless the problem is solved it will simply accompany your child to the next one. A change should only be considered if the teachers seem unable or unwilling to help and your child has *never* gone confidently to that school.

Possible problem 2 – coping with new experiences

A second source of difficulty is your child's need to cope with change and novelty. These include not only the unfamiliar intellectual demands of lessons but the seemingly endless succession of new experiences associated with starting school. Experiences such as getting used to a very different routine, finding classrooms, meeting strangers, discovering where to go for meals, where to wash, leave clothes, learning the school rules – even the most easy-going primary school has at least some of these – developing self-discipline, taking part in group projects and so on.

For a child used to the settled, familiar, and far less mentally taxing routine of home life with Mum all this can prove an overwhelming experience. Although such challenges are present from the first day of term they tend to be less threatening during a settling in period which lasts two or three weeks. Teachers make fewer demands on newcomers and are more prepared to overlook or excuse mistakes. Once this 'honeymoon' period is over, however, they naturally become somewhat less tolerant and more demanding. It is at this point the new school blues may begin.

How you can help

Develop routines at home. Develop a home routine with periods set aside for reading, drawing and playing. Learning to follow a schedule at home makes it easier for your child to adapt to a timetable in school. This also encourages the discipline of studying at set times, especially necessary when homework begins and, later in their school careers, when examination revision starts.

Talk over worries. Encourage your child to discuss any difficulties and help resolve these by talking with their teachers, studying school books and working through lessons together. When talking over problems be sure to remain patient and nonjudgmental. Criticizing your child's intellectual abilities or comparing them unfavourably with another child will only make things worse.

Possible problem 3 – unrealistic expectations

Struggling to satisfy adult expectations is a major cause of stress for some children. This is most likely to afflict children with an overly perfectionist attitude towards their achievements. For some coming second in a class test can prove almost as devastating as being last. If you have always set high standards and, perhaps, been critical of anything less than total success you could be putting your child at risk from this source of stress.

How you can help

Become less demanding. Help by becoming rather less perfectionist. Continue to notice successes but don't show displeasure at setbacks. Remember that making mistakes, and then learning from them, is an essential part of successful studying.

Never give the impression, however unintentionally, that you will love or respect your child any the less if they fail to achieve all you hoped for. Far from undermining performance, the opposite approach encourages the anxious child to work harder and become more relaxed in their approach to learning.

Possible problem 4 – loneliness

When I first met six-year-old Tamsin she was very much a break-time wallflower. While the other children in her class played happily together, she just looked on without making any attempt to join in. Asked whether she wouldn't like to take part in the fun, she just stared down at her feet and silently shook her head. When I asked her why, Tamsin's only response was an even sadder expression, followed by a whispered: 'They don't like playing with me!'

There are many children like Tamsin. Shy, timid, youngsters who, seemingly unable or unwilling to make friends, are condemned to loneliness and rejection. Certain personality traits and behaviours increase the risk of unpopularity. Being regarded as selfish or aggressive, a cry baby or a poor loser are frequent reasons for rejection. On other occasions, however, loneliness is due to events beyond your child's control.

Because children are very conformist, anything which makes a newcomer stand out from the crowd can also become a reason for their rejection. A child who is brighter, or duller than their companions, for instance may be mocked and ostracized. Differences in accent, dress or appearance, or even having an unusual name all increase the risk of social rejection. So too does an absence of shared interests, such as not being able to play football, enjoy pop music or know exactly what's happening in a popular TV soap.

Your child, especially if she is a girl, may also become a casualty of the fickle nature of childhood friendships. Yesterday's 'best friend in the world' can easily become today's 'most hateful person I know', leaving a child abandoned and alone. Although such squabbles are usually soon forgotten, a few children feel so wounded by the rejection that they stop even trying to make friends. Another common cause of isolation is the physical distance between classroom and home. Children from the same form often spend a lot of their time playing together out of school. If your child lives so far away that it is impossible to join in they may be excluded from that circle of potential friends.

Starting at school, changing to a new school, or even moving up in class, for instance, can mean saying goodbye to old friends. Children, especially boys, tend to be clannish, admitting a new child to their 'gang' only reluctantly. It usually takes time for even an outgoing, confident and socially adept newcomer to gain acceptance. For the timid, unsure and less socially competent youngster that admission can be a long time coming. Some shy children become so discouraged by constant rejection that they abandon all hopes of ever joining in. Some youngsters, especially those without brothers or sisters, are shunned by companions simply because they can't play properly. Playing seems such a natural activity, that many adults fail to realize it must be mastered in early childhood.

How you can help

Pinpoint the cause of the problem. If you suspect your child is having difficulty making friends at school (*see box on page 62*) start by identifying the cause of his or her social difficulties. The most obvious way is by asking what's going wrong. Unfortunately many children are extremely reluctant to talk about their feelings, because they are ashamed, fear your criticism, or just can't put into words what is going wrong. Like Tamsin they may take refuge in a usually mistaken generalization, ('Nobody likes me') blame other children, ('They are all too rough') or simply become tongued-tied and tearful.

During such discussions, therefore, it is essential to sound reassuring and be nonjudgemental. A rejected child feels especially unwanted and emotionally vulnerable. Watching your child in social encounters outside school sometimes offers valuable insights into what's causing their isolation.

It can also be helpful, in some cases, to ask a child to draw the playground or classroom, showing themselves in relation to the other children and teachers. No great artistic skill is necessary to produce an often highly revealing portrait of their school life. Sandy, a lonely seven-year-old, for instance depicted herself as a small, solitary figure standing at the far corner of a huge, open expanse of playground, while all the other children – represented by far larger and more aggressive-looking stick men – were enjoying themselves down the far end. Another way of using art to identify problems is by asking your child to draw all the people, children and teachers, they know best. Research has shown that the more detailed such a drawing, the greater the liking for that person. On the other hand where details of clothing and features are barely sketched in, the child feels a negative emotion, either fear or hostility, towards that individual. By comparing the detail of different drawings – which should be completed over a period of days to prevent fatigue – you can usually get a good idea of attitudes towards the subject.

Throw a party. Invite other children around for tea, or games. Even if only one friendship develops as a result of these invitations it will help boost your child's confidence and remove their sense of rejection.

Reduce differences. Where you can reduce or eliminate some of the differences between your child and others, then do so. Sometimes something as simple as a change of hairstyle or clothes makes a big difference.

Teach social skills. Help your child to develop social skills likely to improve acceptance. Encouraging them to be good losers, share toys and co-operate with others will increase popularity.

Teach a leisure skill. Coaching in some popular leisure activity can greatly increase popularity. A child selected for the school swimming team, for example, will make plenty of friends.

Teach them to laugh at teasing. It is important that your child learns to conceal hurt at being rejected. Showing they are upset only increases the risk of further rejection and teasing. A smiling child who can laugh at a joke against themselves, will win many more friends than one who gets angry or sulks.

Provide a playtime game. Giving your child something to play with during break time, such as a model or a puzzle, helps time pass more quickly and disguises their isolation. It also acts as a magnet, attracting children intrigued by such an absorbing activity and eager to join in.

Is your child a playground wallflower?

(Tick any statements which apply.)

Your child . . .

- Has few friends at school.
- Rarely brings anybody home to play.
- Seldom invites friends for tea.
- Dislikes team sports.
- Is very shy.
- Never talks about friends in class.
- Is reluctant to join in games at home.
- Is an only child.

Score Risk factor
0–2 Low
3–5 Moderate
6–8 High

Possible problem 5 – bullying

Sadly the problem of bullying is by no means confined to children starting school. It exists right across the age range and can cause tremendous worry, pain and distress to children. On some occasions chronic bullying has even led to suicide attempts. For this reason my practical suggestions for dealing with this pernicious source of anxiety could equally well apply at middle and secondary level. However, I have chosen to deal with it here because, clearly a child bullied when first starting school is in many ways far more vulnerable. He, or she, lacks the maturity to put even minor incidents of teasing into perspective and may become so frightened by school that their entire educational career is perpetually blighted. The earlier any such difficulties are nipped in the bud, therefore, the better it will be for your child's happiness and achievement.

Bullying is more widespread than many parents realize and need not involve physical abuse leaving visible scars. Silent intimidation or verbal mockery can cause just as much damage to confidence and self-esteem. When Sue discovered her seven-year-old son, Jamie, was being mercilessly bullied by a bigger boy, her first thought was to exact revenge. 'I just wanted to hurt him as badly as he'd hurt Jamie,' she admits. 'Then I realized that by doing so I'd simply be a bully myself.'

The misery of a bullied child can be so heart rending it's only natural for parents to feel like giving the bully a taste of their own medicine. But however understandable, this does not help either child. Although it's obviously difficult for parents to feel much sympathy towards their child's tormentors, the bully is just as much in need of assistance as the victim.

The belief that bullying is something most children indulge in, but grow out of, is untrue. A long-term study of 800 children has shown it may last a lifetime. Adults who were bullied when young are often aggressive and anti-social, more likely to be in trouble with the law and to use violence against their own children. While bullies are usually larger, stronger and less clever than children of the same age, the child who is persistently bullied is usually rather shy, quiet, anxious and submissive. Children who never manage to make friends or join in group play are especially at risk. Equally vulnerable are youngsters who have some physical handicap such as a stammer, limp, or visible birthmark. Shunned by playmates they can easily become the target of a bully. If you suspect your child is being bullied or prone to bullying (*see box on page 62*) here are practical ways to help.

How you can help – if your child is bullied

Build emotional strength. Never encourage your child to fight back by teaching them judo, boxing or a similar form of self-defence since this is merely playing the bully at their own game. It is far more sensible and useful to help your child acquire strong psychological defences, so that they are able to respond with amused indifference instead of the fear and tears on which the bully's ego feeds. The greater your child's confidence and self-esteem the easier they will find it to resist teasing, mockery or threats.

Encourage them to see their would-be tormentors as weak and pathetic, rather than fierce and fearful. Children who refuse to rise to the bait make poor victims who are soon abandoned in favour of more responsive prey.

Develop play skills. If your child lacks play skills, encourage them to learn a sport – not necessarily a team game – and to make as many friends as possible. A child surrounded by allies is most unlikely to be singled out as a victim. The last thing a bully wants is to be ganged up against by a group.

Talk to their teacher. With a child aged eight and over, complaining to teachers or the tormentor's parents should be a last resort only adopted where the bullying is persistent or violent. Bullying should, however, be reported immediately when your child is under eight and regularly bullied. Children of this age find it very hard to defend themselves, especially against attacks by older boys. When discussing the problem, with either the teacher or parents, remain calm and express your concerns firmly but in a nonaggressive manner.

If your child bullies

Now let's look at the other side of the coin. What happens if you discover, or suspect your child is a bully? (*see box on page 65*) Ironically bullying is the one piece of misbehaviour most likely to turn parents into bullies themselves. When Martin learned that his nine-year-old had been tormenting younger children, he marched the boy up to his bedroom, pulled down his pants and spanked him hard with a hair brush. No action could have been more calculated to make matters worse. How can a child ever learn that bullying and hurting people smaller and younger is wrong if they are the victims of identical treatment?

How you can help

Set an example. The essential first step towards curing the bullying child is to set a good example at home. Children copy the way parents respond to situations. Children who are beaten adopt the same tactics on other youngsters. Never physically punish your child – I would say under any circumstances – but especially not for bullying, no matter how much their behaviour may have angered you.

Teach practical skills. Try to discover whether your child lacks certain social skills which prevent them from playing co-operatively with other children. The bully is often a socially incompetent child unable to make an impression or to gain attention other than through violence. Do what you can to teach those missing skills and show them ways of achieving popularity and acclaim – perhaps by mastering a sport – other than through being the school bully. If your child is big for their age, encourage them to join groups of slightly older children with whom size will no longer be a problem.

Is your child at risk of becoming a bully?

(Tick any statements which apply.)

Your child . . .

- Is big for his/her age.
- Is self-willed.
- Demands to be the centre of attention.
- Always wants to get his/her own way.
- Is an only child.
- Is frequently spanked or smacked for misbehaviour.
- Is often in trouble.
- Is disobedient.
- Does poorly in class.
- Has few close friends.

Score: In both cases the higher the score the greater the chances of your child being bullied or bullying. 0–3 Very low risk; 3–6 Moderate risk; 7 + High risk.

Teaching your child independence

A child is less likely either to bully, or become the bully's victim, if he or she has strong self-esteem. This develops from an independent outlook which enables even young children to welcome taking at least some responsibility for their own lives.

In class, the independent child is more likely to use their head and think things through for themselves than to accept a majority view. Such independence of thought becomes increasingly crucial as your child progresses through school and has to accept more and more responsibility for studying and learning. Independence is also closely related to self-discipline, another vital ingredient in virtually any type of achievement. Raising an independent child involves a delicate balance between avoiding needless risks and actively encouraging self-reliance. It is probably one of the toughest yet most essential lessons your child will ever learn. There are three dependency creating traps into which families all too easily stumble.

Carbon copy children are brought up by parents who blindly follow their own childhood experiences. Where unquestioning obedience was required of them, that is what they demand from their child. If no discipline was imposed, their children are raised in a free-and-easy atmosphere. Yet because every child has different emotional needs, and society changes so rapidly, it is essential to adopt a flexible attitude towards all child rearing practices.

Looking glass children are taught to reflect their parent's attitudes, opinions and beliefs. As a result their ability to think and act independently is severely restricted.

Cotton wool children are protected from even the slightest risk. Far from reducing anxiety such an upbringing leads to insecurity and a reluctance to take any chances as adults. The key to independence is strong self-confidence and self-esteem. Children possessing these qualities will automatically want to think and act for themselves. Motivated by a healthy need for achievement, rather than chronic fear of failure they co-operate without becoming overly dependent on the approval of others. While there are no firm rules for raising such a self-reliant child, the following suggestions should prove helpful:

1. Never give the impression that being loved depends on conforming to your wishes. Love must always be unconditional. That doesn't, of course, mean approving every action. But where rules are broken, your disapproval should be directed at the behaviour rather than at the child. Saying, for example: 'That was a bad thing to do . . . ' instead of telling a child: 'You are a bad person for doing that . . . '

2. Family rules should be kept to a minimum but imposed consistently. Few things create greater emotional insecurity than discipline which is strictly imposed one day only to be ignored the next. Both you and your partner must show a united front when imposing agreed rules. If a child realizes they can play one parent against the other, respect for authority is rapidly undermined.

3. Have *Do* rather than *Don't* rules. These are easier for a child to understand and for you to monitor. For instance, the instruction: 'Don't be untidy . . . ' is hard for a child to interpret, since their

notions of what it takes to be tidy could be quite different from your own! As a result they may feel a sense of grievance when scolded for breaking a rule they firmly believed was being obeyed. A rule which states: 'Put your toys away after playing,' avoids any such confusion.

Agree these rules with your child, explaining the reason behind each and, perhaps, pinning the list on your family notice board so there can be no excuse for ignorance.

4. Control the risks in your child's life instead of trying to safeguard him or her from all hazards.

Many things your child will want to do later on, from cycling in traffic to learning swimming, involve certain dangers. The only way to deal with such unavoidable risks is through professional instruction. Help arrange such tuition and, where necessary, check up on the expertise of instructors and conditions under which lessons will be given. If your child wants to learn swimming, for example, a good precaution is to inspect the pool, meet the instructors and find out how many non-swimmers will be supervised at each session.

5. Allow your child a genuine say in family decision making. Some parents pay lip service to such democracy by only taking any notice of a child's wishes when these coincide with their own. This is both frustrating and demoralizing.

6. Encourage your child to tackle challenges just beyond their present grasp. Assessing each new goal demands careful judgement and a good understanding of your child's current level of ability. Consistent failure will lead to a loss of confidence and motivation. Yet success which comes too easily is equally harmful to self-esteem. The child who can honestly say, 'I never believed I'd succeed but I did . . . ' has taken an important step along the road to independence.

The importance of positive emotions

I have discussed the social and emotional aspects of starting school at some length, because these provide the soil in which learning either blossoms or withers and dies. The lonely, anxious, timid child will have very great difficulty in taking those risks on which successful learning and problem solving depend. This is not to say, of course,

How much independence is your child allowed?

(Rate the statements below as follows: 5 = Strongly agree; 4 = Agree; 3 = Neither agree nor disagree; 2 = Disagree; 1 = Strongly disagree.)

Parents should ...
- Make their child's life as trouble free as possible.
- Spare their child disappointments.
- Know how their child feels.
- Know exactly what their child is doing at all times.
- Take all important decisions for their child.
- Expect absolute loyalty from their child.
- Never allow a child to question their judgement.
- Forbid their child to criticize them.
- Demand complete obedience from their child.
- Read their child's private diary to check on them.
- Enter their child's bedroom without asking permission.
- Discuss their child's worries with them.
- Censor any upsetting programmes on TV.
- Ensure their child doesn't get their own way too often.
- Insist on respect from their child.
- Make every sacrifice for their child.
- Inspire some fear in their child.
- Never show emotions in front of their child.
- Put pressure on their child to work hard.
- Always have the last say in any decision.

Score	Independence allowed
20–35	Very High
36–50	Moderate
51–75	Low
76–100	Very Low

The higher the score, the more barriers to independence you are creating. The result, however well intentioned, could do lasting harm to your child's intellectual, emotional and social development. While children need protection they must also be allowed to confront challenges, get into and out of scrapes, suffer disappointments, experience rejection and learn from their mistakes.

that isolated youngsters cannot excel. Indeed some of the world's greatest geniuses were lonely, misunderstood children in school. They may, indeed, have used intensive studying as a means of compensating for their social alienation. But this is not to say that the friendless child will always make such compensations nor that the cheerful, confident youngster who makes friends easily, will be intellectually handicapped by these social skills. On the contrary, in my experience and that of the scores of teachers with whom I have discussed the point over many years, the happy child is more likely to do well in class. The shy, anguished, child genius separated from companionship by intellectual brilliance is more myth than anything else.

The greatest gifts any parent can bestow on their child when they start school, is that confidence and independence which come from a background of unconditional love and positive regard. Let's explore together some of the practical ways you can enhance intellectual and creative development during the important early school years.

Discovering your child's thinking style

How your child learns depends on the way they think. Learning is a process which involves taking ideas and using them to make sense of the world, but the way we *take* and *use* these ideas varies from person to person. Finding out exactly how you and your child learn is important because it enables you to help them get the most from education, both at school and at home. Watching four children tackling the same task can prove very revealing. Take John, Susie, Philip and Mary who are each trying to do a similar jigsaw puzzle.

How John tackles the problem

Six-year-old John is a sociable little boy who makes friends easily. He enjoys working in a group and usually understands other people's points of view. An imaginative child, John enjoys drawing, painting and stories. Given a jigsaw puzzle, he quickly picks out the pieces which are recognizable parts of people or animals. These he groups together and joins up to create a whole figure before moving on to the next. After he has completed the figures and other recognizable objects, he puts each one into the right position, using the picture on the box and joining them together. John prefers to approach the jigsaw by finding *concrete* images like faces, to start from. From there he can approach the problem *reflectively*, thinking carefully of the best way to solve it.

How Susie tackles the problem

Susie, aged seven, does well at school. Even before she started she had a good grasp of numbers and was starting to read. She prefers working by herself to being part of a group and seeks approval for her efforts from the teacher. She gets upset if she makes mistakes or is criticized. Susie works carefully and methodically. She thinks hard before attempting the jigsaw and decides to sort out all the straight-edged pieces first. She joins these up to form the outside edge. Next she works inwards, row by row, studying each piece carefully to make sure they are the right shape and colour before trying to place them. Susie prefers to focus on the *abstract* idea of sorting the shapes first and then build on this *reflectively* and logically, thinking each move through before making it.

How Philip tackles the problem

Six-year-old Philip is a practical boy who can construct complicated Lego models with only a brief glance at the picture. He is impulsive and curious about the way things work – his delight in taking toys apart often gets him into trouble with his parents and elder brother. Philip dislikes being spoon fed answers, preferring to work things out for himself. Faced with the jigsaw, Philip has difficulty knowing where to start and angrily dismisses John's suggestions. He tries to work out in his own mind how the problems should be tackled. He picks out pieces with similar colours, then uses a trial and error approach to fitting the shapes together. Eventually he has pieced a fair number together in twos and threes, but as he is unable to see an end in sight soon gets bored and leaves the puzzle unfinished. Philip tried to find an *abstract* idea with which to tackle the jigsaw, by matching colours, and then carried his method through by *actively* testing it.

How Mary tackles the problem

Mary is six, an impulsive child with a vivid imagination. She enjoys doing rather than thinking, and can't sit still at one activity for long.

Her mother is forever urging her to 'stop and think', and teachers are often delighted by the enthusiasm with which she tackles new projects, while regretting her short attention span. Jigsaw puzzles is one of Mary's least enjoyed activities. She picks up pieces haphazardly and attempts to match them with the picture on the box. When she can't identify any she forces them together into a chain which is then turned into a bracelet.

Mary likes to work with *concrete* experience, which is why she feels unable to cope when she can't identify the pieces. Her reaction is to follow up with *active* experimentation, which leads her away from the real purpose into a game of her own.

Perhaps you recognize your own child among these sketches? In any primary class you are likely to find examples of each type, while many more combine characteristics of two or more thinking styles. And no one is necessarily more or less intelligent than any of the others. The teaching methods used in primary schools today ensures that all four styles are equally valued and developed. A good teacher encourages each child to work with both their senses *and* their intellect, to reason *and* to experiment in order to learn. Project based work gives scope for all the child's various talents to be used.

Unfortunately, in the more formal learning environments of most middle and secondary schools, certain thinking styles can place children at a disadvantage. Teachers may place more emphasis on the ability to think abstractedly and reflectively. It is for this reason, rather than lack of effort or intelligence, that Susie has the best chance of doing well in school, and of gaining the examination grades required for a university place. John may do reasonably well, especially in arts subjects, but Philip and Mary are at risk of being branded dunces. If so they will be victims of neither idleness nor stupidity but a profound conflict between the demands of school and the way their minds work best. They are in the unfortunate position of favouring styles of learning poorly suited to the way most lessons are taught.

How thinking styles arise

There are two main differences in how children, and adults, most like to learn. The first lies in the way new information is perceived. The second in how the brain then processes that knowledge.

Some children, like John, prefer to stay in close contact with reality.

They think best when able to reach out and touch the things they are thinking about. Children who are good at making models, drawing or painting, talking to people, and using construction toys come into this category. These are *concrete* thinkers. Other children, like Susie, create and work with an abstract model. Children good at *abstract* thinking enjoy doing sums and solving logical problems. As they get older they may be especially attracted by intellectual games such as chess. Such differences may be viewed as the end points on a line.

Every child, and adult, stands at a different point on the line which represents their preferred perceptual style. Each has its own particular strengths and weaknesses. Unfortunately, except in very young children, most schools either neglect or actively discourage intuitive learning.

CONCRETE ———————— ABSTRACT

How information is dealt with

Once information has been taken in, the brain can work on it in one of two main ways – either *actively* or *reflectively*. Children who think actively are spontaneous and impulsive, they like to jump right in and act on what they have just learned. Philip and Mary are *active* thinkers. Others, like John and Susie prefer to observe and reflect before deciding what action, if any, they should take. As with perception, these two styles can be viewed as end points on a continuous line.

ACTIVE ———————— REFLECTIVE

'In processing experience and information some of us are watchers, while some of us are doers,' comments Bernice McCarthy, a leading American educationalist and creator of the 4-Mat System of learning. 'Both ways of processing information and experience are equally valuable. Both kinds have their own strengths and weaknesses.'

This style determines how your child will acquire knowledge most comfortably, easily and effectively. At the top right of the diagram is a child, like John who combines a concrete and reflective approach to produce what I term an involved thinking style. Research, in the UK and United States, suggests around a third of children favour this style. Susie's preferred way of learning places her in the lower right quadrant of the diagram. Like John she is reflective but, unlike him, she prefers to deal with abstract ideas. These intellectual thinkers rep-

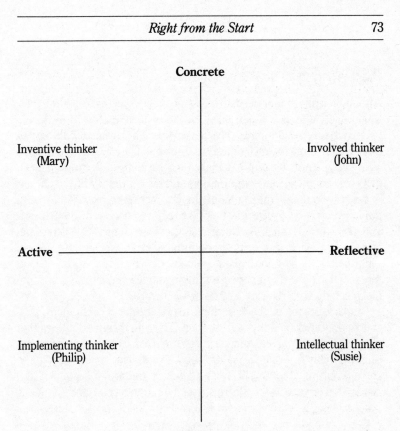

Concrete

Inventive thinker
(Mary)

Involved thinker
(John)

Active ———————————————— **Reflective**

Implementing thinker
(Philip)

Intellectual thinker
(Susie)

Abstract

*Combining the different ways of perceiving and processing information
produces four thinking styles.*

resent about a quarter of school children. Youngsters like Philip also use abstractions but, instead of reflecting on them, perform active experiments to discover how those ideas will work out in practice. Around 17 per cent of children appear to favour this implementing thinking style. Finally there are those who, like Mary, combine a concrete and active approach to learning. I call these inventive thinkers and believe they comprise around a quarter of pupils.

The thinking styles most schools favour

Although many children, and adults, can to some extent alter their thinking style to meet a particular mental challenge, most of us have a preferred way of thinking. Teachers, especially from middle school upwards, favour abstract/reflective thinkers. They expect children to sit quietly, watching and listening, then carefully reflecting on what has been taught before coming up with their answers. This, of course, is perfectly suited to the style of the intellectual thinker. As a result pupils who prefer to learn in this way, enjoy school and feel comfortable with their lessons. As Bernice McCarthy comments: 'When someone is teaching us in our most comfortable style, we learn. But, more importantly we feel good about ourselves.' Which is hard on around three-quarters of children whose thinking styles make them less capable of coping with the way lessons are structured.

Primary school is the best time to identify and work with your child's preferred thinking style since it is during these early years that their self-image, as a competent or ineffective learner is formed. Children who transfer to middle school confident of their ability to solve problems are more likely to persist in the face of set-backs, and sustain motivation to learn despite confusions and failures. Furthermore the earlier you work with your child's favoured style the easier it is to identify and take practical steps to prevent barriers arising further down the educational road.

Conflicts in the family

Difficulties can also arise at home if one or both of you have different thinking styles to your child. Conflict is most likely to occur between involved/implementing and intellectual/inventive thinkers. A parent who favours an abstract/reflective approach to thinking, for example, may condemn the inventive child as being impetuous and illogical. 'For goodness sake stop and think,' I heard one father tell his impulsive eight-year-old son irritably. 'You're just being silly.'

While it is very important for children to allow themselves ample thinking time, a point we shall be exploring later in the book, criticizing a child's favoured thinking style is not the way to help them become more reflective. The most likely outcome, is in fact to reduce confidence in themselves as capable learners. They come to believe that *any* problem which demands abstract thinking must be beyond them. Similarly a parent favouring the intuition style of thinking can find a child who favours the intellectual approach, over-analytical and objective. 'My daughter rationalizes everything,' the mother of an eight-year-old complained to me. 'She seems completely out of touch with her feelings.'

Having identified your child's preferred style, using your own observations of their approach to learning and problem solving together with results from the assessment on page 77, take the following practical steps to help:

If your child is an involved thinker

If your child is an involved thinker, they want to find out *why* things happen. Because they tend to rely on their emotions they may be easily distracted if you don't listen carefully and respond in a positive way to their ideas. Your child will be sensitive to your feelings about them, so avoid offering too lavish or undeserved praise, as this will devalue your judgement in their eyes. Encourage them to talk about the way they feel – it is the most appropriate way to develop their language skills.

When they start learning to read, focus on characters and situations in the story – their interest in these will motivate them to want to make sense of the words. Don't worry about a vivid imagination or tendency to respond intuitively. Even if you find them difficult to relate to, don't stifle your child's natural creativity but let them explain their way of thinking. Never be over-critical, even when you consider this deserved, since such comments reduce self-confidence and increase anxiety.

If your child is an intellectual thinker

They will take learning seriously and respond well to formal instruction, even at an early age. Guide them towards sources of information, by providing plenty of books and library visits, instead of spoon-feeding facts. Present information in a logical, structured way. Give hints about the best way of solving problems, instead of giving the answer. Allow them time to reflect without pushing them to speak or act all the time and never be in a rush to provide answers. Your child's mind will develop most efficiently if allowed to think things out unaided. Try not to talk down or patronize with comments like, 'You're too young to understand.' They want their intellectual skills to be recognized and valued. Be patient with tendencies to think things through step by step.

Because intellectual thinkers tend to have a great deal of respect for authority, don't be surprised if your child seems to believe their teacher's words are law when first starting school. Gently remind them that there are other points of view.

If your child is an implementing thinker

They will be very curious about *how* things work. Feed this curiosity by providing access to practical resources such as modelling materials, paper, paint and construction kits. Try and be patient with a fascination with taking toys apart, this is a good way of learning. Explain learning points that they find difficult to understand with a drawing or model rather than just words.

Let your child have a wide range of opportunities for experimenting and exploring and try to find ways of presenting abstract problems in a practical way. Today a majority of primary schools emphasize this form of learning, but if your thinking style is more reflective try and see their point of view when teaching at home. While still young, lack of physical strength and limited manual dexterity may lead to frustration and temper, so do try and stay calm. When teaching let your child lead the way. If they are eager to construct something from Lego, you might introduce simple maths concepts (*see page 122 onwards*) involving counting and comparing so that they can relate abstract theory to practical problem solving which they enjoy.

If your child is an inventive thinker

You must provide plenty of scope for practical play. Since they learn best by trial and error, offer just enough supervision for them to satisfy their curiosity without being intrusive. You might, for example, organize a short cooking session to make biscuits. Prepare a simple picture recipe for them to follow and help measure the ingredients. Talk through the practicalities as they carry them out so they can relate them directly to the activity, but don't insist on a perfect end product.

Don't criticize your child's ideas however ridiculous they sound to you. They are most interested in trying to transform a vivid idea into reality, regardless of the practicality of the experiment or the end

Discovering your family's thinking style

This brief test provides only an indication of your child's preferred learning style. Careful observation is the most accurate way of arriving at a conclusion. Watch your child at work and play. Notice how they respond to mental challenges. Do the questionnaire twice – once for yourself. Only tick statements with which you *strongly agree*.

- ☐ ☐ I become deeply involved in tasks which interest me.
- ☐ ☐ I blurt things out without thinking.
- ☐ ☑ I think carefully before voicing an opinion.
- ☑ ☐ I enjoy finding out how things work.
- ☐ ☐ I dislike being alone.
- ☑ ☐ I enjoy trying anything new.
- ☐ ☑ I would sooner work things out for myself than be given the answer on a plate.
- ☐ ☑ I am quickly bored by routine.
- ☑ ☐ I have a vivid imagination.
- ☐ ☐ I have a strong need for approval.
- ☐ ☐ I am impatient.
- ☑ ☐ I lose interest when something takes longer than expected.
- ☐ ☐ I am very creative.
- ☐ ☐ More than anything I want to be considered clever.
- ☑ ☐ I dislike being told what to do.
- ☐ ☐ I solve problems by trial and error.
- ☐ ☐ I enjoy trying to repair things.
- ☐ ☐ I pay close attention to details.
- ☐ ☐ I am very concerned about other people's problems.
- ☐ ☐ I get upset when things don't go my way.

How to score

Total the number statements ticked against each heading.

Involved	Intellectual	Implementing	Inventive
1.5.9.13.19	3.6.10.14.18	7.11.15.16.17	2.4.8.12.20

The thinking style with the most ticks suggests your own and your child's preferred style. If two or more columns have equal scores, it means you or your child use a combination of styles. Look out, especially, for high scores under just one heading especially if this indicates a potential conflict between you and your child.

result. Inventive thinking is the style most likely to annoy adults, especially intellectual thinkers. They can be frustrating to teach, especially if expected to concentrate for long periods of time. Keep this in mind when helping your child learn at home by arranging short bursts of practical activities.

Encourage your child's problem solving skills

Being good at solving problems will help your child at school by making many lessons easier and more enjoyable. So lets explore the way a child might tackle a problem to see what can be learned about problem solving in general.

Jenny, aged six, wants to play snakes and ladders but she's lost the dice. Instead of giving up and finding another game, Jenny finds a sheet of paper, crayon and sellotape to make her own dice. At the first attempt she cuts out only five squares and they are all different sizes. Realizing her mistake she cuts six squares of the same dimensions. But when she tries to stick them together her flimsy cube collapses. Determined to play her game, Jenny finds stiffer card which she finally fashions into a crude but serviceable dice.

Most young children are natural problem solvers. Because the instinctive curiosity of a young child is often infuriating and sometimes dangerous, many parents are tempted to discourage inquisitiveness for the sake of their own peace of mind – and the child's safety. But a child like Jenny, who has been allowed access to a variety of materials and encouraged to discover things for herself by trial and error, is far more likely to do well in class and everyday life than children spoon-fed answers.

You will find that today most primary schools place far greater emphasis on coming up with original ideas for finding solutions and thinking them through to a satisfactory conclusion than they do on the old-fashioned skills of memorizing facts and figures and repeating them parrot fashion. In some schools it is considered so important it is dealt with as a separate subject, with problem solving sessions a regular feature of the timetable. Problem solving is a skill with relevance across the whole curriculum – in arithmetic, languages, science, art and technology as well as play. While solving problems obviously demands intelligence, this does not mean that a child who is poor at finding answers necessarily has a below average IQ.

Because her five-year-old son Billy had a good memory and was able to read well before starting school, his mother assumed he'd do well. To her disappointment he quickly fell behind the others. Billy's difficulties lay in the fact that he lacked the strategies needed to turn his knowledge to good effect when presented with an unfamiliar problem. Five-year-old Julia fell behind in lessons for a different reason. Instead of giving herself time to think, anxiety made her blurt out the first answer which came to mind. Peter was able to come up with answers very quickly, but if these failed to work, he got bogged down and couldn't find alternative, less obvious, solutions.

Such barriers to success are widespread and can seriously handicap a child starting school. Fortunately, there is much you can do to enhance your child's problem solving skills.

The building blocks of problem solving

While the make-up of a problem may be obvious to you, it can easily confuse your child. In order to solve any problem your child must identify the three building blocks from which all are constructed.

Building block one – The facts *given* or implied. These can be summed up as: 'What do I know?'

Building block two – The *operations* which must be performed on those facts. This can be summarized as: 'What can I do with what I know?'

Building block three – The *goal* they are expected to achieve. This can be summed up as 'Where do I want to go?'

Taking problems apart
Imagine your child has been given two very different problems:

1. Multiply 4 by 6 and subtract 8.
2. Create a fancy dress for a party.

With the first problem the *givens* are the numbers 4, 6 and 8 together with the instructions about what to do with them. With the second problem, not all the facts have been given, but your child is expected to use their knowledge about fancy dress in general and imagination to come up with items such as cloth, silver paper, paint and so forth.

The operations in the calculation are multiplication and subtraction.

The operations needed to make a fancy dress outfit may include cutting, stitching, gluing, painting and so on. The calculation has only one correct goal or solution, which is 16. For this reason it is called a *convergent problem*.

With the fancy dress, however, there can be a wide range of satisfactory 'goals' although some will be better than others. If your child comes up with the wrong answer it's because one of these has been either misunderstood or misapplied. They have failed to understand, or discover, all the *givens*. The wrong operation has been used, or the right one employed incorrectly. The wrong goal has been set. This often happens during exams when candidates provide excellent answers to a question which was never actually asked! When a mistake has been made, start by asking: 'Does my child understand the givens correctly?' If so, have all the givens been identified? Often problems require your child to draw on previous knowledge or seek additional facts before attempting to find a solution. If this seems like the source of error, help by explanation and demonstration.

Tom, aged three, is trying to make a car from Lego. He hasn't grasped that, if the pieces are to fit securely together, pegs and holes on the brick must be carefully aligned. Because of this his car keeps on falling to pieces. His mother *could* simply tell him: 'Do it like this . . .' while demonstrating the way Lego bricks slot together. A far more useful and constructive approach would be to teach her son important general lessons about solving problems: 'Mmm, seems as if the bricks don't fit properly,' his mother says thoughtfully. Then, instead of immediately providing the solution, she playfully experiments with various ways of fitting two bricks together. Tom, who has been watching intently, suddenly understands where he's been going wrong. 'No, Mummy, like this . . .' he says triumphantly and joins two bricks perfectly. In that flash of insight Tom will have discovered much more than just how to build a toy car. He has also learned not to worry when he doesn't find an answer immediately. Even Mums can't solve every problem instantly, and that persistence is essential. Sometimes you must try several approaches before discovering the best, or right, solution.

Persistence – the key to learning success

Persistence is probably the single most vital ingredient in problem solving success. Impulsive children often fail simply because they refuse to give their brains a chance to work on the problem. If the solution is not always immediately apparent, they rapidly conclude the problem must be beyond them. These are not so much 'don't knows' or 'can't knows' as 'won't knows'. They stubbornly refuse to persist long enough to achieve the intellectual insights needed.

Taking time over problem solving is central to success. Unfortunately the popular view of intelligence is that it means finding answers instantly and effortlessly. Indeed speed of answering is often equated with a high IQ. Yet even the world's greatest geniuses must often have wrestled long and hard with complex problems, struggling for days, weeks, months, sometimes even years, before an answer is found. When he was inventing the light bulb, for example, Thomas Edison is said to have tried out more than a thousand different materials for use as filaments before finally hitting on the right one. Asked if this meant he had failed a thousand times, the great American inventor simply smiled and replied: 'Not at all, I have discovered more than a thousand ways you cannot construct a light bulb!'

Problems arouse emotions

Part of the difficulty stems from the negative feelings which problems arouse. The longer some children take to come up with a solution, the more uncomfortable they become. After a while, and the period varies according to the degree of discomfort experienced, they would sooner abandon the task than continue to feel tense and uneasy. Ending the attempt by concluding that the task is beyond you, reduces this tension.

'Problems, depending upon their nature, evoke in us frustration or grief or sadness or loneliness or guilt or regret or anger or fear or anxiety or anguish or despair,' says psychiatrist Dr Scott Peck.* 'These are uncomfortable feelings, often very uncomfortable, often as painful as any kind of physical pain.'

Faced with such pain, a child may resort to avoidance, or denial, insisting the problem is trivial and unimportant. To persist in the face of distress demands self-discipline and assurance plus sufficient self-confidence to encourage the child in the belief that they will be able to find an answer. Unfortunately two things work against the learning of persistence. The first is the 'instant' nature of our society. The notion that one must work hard and long to achieve important goals is cur-

---

* M Scott Peck *The Road Less Travelled*, Random Century.

rently unfashionable. These days instant gratification is more and more the demand for any task. Courses offer 'painless' and 'instantaneous' ways for acquiring any skill from driving a car to speaking a foreign language. The food we eat is designed to be prepared and served with a minimal amount of time and effort.

Television programmes are written, directed and edited to put across even complicated ideas in such a way that they make minimum demands on the viewer's intellectual processes. Teachers strive to make their knowledge available with a minimum of effort. It seems unlikely that Winston Churchill's famous wartime offer to the British people of 'Blood, toil, tears and sweat' would find many takers today. In education there are easier and harder routes to knowledge and understanding, but there is no *easy* way forward, and any child who comes to believe this in primary school is unlikely to succeed.

Teach persistence not mastery

The second problem is that adults are inclined to teach a mastery rather than a persistence model when demonstrating how something should be done. A father shows his small son how to tie shoe laces quickly, deftly and easily. The child looks on in awe. The movements were made too swiftly for him to follow exactly. He makes a few fumbling attempts and, having failed to reproduce his father's neatly tied laces, concludes he is 'too little' to achieve the same result. This is not necessarily because adults are conceited or insensitive, although many like nothing better than showing off to their children.

Mainly it is because once a problem has been solved and the skill perfected it can be very difficult to put yourself back in the position of a beginner. To the experienced driver there is nothing to moving the gear stick, pulling away on a slope or reversing into a parking space. They all too quickly forget their own, early, incompetent efforts and grow impatient when a learner under their tuition continues to make similar errors. This is why some grown-ups become so impatient when a child appears incapable of accomplishing something they are able to do with ease. There is a tremendous temptation to snatch away the partly completed task with an irritable: 'Oh, let me do it . . .'

Try to view the problem through the child's eyes and teach patience and persistence. Never make a task your child finds difficult appear too easy. Let them learn, as early on in their school career as possible, that there are no instant ways of acquiring new skills and knowledge.

Divergent and convergent problems

Having satisfied yourself that the givens are understood, next consider the operations. Does your child understand the various ways in which the givens can be manipulated? When both givens and operations are understood, consider whether the correct goal has been identified. As in the calculation above, one class of problems can have only one correct answer. Because several ideas converge to provide that solution these are known as *convergent problems*. All the thoughts buzzing around in your child's head as they try to find an answer, must converge on a single point to reach an answer. Convergent problems require a logical approach. The majority of questions asked in school come into this category.

The second class of problems are those which have a number of equally satisfactory or viable solutions. Since ideas can spread out along many pathways to provide a host of solutions these are termed *divergent problems*. Divergent problems require imagination and creativity. They are most likely to be asked in art or English lessons: 'Paint a picture of your favourite animal', or 'Write an adventure story'.

Because each is important, it is necessary to develop both your child's ability to tackle each type, so that they use both logical and imaginative problem solving skills. If they do best at convergent problems, enhance divergent skills with games demanding creativity, such as inventing stories, play acting and day dreaming. If your child is good at divergent problems, but less successful using logical reasoning, ask lots of questions starting with: 'What?', 'When?' and 'Where?' 'What happens if we add flour to water?' Then solve it by trying an experiment. 'When does the clock chime?' Then solve it through observation. 'Where do lions come from?' Help find the answer in a book.

Provide a rich environment

Encourage your child's natural curiosity by allowing plenty of scope for exploration and discovery. Keep rules to the minimum necessary for safeguarding your child and protecting their surroundings. Rather than confine toddlers to a play pen, for instance, make an entire room safe by removing anything breakable (never underestimate the reach of a toddler) and capping all power points. Be sure that cupboards with glass, china, knives, alcohol or cleaning liquid are locked or their contents temporarily removed. Provide ample opportunities to solve problems by doing things to find a solution instead of merely telling children the answer. Be alert for every opportunity to say: 'Let's see . . . ' Then devise a simple way of allowing your child to find out. But don't make it a game of you do while they look on as this is both boring and teaches little or nothing.

Learning from mistakes

Encourage your child to learn from mistakes by seeing them as just one step along the road to the right – or best – answer. Never scold or criticize, however silly the error seems. Youngsters encouraged to learn from their mistakes without feeling foolish, grow into assured and enthusiastic learners. But where early attempts at solving problems are met with disinterest or discouragement, the child is likely to become cautious and apprehensive when faced with any unfamiliar challenge. When his teacher asked: 'Where does milk come from?' four-year-old Stephen immediately replied: 'From a milk float.' To his surprise and dismay the teacher looked annoyed. 'That's a silly thing to say, Stephen,' she told him impatiently. 'Now can somebody give me the right answer?' The other children giggled and Stephen felt ashamed and puzzled. He knew each morning a van delivered milk to his house. Yet this 'right' answer had made him look and feel foolish and made him reluctant to raise his hand again. Instead, locate the point at which your child's confusion has arisen. This is best done by means of diagnostic listening (*see page 218*).

Check your child's understanding of the goals, operations and givens before taking whatever practical steps are needed to help them discover why the answer was wrong. Insight learning, what is sometimes called the 'Ahah' phenomenon is the most exciting and powerful way of acquiring new knowledge. Offer encouragement by first noticing and commenting on anything done well. Next consider everything interesting in the answer, whether or not this is correct. Only then should you point out and help correct mistakes. Starting with a positive response catches a child's attention and reduces anxiety.

Avoid being over perfectionist. Complex skills can only be acquired through a process called 'successive approximations'. In other words by progressively doing them more and more accurately. If your child writes a story, for instance, don't criticize the handwriting or spelling. Instead, encourage the flow of imaginative ideas. Messy handwriting can be dealt with later. Let your motto be: 'If a job's worth doing it's worth doing badly!' That's the only way your child will ever learn how to do it well.

Become a learning resource

Remember that *you* are the most important learning resource in your child's life. Never make them anxious or reluctant to seek advice and guidance. This doesn't, of course, mean solving every problem and handing the answer on a plate, as nothing is more calculated to destroy curiosity and a desire to solve problems for themselves. It does mean being willing to offer constructive advice and point your child in the right direction.

Encourage your child to approach problems methodically by asking him- or herself: 'What plan must I have to find an answer?' Having come up with some possible plans, they try these out and observe the result. By providing a route map to the right or best answer, plans boost confidence and reduce apprehension. Every so often they must check they are following their plan and that it is taking them in the desired direction. When teaching problem solving always keep in mind the ancient Chinese proverb: 'I am told and I forget. I see and I remember. I do and I understand.'

Helping your child to read

Reading is the essential passport to learning and discovery. Children who are confident readers gain knowledge and understanding far more easily and swiftly than those who must struggle to make sense of the written word or, having learned to read, remain reluctant readers. Although I have included this chapter in the Primary School section, this does not mean that you need to wait for the start of formal education before helping your child learn to read. Indeed, the earlier children experience the joy of reading the more likely it is that they will start a life-long love affair with books.

Tragically, there are indications that literacy levels are at best static, at worst declining, on both sides of the Atlantic. Studies in the UK have shown as many as 28 per cent of seven-year-olds are unable to

Is your child a good problem solver?

(Tick any statements which apply on most occasions.)

My child ...

• Has lively curiosity.

• Gives up quickly when an easy solution cannot be found.

• Likes to work things out for him/herself.

• Quickly gets frustrated by set-backs.

• Possesses a vivid imagination.

• Behaves impulsively.

• Finds unusual uses for everyday objects.

• Persists in applying obviously unworkable solutions.

• Enjoys unfamiliar challenges.

• Becomes upset over mistakes.

How to score
Total ticks of *odd* and *even* numbered statements separately.
Now subtract *even* from *odd* total to produce your child's rating
as a problem solver. For example:

    4 *odd* statements and 2 *even* statements ticked. Rating = +2
    1 *odd* statement and 5 *even* statements ticked. Rating = – 4

Rating +5 to +4: Your child has a positive attitude towards problem solving. This provides a sound basis for developing further
skills.

Rating +3 to +2: Your child has a reasonable foundation on
which to build further problem solving skills.

Rating +1 to 0: Your child needs help to develop more effective
problem solving strategies.

Any minus score suggests your child has difficulty solving problems and probably dislikes them. Use the practical procedures
described to overcome this attitude. Never assume, however, that
failure here reflects low intelligence.

read without help. Even when children know how to read they may not want to become readers. A survey commissioned by the Adult Literacy and Basic Skills Unit found that more than four out of ten children never or rarely read books and one in eleven hardly ever reads a newspaper or magazine.

One of the most comprehensive studies of language skills ever undertaken of British school children[*], by researchers from the Government's Assessment of Performance Unit, found while 87 per cent of girls and 76 per cent of boys claim to enjoy reading, there is a hard core of 10 to 20 per cent who hate it. A similar proportion said they would only read if they *had* to, and could not recall ever reading anything they enjoyed. The proportion of those 'turned off' reading and writing increased by secondary school.

In the United States a current educational buzzword is 'aliteracy', used to describe adults who although able to read seldom do so. A study by John P. Robinson, a sociology professor at the University of Maryland, shows the average adult devotes just 24 minutes a day to all types of reading, including newspapers and magazines, a decline of 25 per cent since 1965. According to research by the advertising agency Young and Rubican, this compares with a daily average of 3 hours 48 minutes watching television and 3 hours 21 minutes listening to the radio. Roughly half of all American adults never read books or magazines, while even newspaper sales are declining.

According to UK researchers, negative attitudes are established long before pupils reach the age of 11 and probably date back to when 'children are first being taught to read and write.' This view is supported by the Adult Literacy survey which found that although a million teenagers were unable to read well enough to understand a job application form, only a third of 16- to 20-year-olds showed any interest in being helped.

The failure of schools to foster a joy of reading alongside the mechanics of reading is forcefully made by Liz Waterland, author of *Read With Me* and deputy head of an infants' school. She points out that while there *are* some very poor readers, the majority of children have reading ages close to their chronological ages, while a few have scores two or three years ahead of their actual age.

'The problem is, rather, the qualitative one of children who by objec-

[*] Assessment Matters: No. 4 Language for learning report to the School Examinations and Assessment Council.

tive criteria can read but who in practice seldom do, or who read poorly, stumblingly, without apparently realizing that they are supposed to be making sense.'*

Yet reading is more than communicating information by means of the printed or written word. Because reading involves an imaginative dialogue between text and brain, it also helps your child to think better. Studies show the greater a person's reading skills the higher their professional achievements are likely to be. As the 18th-century writer Sir Richard Steele commented: 'Reading is to the mind what exercise is to the body.'

Your role in reading

You play a vital part in developing your child's reading skills and enjoyment of books. Research has shown that six- to nine-year-olds, whose parents take an active role in reading progress by leaps and bounds. Unfortunately while parental involvement is essential it is not always welcomed by schools.

In a survey among 500 parents belonging to the Red House Children's Book Club, only 57 per cent reported their child's school looked favourably on parental help. Twenty-one per cent said they were explicitly discouraged from helping, while a fifth had no idea of their school's policy on helping. In part this reluctance may be due to the variety of teaching methods used. Some teachers may fear that by adopting a different approach at home your child could become confused.

How your child may be taught to read

Although most schools use a combination of methods, one or two are usually emphasized.

Look and say. Over the past years this approach, also known as 'wholeword', has become the dominant teaching method. The child first learns, usually with the aid of pictures, to recognize words by their shapes. They might, for instance, be shown a card with the word 'dog' on it and be expected to remember that shape when they next come across the word. The method helps to build vocabulary since

* Liz Waterland *Read With Me – An Apprenticeship Approach to Reading*, Thimble Press, 1989.

children usually find it easier to recognize words by shape than by sounds.

Those in favour of 'look and say' say it is the most efficient way of learning to read, since fluent readers see words as whole units, rather than sequences of letters or sounds. They also claim the method is more enjoyable and therefore more motivating. The main difficulty in this method is that it offers no help when your child encounters an unfamiliar word.

The phonic method. The child learns the sounds of all 26 letters, plus some 40 letter combinations, then starts to read by 'sounding out' each letter. This enables children to tackle unfamiliar words by sounding each letter individually, 'c-u-p' for example, and is helpful once they have a small vocabulary. While this can be useful with some children, many teachers regard phonics as an old-fashioned and outmoded 'drill and discipline' approach. They worry that the tedium of having to remember hundreds of words stops children developing enjoyment from their reading. They also claim it encourages children to guess unfamiliar words from their context, a process which can result in the sort of 'word blindness' found in dyslexia (*see The ABC of Learning*).

To make matters worse not many English words are spelt phonetically, while some letters create confusion by having more than one pronunciation. George Bernard Shaw, a lifelong campaigner for more rationale in spelling, would ask the unwary to pronounce *ghoti*. After they had struggled for a while with various possibilities, he announced that according to the rules of English pronunciation it should be *fish*! The *-gh* is pronounced as in *touch*; the *-o* as in *women* and the *-ti* as in a word ending with *-tion*. If you find that confusing just think what this must do to the confidence of a struggling young reader! Moving on from the teaching method to the choice of books, schools may operate a number of approaches.

DART. Many school now use DART, which stands for Directed Activities Related to Text, based on the work of Professor Derek Lunzer and Dr Keith Gardner. The idea is to encourage children to think about what they read through an active involvement with the text. Techniques include:

Sequencing. Children rearrange portions of the text into the correct order. This is especially important in subjects like art and history.

Matching. Involves pairing up pictures or diagrams with the words. This is helpful with a range of subjects including maths (eg area and shape) and geography.

Predicting. Making an educated guess about what will happen next is valuable in subjects as varied as science and English.

Modelling. Here your child makes a drawing or creates a model on the basis of what has been read. This helps with a range of subjects including Craft-Design-Technology (CDT) and project work.

Cloze. Activities in which children must fill in missing words. Used in many school subjects, especially on worksheets.

Questions. Instead of being asked traditional comprehension questions, children are encouraged to think about different aspects of what they read. This is helpful with creative writing projects.

As you can see, many of these aspects of DART could easily be implemented at home, to make reading a richer and more stimulating experience.

Structured reading schemes. These involve groups of books whose vocabulary starts simply and increases in complexity as children move from one level to the next. They can be read with 'look and say' or phonic methods. Progress is easily measured and repetition builds a core vocabulary, but texts are limited and the unnatural language rarely makes much sense.

Real books. Involves favourite books written especially for children. These can be grouped and colour-coded depending on difficulty. Real books increase reading enjoyment but if there is no overall structure progress will be slower and less confident children may feel intimidated. It is also difficult to find enough suitable books for the emergent reader. One teacher gets around the problem by using the Oxford Reading Tree, a structured series her children enjoy, but *not* in sequence.

Parent participation. Some schools encourage involvement by providing books which children take home to read with their parents. On the plus side, as mentioned above, research shows that children learn more quickly with parental involvement. But problems arise either if there is a lack of interest in the home or if over-zealous parents spoil the fun by forcing a child to read when they would sooner be playing.

Reading is a developmental skill

Both reading and writing, which I shall discuss later on are developmental skills with various stages all of which must be passed through.
If there is an overemphasis on in-appropriate skills at the wrong stage,
conflict can arise and your child may lose confidence and opt out.
Learning to read and write need be no more difficult than learning to
speak and should be approached in the same way. As Frank Smith,
author of *Understanding Reading** put it: 'Learning to read involves no
learning ability that children have not already been called upon to
exercise in order to understand the language spoken to them at home.'

And how is language learned? Many experts believe this occurs
mainly through imitation. As totally immersed in speech as a swimmer in water, a baby slowly but surely extracts meaningful sounds,
starts joining in and is encouraged to continue and build on those
early attempts. 'You encourage them by responding and they learn to
talk by talking,' says Margaret Meek.†

The link between speaking and reading is the fact that the best way
for your child to acquire a reading vocabulary is in the same way they
developed a spoken vocabulary, by being exposed to new words in a
way which is interesting and familiar. Liz Waterland describes this
process of imitation and encouragement as the 'apprenticeship
approach'. She believes this to be the most natural and effective way
of developing both skill and enjoyment in reading. 'Essentially,' she
says, 'reading cannot be taught in a formal sequenced way any more
than speech can be.' She regards reading as a process through which
your child gains meaning, rather than 'a series of small skills fluently
used.' The process she advocates, and one with which I am in whole-
hearted agreement, is to observe your child's development as an
apprentice reader through the following stages guided by your child's
development. The plan below is adapted from that developed by Liz
Waterland, whose book I thoroughly recommend to any interested
parent.

* Frank Smith, *Understanding Reading*, Holt, Reinhart & Winston, 1978.
† Margaret Meek *Learning To Read*, Bodley Head, 1982.

Your role in reading

It is essential to bear in mind that your child is never at just one reading stage at any given time. He, or she, may show several different ways of reading even from the same book, because skills vary according to the difficulty of the text rather than ability. Although the stages are generally arranged in a hierarchy there is no time pattern. Even a competent reader will revert to an earlier stage to make sense of a difficult text.

Stage 1 - you do the reading

Your child listens to the story, apparently making no contribution to the reading. In fact they will learn a lot about what reading is all about and what the reader does, while attaching meaning to the words as they would if reading independently. At this stage they will be listening to the story while observing both text and illustrations.

Assess their understanding by encouraging them to discuss the story. Watch their eyes – easier when the child is seated sideways on your knee – to see what they are making of the text. This also helps you evaluate how much effort and concentration is going into the session.

Stage 2 - your child reads with you

'This is a very curious feeling,' comments Liz Waterland, 'rather like having a tape recording of the book just out of phase.' As well as joining in your child may anticipate what words or phrases will be coming next. When your child is confident enough to take over, they give a signal, such as touching your hand, and carry on alone. Repeating the signal means it's your turn again. The advantage of this approach is that the child can dictate the reading pace and amount of support provided.

At first they may just make up the story, without even glancing at the text. Later retelling becomes more accurate. They may follow a line with a finger, matching the start and finish of each with both voice and gesture. As progress continues, fluency and word/sound match increases. As with Stage 1, encourage discussion of the text and listen to ideas. But don't make this into a formal 'question and answer' session or you'll spoil the fun.

Stage 3 - your child begins to take over

As confidence increases, your child will want to do more and more of the reading, and will understand the meaning of a large amount of text. At this stage, expect them to pick out familiar words or phrases – such as 'Once upon a time . . . ' or point to a recognized letter and say: 'That's in my name!'

Sounding words is helpful at this stage as they help your child identify unfamiliar words from the context. For instance when Julia was reading: 'Dad went to the g(arage) in his car . . . ' she stuck on 'garage' which she confused with 'garden'. Glancing ahead she saw the word, 'car' and this, together with the sound of the awkward word, gave her the correct answer. Be flexible and follow your child's lead. Where appropriate read part of the story, letting them take over as and when they like. Or allow them to do most of the reading, smoothly filling in the gaps if they falter to ensure the story moves along at an entertaining pace. Reverse roles by allowing your child to ask you questions, or make deliberate mistakes and see whether they spot them. This improves reading skills by allowing your child to practise thinking carefully about what is read. It also makes the game more enjoyable – children love getting their own back!

Stage 4 - your child reads independently

At this stage knowledge gained in the three previous stages is brought together, bringing meaning to and drawing meaning from the text. But reaching this stage does not mean the earlier ones can be abandoned. The process, Liz Waterland points out, is not sequential but cumulative. 'In other words, children create a total process by the accumulation of behaviours; they do not acquire one at the expense of the one before.'

Television is often seen as the enemy of reading, but it doesn't have to be. A study by psychologist Daniel Anderson, of the University of Massachusetts at Amherst, found no consistent proof that television viewing interferes with intellectual development. Educational programmes can actually improve attention span and vocabulary skills. Family life, Dr Anderson believes, is more important to intellectual growth than television. 'Kids actively learn from what they see on TV,' he comments, 'whether they learn something relevant depends on the message.'

This view is supported by Margaret Meek of London University's Institute of Education: 'Television lets reading children discover that language doesn't just describe things,' she says. 'It determines how they are to be seen. The social strength of TV is that it enlarges and encourages talk, which helps reading at every stage.'

Use television to generate an interest in reading by:

- Getting books based on popular TV series.

- Encouraging your child to read the programme listings and notes in TV magazines and newspapers. Ask questions like: 'What's the film about tonight?' 'What time does the show start?' 'Guess what I'll be watching tonight?'

- Comparing television programmes with printed versions of the same thing. Your child may be surprised to discover how much TV leaves out, or adds on, to the original text.

- With older children watch television news and then compare it with the same story published in the newspapers.

Improving reading attitudes

Focus on any special interests your child has and encourage them to read about them. Check with the local library to find out what books there are on the subject, and at your newsagent to suggest relevant magazines. Try and share their interest (*see building a learning ladder on page 177*) even when you are not particularly enthusiastic about mountain bikes or the Top Ten! Play games using magazine articles. One of you opens a magazine and reads aloud a few lines from any article. The other then scans the contents listing to identify where the extract came from. By encouraging intelligent guesses, this game helps your child to think about both content and title.

In another version of the same game, the person listening has to find the paragraph or sentence chosen. With older children you can increase the excitement by setting a time limit. When cooking or assembling a kit, ask your child to check that the instructions are being followed in the correct order. Read from a book where each chapter has a cliff-hanger ending so that your child will be begging you to read some more.

Measuring your child's progress

This is often difficult to assess accurately since many different skills are involved. The Primary Language Record, developed by the Inner

London Education Authority, was recommended for use by *all* schools by the Cox report which advised on National Curriculum English. This established five levels of reading competence and can be used for children up to around eight years old.

1. *The beginner reader* depends on adult help.

2. *The non-fluent reader* copes with familiar and predictable texts, but requires help with new material. He, or she, is developing strategies for testing predictions about what words may mean, for instance by picking up clues from the illustrations.

3. *The moderately fluent reader* is starting to read silently and tackles new texts confidently, returning to familiar books occasionally for extra practice.

4. *The fluent reader* is entirely independent and draws their own conclusions from the reading material.

5. *The exceptionally fluent reader* is avid and independent, tackles new material easily and with complete confidence, appreciating nuances and shades of meaning.

Additional reading skills which the fluent reader should acquire are skimming and scanning a text in order to speed the rate at which information can be acquired. As these are more appropriate to older age groups, I shall be discussing them when we look at Middle and Secondary schools.

Choosing the right books

This is one of the most crucial aspects of learning to read and learning to enjoy reading. In *Teacher** Sylvia Ashton-Warner makes a distinction between what she calls *organic* and *inorganic* language in books. Organic language is a living form, drawn from your child's special interests, ideas, and emotions. Inorganic language is often meaningless to the child because it is a dead thing, imposed on them from the outside.

This is a point emphasized by specialists in the teaching of reading: 'The material that children are asked to read should be closely linked to their own interests and experiences,' says David Mackay and his co-

* Sylvia Ashton-Warner *Teacher*, Virago, 1983.

authors in *Breakthrough to Literacy*.* 'The personal words a child accumulates will depend on his interests.'

Predicting these interests can prove tricky and there is often a yawning gulf between what teachers and child experts *think* children will enjoy reading and what they *actually* want to read. There can also be difficulty over the word 'enjoy'. 'Many children enjoy authors who offer easy and sometimes offensive stereotypes in both character and storyline,' points out Sue Bates†, 'The phenomenon of reading books with the same genre or by the same author goes unchallenged in adult circles. But something deep inside us finds this enjoyment in the child's reading experience worrying, and it is often described as limiting.' Children are extremely conservative in their choice of reading, steadfastly loyal to one particular author, genre or character and reluctant to try anything different. Peer group pressure may also play a role in determining which books will become childhood best sellers. Once again the key is to be guided by your child and not to impose too many restrictions on the type of material they are allowed to read. Even comics can be acceptable as a way of encouraging enjoyment provided they don't dominate reading.

Ideally, the books chosen should meet as many as possible of these criteria. The story should . . .

- Engage and hold your child's attention. They must *want* to go on reading it.
- Create an atmosphere that stimulates the imagination.
- Be relevant to things in his or her life while offering reassurance and comfort. Bad things may happen to the characters but it all comes out right in the end.
- Explore a new and unfamiliar world.
- Arouse strong emotions, whether laughter or tears.
- Have attractive illustrations which are meaningful and closely related to the text.

Six rules for helping your child

1. Make sure reading sessions are always fun. Your child must look

---

* David Mackay, Brian Thompson, Elizabeth Shaub, *Breakthrough to Literacy*, Longman, 1970.

† Sue Bates, 'What Makes A Good Book?' *Child Education* June 1990, pp34–35.

forward to them, not dread them as ordeals where reading skills are put on trial. Share reading to the extent your child prefers.

2. Discuss the story afterwards. Expand their understanding by asking the right sort of questions. For instance in a story about a child living in a town, who has to leave his dog at home when going on holiday to France, a rather limited question might be: 'What colour front door did his house have?' Although starting with simple questions like this can build confidence, you should quickly move to more complicated questions which explore their understanding of the story: 'How was he feeling at the start of the holiday?' or 'Why did he have to leave his dog at home?'

   Finally, ask searching questions in which your child has to evaluate what was read: 'Do you think the writer successfully described the boys feelings when he said goodbye to his pet?' But avoid the testing type of questions, such as 'What does that say?' used by many parents. Words don't 'say' anything, worse luck, and your child will become confused. Instead ask: 'I don't suppose you can point to . . . ' and then mention a word.

   Before asking any questions, find a book your child really enjoys. Many schools run a book shop and operate book clubs, and think about the various types of questions you could use.

3. Don't interrupt by correcting any words your child mispronounces or stumbles over. The great thing is to maintain the pace so the story remains interesting and fun. Don't become irritated if they are unable to remember all the words from one book. Allow your child to develop at their own speed.

   Ask whether mistakes make sense. For example if they read 'nobody' rather than 'no one' it suggests that instead of reading each word in sequence they are giving meaning to the text, something fluent readers do. If they get stuck provide clues rather than the actual word. This will help your child learn to pick up meaning from context.

4. Never apply too much pressure to read independently. Some children deliberately stop reading by themselves because they fear they'll no longer be able to. If this happens, go back to reading aloud for as long as it takes to persuade your child to join in again.

5. Don't go too quickly. Allow your child to consolidate their understanding at one stage of reading before progressing to the next. If your child gets stuck after moving to more complicated stories drop

back to simpler ones for a while. Don't prevent your child from reading the same story again and again. Rereading helps in two ways. Firstly it improves reading attitude by presenting a familiar and reassuring text. Secondly, the familiarity aids a child to practice reading fluently, so enhancing reading skills.

6. Build up a library at home of a wide range of books, encourage your child to look up facts when stuck for an answer. Visit the local library regularly so that your child becomes accustomed to choosing their own books.

Does your child have trouble reading?

Watch out for these warning signs and act promptly, using the suggestions above, *if your child* ...

- Lags behind classmates in the number and standard of books read.
- Reads in a stilted way with poor understanding of meaning.
- Is reluctant to read aloud to you, however reassuring the invitation.
- Becomes impatient with an unfamiliar text, maybe even throwing the book to the floor.

Helping with your child's writing

Provided it's easy to read it shouldn't matter what your child's handwriting *looks* like. But it does! In a recent study, several children copied out an identical essay. These were marked by teachers who had been asked to ignore the handwriting and award marks solely on the quality of the ideas. Despite this, messily written scripts were given significantly lower marks than those in an attractive script. Which suggests that in an exam, untidy handwriting might even make the difference between a passing and failing grade.

It's important to distinguish between poor writing and script containing 'intelligent simplifications'. These arise as your child's handwriting becomes more sophisticated. By doing away with unnecessary pen strokes, simplifications make writing faster. Far from revealing a lack of ability, they are associated with an above average IQ. Your child is thinking so rapidly they have to simplify their script in order to get ideas written down fast enough. If their handwriting is poor you may blames laziness or lack of attention. Many children with poor handwriting feel ashamed of their writing and would like nothing better than to produce neat, elegant script.

In most cases, the cause lies in a failure to perfect two key writing skills.

1. Selective attention – concentrating on one task to the exclusion of all else – is essential for well formed, attractive, handwriting.
2. Hand eye co-ordination. Neat writing demands very precise muscle control and a high degree of co-ordination between hand and eye.

Selective attention refers to a person's ability to identify aspects of their surroundings most crucial to the task in hand. A learner driver, for example, often spreads their span of attention too widely, attempting to take in not only road conditions but readings from various dashboard instruments. An experienced motorist can attend only to key aspects of driving, switching from the road ahead, to speedometer, and then rear view mirror as conditions demand.

When they first begin to write children are expected to pay close attention to the fine movements required for producing letters and words. These sequences are so precise they are seldom rivalled in complexity by anything else we ever have to learn throughout life. Selective attention, like all developmental abilities, improves as your child grows older and is acquired at a different rate by different children. As with such physical attributes as height or the start of puberty, so children lag behind their peers before closing the gap in a matter of only a few months. By this time, however, handwriting may have been permanently damaged through effects on motivation, self-image and anxiety.

Why repetition fails. The key to improving selective attention is to train the brain centres responsible for filtering incoming information. Training which fails to do this is not only useless but can undermine performance even further. This is why the usual remedy for poor handwriting, of obliging a child to copy words and phrases over and over again is ineffective and harmful. Far from discovering how to focus attention more accurately on the formation of letters, the child simply practises writing inaccurately!

Suppose when learning to play golf, a novice receives inadequate professional coaching. As a result they acquire the bad habit of bending the elbow on the swing. Aware that the swing is at fault, but not certain why, the novice decides to spend more time on the driving range from the belief that 'practice makes perfect'.

The false reasoning behind this approach is obvious. The more time the novice spends driving ball after ball into the net using a faulty elbow action, the more firmly the incorrect swing will become established. Until they have been told what is going wrong, and what can be done to prevent that mistake no amount of practice can possibly improve their game. Yet this is exactly the same position a child finds itself in if forced to copy line after line of writing from the mistaken belief that practice alone is sufficient to correct bad penmanship.

Hand-eye co-ordination as with selective attention, develops as children get older and not all acquire the skill at the same rate. A high level of co-ordination between hand and eye is obviously essential for good writing. The child who is constantly criticized or scolded for having untidy handwriting loses confidence and comes to see him- or herself as a naturally poor writer. This then creates a third barrier to writing in general – a negative attitude. When children are told to write something, adults often make the task more complicated than it need be by insisting some or all of these conditions are satisfied.

1. The writing should be neat – not simply legible.
2. The writing should be quick. Children are expected to produce quite a lot within a given amount of time.
3. The writing should be accurate, without spelling or grammatical errors.
4. The writing should be interesting or creative, telling the reader an imaginative or accurate story.

Given such pressures – how would *you* like to satisfy all those demands! It's not surprising that even children who write well are often reluctant to make the attempt.

How reading and writing differ

Good handwriting is the technical skill which aids the main purpose of writing, which is to communicate. Although closely linked to reading, writing has two additional, and important, ingredients.

A purpose – there must be a reason for wanting to write, since few people do it purely from enjoyment.

An audience – the writing is intended to be read by somebody.

These determine the type of writing needed. So far as neatness is concerned, this should always be sufficiently legible for the *intended reader*. This means your child must be able to write neatly, when there is a need to do so, for example in an exam, or if sending off birthday invitations.

How to teach writing

Never place too much emphasis on neatness, spelling or grammar. Although all are important, at this stage of learning what matters most is for writing to be fun.

Copying is NOT writing. Jane, a teacher in a reception class, describes how for several years she followed a tightly structured system in which children wrote over writing, then progressed to copying *under* it before moving to the final stage of copying onto another sheet of paper. They were then ready to move on to using their own word books, gradually becoming independent. She also placed great emphasis on correct letter formation. 'The shock came when I asked the class to write on their own,' she recalls. 'They looked horrified and said "we can't write yet!"'

Jane knew her class were always 'writing' messages on the board and making books during their lunch breaks which meant she was facing a crisis of confidence, brought about by an over-emphasis on secretarial skills. She solved the problem by introducing a personal journal called the Early Bird book in which they were allowed to write, or draw, completely independently. These books are never marked, but questions and comments are written inside, and difficult passages translated, in pencil, for future reference. Each term she keeps back one page for their records and to monitor progress. Apart from improving handwriting, this has encouraged the children to become far less inhibited in what they write. They no longer feel it necesary to stick to 'safe' (ie known) words but will experiment by using a far more adventurous vocabulary. The method also enables Jane to find out what each child knows about writing and to analyze their spelling. This is an idea any parent could introduce as a way of both

encouraging creative writing, and drawing, while being able to keep
an eye on developing writing – and reading – skills.

Ten ways to encourage writing

1. Children often find it easier and more enjoyable to write when there
   is a practical purpose. So encourage writing about *real life* situations and things they are interested in such as a hobby or leisure
   pursuit.
2. Suggest keeping a scrap book or diary. On trips collect snap shots
   or postcards for illustrations.
3. Read your child's stories aloud, or encourage them to do the same.
   When this happens *never* make an immediately critical comment.
   Only after being positive should you ask whether your child would
   like help in correcting anything.
4. An old carton with a hole cut in the front can be turned into a 'television' for fantasy play which involves writing and then performing either a popular show or programme of their own invention.
   Alternatively suggest your child writes a play for finger or glove
   puppets and performs it for the family.
5. If you possess a video camcorder suggest your child, perhaps in collaboration with others of similar age, prepare a 'shooting script'
   which can then be turned, either with your help or independently,
   into a movie for showing on TV.
6. Where there is a typewriter or computer with a word processing
   program in the family, allow your child to use this to type either
   original material or something already hand written. This is especially helpful for children anxious about their handwriting.
7. Encourage letter writing – suggest finding a pen friend. Writing to
   television stations about a programme they enjoyed, or disliked, is
   also a good idea since it encourages more critical viewing.
       With younger children you can create a fantasy figure with
   whom your child corresponds – you provide the 'replies' of course.
   In her class, Jane and the children constructed a life-size dummy
   with a balloon for the head. As time passed and the head began to
   shrink she suggested the children write to ask whether he wanted a
   new balloon head or a paper bag head instead. All eagerly did so,
   and were delighted to get a personally addressed, individual letter

in reply saying he wanted a new balloon head! Imaginative games like this give writing both purpose and audience.

8. Ask older children to write something specially for younger ones. Anxious writers are reassured by the fact that, not being able to read or write as well as they can, the youngsters won't laugh at mistakes. Enlist the assistance of younger brothers, sisters, cousins and the children of friends.

9. Encourage your child to prepare a rough first draft of written work. Discuss the subject matter first, and explain that the draft can include drawings, notes, different spellings and various ideas. You might take a story and suggest they provide a new ending. The rough draft is written on the left side of the page, a final polished version on the right. Stimulate their interest by asking questions such as, 'How did the hero escape?' 'Where did he go?' 'What happened next?' 'Why was the dragon scared?'

   In the draft any words which your child finds hard to spell can be underlined in pencil. Your child can also indicate any other problems. When finished see where help has been requested and only offer it with those problems they identified. Encourage the writing of a second draft where necessary before tackling the final version. The advantage of this approach is that your child remains in control of the learning process. *They* determine what assistance is needed and you only intervene when asked to do so, so reducing anxiety and boosting confidence.

10. Play games like consequences, in which you write a few lines, fold the paper over and get your child to write the next part of the story. There are many ways in which this game can be structured. One is to tell the story of Mr and Mrs . . . (your child or you complete), who went to . . . (your child or you complete), where they met . . . (your child or you complete), and . . . (your child or you complete), who were . . . (your child or you complete) and the consequence was . . . (your child or you complete).

   Once your child feels confident about writing, and enjoys doing so, the time has come to turn your attention to improving the legibility and look of their script, while also correcting spelling and grammatical errors.

Identifying handwriting problems

These can arise for a number of reasons:

1. Your child may deliberately write illegibly to conceal the fact they are unable to spell certain words. Research shows a close link between poor handwriting and poor spelling.

2. The pen is held incorrectly. Too tight a grip, possibly caused by anxiety, impedes the writing movement. A related fault is pressing too hard on the paper, sometimes when such force is used the paper actually tears. The pen or pencil should be held lightly, about an inch (2.5 cm) from the tip, between the thumb and the first two fingers.

3. Your child feels under too much pressure. It isn't possible to say exactly when a child should start using proper letter formations, but one who is still at the scribbling stage lacks the necessary control to produce accurate letters. Games like joining the dots and tracing, together with the exercises described below, help develop muscle control while encouraging the belief that writing is enjoyable.

4. Capitals were taught first. Although these are easier to write, one reason why many children start this way, the process is hard to unlearn. In moments of stress or tiredness older children may revert to capitals or suddenly insert a capital, instead of a lower case letter, in the middle of a word. Although some teachers advocate teaching 'cursive' or joined-up writing from the start, regarding it as a natural development and extension of scribble writing, others feel it is better left until a child can:

   (a) Recognize the need for spaces between words.
   (b) Form lower case letters confidently.
   (c) Write on the line.

   Unless you do there is a risk of the child joining everything in sight! Help your child by using the approach adopted in their school.

5. Children often find certain letters harder to form than others, 'd' and 'b' are notorious. It helps if, early on, they learn that 'd' starts with a 'c' and that to form a 'b' you go *down* the *bat* and *up* and around the *ball*. If your child has trouble with these letters, short, intense practice can help. But make it seem like a game, for instance by asking them to see how many 'c's they can write in one minute.

Writing through drawing

As soon as your child shows an interest in drawing and writing, provide paper and crayons, pens and pencils with which to experiment. As your child starts to write enhance selective attention and co-ordination with these six drawing games. They can help eliminate the major causes of poor script: legibility; letter crowding; excessive rigidity; sharp angles and variability in letter height and slant. When playing the games with your child follow these rules:

1. Prepare by creating the basic design as shown in the examples.

2. Work with your child to provide encouragement if difficulties are encountered and praise when they do well.

3. Do not expect a sudden improvement. Getting rid of bad writing habits takes time.

4. Keep the sessions short. Your child should be left wanting to do more drawings.

5. Be patient. If you are feeling especially tired, stressed or irritable, postpone the session to another time.

Game 1 - Draw a Dragon

What to do: Start by copying the dragon's skeleton as illustrated below. (*See illustration 1a.*) Next draw half a wavy line dragon as shown below. (*See illustration 1b.*)

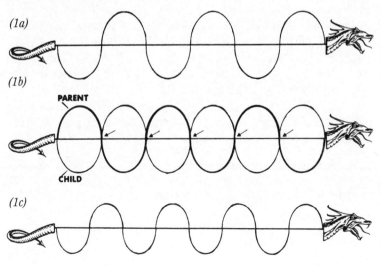

(1a)

(1b)

PARENT

CHILD

(1c)

Now tell your child to complete the dragon's body by drawing a corresponding wavy line which must pass through both the backbone and your own line. (*See illustration 1c.*)

These are shown in illustration (1b) with arrows indicating the intersections. Start with just a few loops and tell your child to draw slowly at first. As accuracy improves, the rate at which the line is drawn should be increased until it matches normal handwriting speed. When your child can intersect a few lines accurately at handwriting speed, increase the number of waves, as shown in illustration (1c) to make the task more challenging. Once again your child should go slowly at first, gradually increasing speed.

When your child has mastered large loops draw the wavy line so that it corresponds to the size of the normal upper and lower letter strokes, for instance those used when writing 't', 'l' or 'h', and 'y' or 'p'. Do not expect your child to achieve perfect accuracy in just one or two sessions. As the number of wavy lines increases it becomes more and more of a challenge to intersect them correctly at normal writing speed – try for yourself!

What to tell your child: 'We are going to draw some dragons. This is the dragon's head, here is his tail and this is his backbone.' (Point out the parts.) 'I am going to draw half his body (put in the first wavy line) and I want you to complete the picture.' With a young child it is often helpful to complete the first dragon yourself, so that they can see exactly what is required. 'The important thing is to make sure your lines cross mine as well as the dragon's backbone,' (indicate some of the crossover points) 'so that he looks right. Start slowly and try to make your half look as much like my half as you can.' If some crossing points have been missed, say: 'That's good. But look, you didn't draw your line through his backbone here . . . let's try another dragon.' Continue in this way until a number of drawings have been made. You can turn *Draw a Dragon* into a family game, with children competing on speed and accuracy. But only do so when they are equally matched in age and ability.

*How **Drawing a Dragon** helps*: This game is especially helpful if your child's handwriting shows these faults: poor legibility. letters crowded too close together, angular script.

Game 2 - Finish a Face

What to do: The task is to complete the face in one of the five ways shown without touching any of the features which you should first draw out on the sheet of paper. Gradually make the features smaller and smaller to make the task trickier and enhance fine muscle control. I suggest your child attempts all five ways to finish the face in one session. When your child is able to accomplish this with large faces, make the drawings smaller. Increase the rate of completion until it matches normal handwriting speed. (*See page 108*.)

What to tell your child: 'I'd like you to finish drawing some faces for me. Here is a row of them,' (point to illustration 2a) 'and I want you to complete each one like this.' (Demonstrate the first method of completion by following the arrows shown. Take care not to touch any of the features at any point.) 'You mustn't let your line go over any part of the face, and I want you to move your pencil in the same direction I did. Go slowly at first . . . ' (It is sometimes helpful to guide your child's hand during early sessions.) (*See illustrations 2a–2e.*)

*How **Finish a Face** helps*: This will help your child if their handwriting shows signs of: poor legibility, letter crowding, variability in the height of small letters and angular script.

Game 3 - Sketch a Snail

What to do: As I explained above, good writing demands very fine muscle movements, because shaping letters accurately involves working to fine tolerances. This game trains your child to achieve these tolerances both by improving hand-eye co-ordination and, just as importantly, increasing selective attention. Illustrations (3a) and (3b) on page 110 show you how to form the snail's shell during the training period. In (3a) a left-facing snail is drawn by forming the shell spirals with the pen moving from left to right. In (3b) a right-facing snail is drawn by forming the shell spiral with the pen moving from right to left. Demonstrate how to play *Sketch a Snail* by drawing two snails facing one another. Now ask your child to complete several rows of snails on their own. During early sessions your child can draw the spirals as they please providing the circling movements are made in the correct direction. That is from left to right for a left-facing snail (3a) and from right to left for snail facing towards the right (3b).

In later sessions, however, your child must be encouraged to draw the spirals closer and closer together without ever actually touching.

The faces are to be completed by moving the pen in the direction shown by the arrows in the five drawings below.

(2a)

(2b)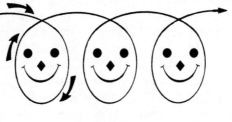

(2c)

(2d)

(2e)

Notice how, within a period of just nine weeks, a child can move from sketching a snail with just a few widely separated loops to a complicated shell involving many more loops closely drawn. When your child is proficient at this game, make it harder by asking them to draw the spiral from the inside of the shell working outwards.

*How **Sketch a Snail** helps*: This game greatly enhances your child's ability to produce accurate movements when shaping letters. It is especially helpful if your child's handwriting difficulties include: poor legibility, crowded letters, angles in the script and variable heights of small letters.

Game 4 – Looping the Loop

What to do: Your child creates this design by moving their pen in the direction shown. It's a tricky challenge so do not worry if they only complete part of the design at first. (*See page 111.*)

Your child learns to draw this shape by making the pen movements shown in (4b). The arrows indicate the direction of travel to create the four loops. Some children find this a difficult design to master all at once. If this happens, ask them to draw only part of the design as shown in (4c).

What to tell your child: 'I am going to show you how to draw this picture.' (Point to the completed drawing 4a.) 'You do it like this . . . ' (Demonstrate the movements involved by following the direction of the arrows in 4b.) 'Now you have a go. I want you to draw the loops as smoothly as you can. Just relax your hand and let the pencil flow across the page. Imagine you are gently stirring a pail of water.'

During these sessions encourage your child to relax their hand, wrist and arm muscles as much as possible. If this proves tricky, carry out the following simple relaxation exercise. Ask your child deliberately to tense these muscles by clenching the writing fist as hard as they can, then trying to touch the back of the hand to the shoulder. This tension is held for a count of five, then the muscles must be allowed to 'flop out' and unwind. Ask them to notice the difference between tension and relaxation in the hand and arm. Explain that, anytime their hand, wrist or arm feels stiff after writing this will make it easier to carry on writing.

*How **Looping the Loop** helps*: This game is designed to enhance hand-eye co-ordination and reduce unnecessary muscle tension when

(3a) A left-facing snail is drawn by forming the shell spirals with the pen moving from left to right.

(3b) A right-facing snail is drawn by forming the shell spirals with the pen moving from right to left.

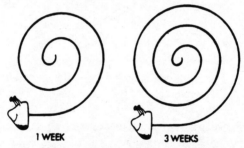

(3c) The progress which is, typically, made in creating shell spirals. At one week only a few, widely spaced lines are drawn.

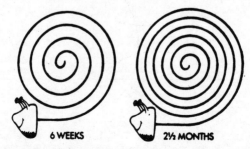

(3d) As the weeks pass the spirals increase and are drawn closer together.

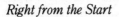

(4a) The design you want your child to create is shown above.

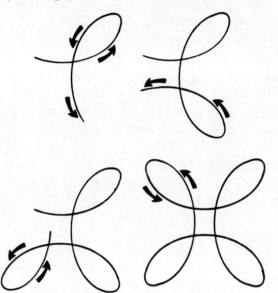

(4b) This must be formed by moving the pen along the lines indicated by the arrows.

(4c) If your child has any difficulty in producing the whole design, start with just half of it, as shown above. Once this can be drawn without difficulty your child should have no problem in completing the whole drawing.

forming the letters. It helps your child's writing to flow and is especially helpful when problems include poor legibility, rigidity and angles in the script.

Game 5 - Complete a Caterpillar

What to do: Partly draw a caterpillar as shown opposite.

Your child's task is to complete the caterpillar by forming a series of loops, all the same size. When this has been mastered ask them to draw the humps underneath the line. Then vary the height of the loops. Finally make the loops very small to develop good hand-eye co-ordination.

How *Complete a Caterpillar* helps: This game overcomes the problem of variability in the height of small letters, while providing practice in the movements required to form the letters 'm' and 'n' accurately.

Game 6 - Building a Fence

What to do: The drawings are produced on a blank sheet of paper in three stages.

Stage One: Your child draws a series of vertical and parallel lines moving left to right across the page.

Stage Two: Explain that the next step is to draw cross-bars on the fence. These must be horizontal and parallel. Demonstrate, moving your pen left to right across the page.

Stage Three: When your child is able to draw more or less accurate vertical and horizontal lines, repeat the game this time asking them to try and make sure that each of the squares formed by the criss-crossed lines are as nearly the same size as possible.

What to tell your child: 'I want you to draw a fence. Start by putting in the upright posts. Make these as straight as possible and in line with one another. (Demonstrate what is required.) When your child has done this say: 'Good, now let's draw in the wires across the posts.'

How *Build a Fence helps*: It enhances a smoothly flowing script while producing straight lines horizontal to the writing line, as with the cross strokes of 't', 'f', 'h' and 'z'. You will find it especially helpful if your child's handwriting shows signs of poor legibility, rigidity and angles in the script.

(5a)

When completing the caterpillar, the important point is to ensure that all the humps are drawn the same size.
When your child has completed several sheets correctly, move to the second part of the project in which humps are drawn on the upside down caterpillar shown in (5b).

(5b)

Once both these designs have been mastered successfully, and your child is consistently producing humps of the same size, proceed to the more challenging tasks shown in (5c) and (5d). Here the humps alternate in size, first on an upright and then on an upside down caterpillar. This provides practice in maintaining the size of small letters when larger ones come between them.

(5c)

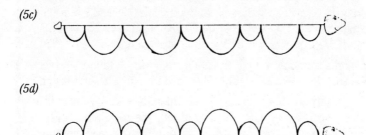

(5d)

The final stage of practice is to reproduce the caterpillar shown in (5e) where the humps are half the size of thoze drawn previously. This gives valuable training in producing small letters of consistent size.

(5e)

Assessing your child's handwriting

If any of the errors below are consistently present in your child's *best* handwriting you should follow the practical suggestions contained in this chapter to help put matters right.

- Inappropriate capital letters – a common error. These will disappear with practice.
- Variations in letter slant or the height of letters suggest your child has yet to find their own particular handwriting style. Inability to control the writing implement could be another cause of the problem.
- Uneven letters. The 'a' and 'r', for example should be the same height, and the 'g' and 'y' extend the same length beneath the writing line.
- Letters are not on the line. Children sometimes write a 'y' for instance with the whole letter resting on the line rather than extending below it.
- The letters are excessively large or small. When very large it means your child is having difficulty forming and controlling the writing. The drawing games (*see pages 105–13*) will help here. Very tiny letters indicate a lack of confidence.
- Words running into one another reveals a failure to plan ahead. So too do words squashed into the end of the line to fit.
- Legibility. Can someone who is unfamiliar with your child's handwriting read isolated words with the remainder covered up? After a couple of weeks can your child still read their own handwriting?
- Mirror writing. Words or even whole letters are reversed. This is very common during the first year of writing and is no cause for concern. It will disappear once your child learns to read fluently.

Helping with your child's spelling

Of course it's important for your child to spell correctly. Poor spelling, especially of common words, makes a bad impression on teachers and may cost marks in an exam. But too much emphasis on correct spelling inhibits your child's creative writing and leads to a loss of confidence. I remember reading a story by an imaginative seven-year-old. It was a wonderful tale, full of interesting ideas and observations. Yet the only comment her teacher had made was to underline the five spelling mistakes in vivid red ink adding a terse message warning against such carelessness in future! What a way to destroy enthusiasm and extinguish the creative spark.

Why spelling is tough

'The conventional spelling of the English language is archaic, cumbersome, and ineffective. Its acquisition consumes much time and effort. Failure to acquire it is easy of detection.'

Little has changed in the 80 years since American teacher Thorstein Veblen wrote those words. Many children at all levels of education not only find difficulty in spelling even simple words but feel deeply pessimistic about ever being able to do so. One of the main problems is that the relationship between speech and spelling is not simply between sounds and letters. The letter 'c', for instance, does not by itself *say* anything. Only when placed in a word does 'c' possess any sound and this differs in different words, as in 'cynic – cat – choose – face – ache' and so on. This confusion makes the common practice of *sounding out* words an unreliable method to adopt. The 'a' sound in *was*, for example, could be made equally well using an 'o'. Unfortunately children are often encouraged to use this highly unsatisfactory strategy when learning to spell.

It is *very important*, therefore, that when supplying words for children writing at home you do not just say them aloud but write them down as well. For example, your child asks, 'How do you spell banana?' Without glancing up from other work, you reply: 'B-A-N-A-N-A'. The effective response is to take time to write it down clearly, and get your child to memorize it using the three step strategy described below.

How your child learns to spell

The traditional 'drill and discipline' method for learning how to spell, where children have to learn lists of words, is tedious and uninspiring. Classroom tests, which often follow this exercise, make poor spellers even more gloomy about their chances of eventual success. Spelling rules are also taught in some schools. But these are of little practical value, being complicated and having many exceptions. If you learned to spell using rules, how many – apart perhaps from '*i* before *e* except after *c*' – do you clearly remember and regularly use?

Teaching your child to spell

Encourage your child to adopt this three step procedure whenever they learn a new word.

First – STUDY the word carefully. Special attention must be paid to parts of the word which appear tricky. Having looked carefully at the word, your child closes their eyes and tries to imagine it written down, at the same time saying the word aloud and pretending to write it by moving a finger across the paper.

Second – ATTEMPT to write the word while keeping the original covered. The word should always be written from memory, *never* copied. Tell your child to think about what the word looked like, how the letters sounded, and the way their fingers moved when pretending to write it.

Third – CHECK whether the spelling is correct. If a mistake has been made, get your child to circle the incorrect letters with a red pen, then study them carefully for a few moments before trying again. This time the tricky letters should be written down extra large. You might like to monitor the spelling progress of a young child, from early experimentation through to fairly reliable spelling, by means of the chart on page 120.

Here are ten practical ways to improve spelling by means of enjoyable activities and games:

1. **Spelling Magic**. Encourage your child to play around with words to find easier ways of learning them. It doesn't matter how silly these 'tricks' are so long as they make recall easy and accurate.

Island   An island *is land* surrounded by water.
Occasionally You're an ass to spell occasionally with more than one 's'.
Friend   *Fri*day is my *end* of the week friend.

Mnemonics can be useful too. This involves inventing a sentence using words which start with letters in the word your child must spell. Many children, for example, misspell Wednesday. They can be helped to remember the correct letter sequence by remembering the phrase:

We Eat Damp Noodles Every Suppertime on Wednesday.

2. **Hidden Words**. Your child searches for words 'hidden' inside a longer one, eg 'car' inside *cartoon*; 'moth' in *mother*; 'eat' in *meat* etc. Most children are amused to discover that father is really a fat – her!

3. **Kim's Game**. A party favourite which improves memory and spelling. A variety of objects are placed on a tray and covered with a cloth. The cloth is removed for a few seconds and the player has to remember, and write down, as many objects as possible. The number of objects is gradually increased.

4. **Pelmanism**. Is played in the same way as Happy Families. Prepare by writing pairs of words with the same letter pattern on separate cards. For example one card might have 'bad' and the pair 'sad', or 'said' and 'paid' might be paired up. The letter pattern should be underlined or written in a different colour to make certain it stands out. The cards are shuffled and placed, face down, in rows across the table. Your child turns over any two cards, studies them carefully and keeps both if the letter patterns are the same. If they are different the cards are turned face down again. Then it is the next player's turn. The person who collects most pair cards wins.

5. **TV Tests**. Based on favourite advertisements are an excellent way of catching a child's interest. When a word or phrase appears on the screen, tell them to study it carefully. The word or phrase is written down, and checked next time it appears.

6. **Invisible Tracing**. Is helpful with words your child finds particularly tricky. The awkward word is written on a card and your child traces the letters with one finger to get the 'feel' of it, speaking the word aloud while doing so. The card is turned over and your child tries to write the word from memory. If correct offer plenty of praise. When wrong, repeat the tracing process. Keep the cards and gradually build up a collection of learned words. These can be looked at occasionally to refresh your child's memory. A child may have to practise certain words several times over before they become firmly fixed in their mind.

7. **Hidden Treasure**. Grids, like the one on page 118, can be constructed fairly quickly and easily. Your child has to discover, and circle in red, a hidden 'treasure' word concealed within other letters. This is always the longest word in the grid, which will usually contain several

shorter words as well. Having found the treasure word your child should be rewarded with a small treat. Start with simple grids increasing their complexity as your child's skill and confidence increase. When they feel sufficiently confident, they can make Hidden Treasure charts for you to solve.

```
G  H  D  I  B  T  B  D  X  C
D  Z  C  H  O  P  R  Y  U  I
R  W  E  R  X  M  B  V  Z  Y
Y  T  W  Q  E  Y  T  F  G  X
L  K  Y  M  R  U  D  F  L  K
```

Here the treasure word is BOXER. Points can also be awarded for every other word identified. The treasure word selected should be written down first, then other letters formed around it. All the letters of the treasure word must be in a straight line, running horizontally, vertically or even diagonally.

8. Keep A Spelling Journal. Suggest your child keeps a notebook of new words they want to spell. This is far better than giving them words *you* think they ought to learn.

9. Spelling Die. Prepare for this game by writing down and numbering, from 1 to 6, six single letters and six groups of letters. For example:

(1) T　(2) H　(3) L　(4) R　(5) D　(6) F
(1) AUGHT　(2) ABLE　(3) OAST　(4) IGHT　(5) AIL　(6) AKE.

The Rules:
Your child can play this alone or with a friend. They start by throwing a die twice. The first gives the starting letter of a word. The second a possible ending. Given the first letter and letter groups above a (3) gives 'L' and a (6) 'AKE' making 'LAKE'. If a word can be made up, and your child spots it, they win a point. If they miss seeing a word but their friend does, then a point goes to them. If no word can be made no points are awarded. The first player to score six points wins.

10. First and Last. This is a game for two players. One person writes down a word and the other has to think of, and spell, another starting with the *last* letter of the preceding word eg: Mouse – Elephant – Trip – Pail – Letter – Red . . .

Whichever games you decide to play, and many are an excellent way of passing the time during a car, train or air journey, never turn them into a chore. Keep the atmosphere light and relaxed. Your child must enjoy and look forward to playing if the spelling lessons are to be learned successfully.

Helping your child with mathematics

You don't have to be an Einstein to encourage your child to become more proficient and confident in maths. Indeed help at home is usually essential since this subject causes greater difficulty to more children than any on the timetable. As a result many develop such a negative attitude towards numbers they firmly believe even the simplest calculations must be beyond them.

If you promote maths as interesting and valuable then chances are your child will also see it as a worthwhile skill to master. Unfortunately, as a result of their own unhappy experiences in class, some parents are more tolerant of innumeracy than they would be of poor reading or writing skills. Imagine the outrage if a ten-year-old admitted they could hardly read or write! Yet a child of the same age who confesses to being baffled by maths often finds sympathetic agreement: 'I was hopeless at sums too!'

One barrier is that maths is often viewed as a deeply mysterious subject, involving daunting entities like decimal fractions and quadratic equations. A classroom-bound topic which has little relevance to real life. In fact, of course, maths is as much a part of everyday living as reading or writing. How many times do you . . . Estimate the amount of petrol needed for a trip by car? Work out how much paint to buy when decorating a room? Calculate the dinner money your child will require to see them through the week? Estimate the cost of your shopping trolley so as not to run short of money at the checkout? Decide what time you must leave home to catch a train?

In all these commonplace activities, you are drawing on mathematical knowledge and thinking. As a government report put it: 'Mathematics has a crucial role to play in equipping young people to meet the responsibilities of adult life – as citizens, employees and members of households. At home, for example we use mathematics daily – in managing the family budget, in comparing price and quantity of goods in the shops, in assessing the real cost of hire purchase agreements and of insurance policies, in measuring up for carpets and

Date:

Progress chart for spelling development

1. *Experimentation:* Marks scattered randomly on page, but showing some pencil control and awareness of letter formation (ie some known letters may appear).

2. *Letter strings:* No word spacings yet – some letters representing ideas and meaning (ie some initial consonants representing words, interspersed or followed by other letters at random).

3. *Groups of letters:* Word spaces begin to appear but may not relate to actual words. A few known words distinguishable, interspersed with consonants or groups of consonants (eg tbl for table).

4. *More recognizable word units:* Made up of initial consonants/consonant blends and some vowels, plus a growing number of familiar known words.

5. *Becoming more reliable:* In use of initial letters/blends, and more accurate in use of vowels and approximation of vowel digraphs etc. Gaining wider vocabulary of correctly spelt known words and common letter patterns.

6. *Spelling:* Of most common words and letter patterns now fairly reliable. Beginning to apply knowledge of common letter patterns (both consonants and vowels) consistently and make appropriate use of spelling rules.

Comment:

curtains and in working out a car's consumption of petrol. As citizens we need to make sense of a growing volume of statistical information, for example about the country's economic position, crime rates, house prices, and trends in average earnings.'*

How modern mathematics is taught

For some parents, novelist L F Hartley's observation that the past is a foreign country where 'they do things differently' might have been written with the modern approach to teaching maths in mind! In the not so distant past school maths was divided into three major branches:

Arithmetic – which involves counting with numbers.

Geometry – which is concerned with shapes.

Algebra – which uses letters like 'x' and 'y' to express the relation-ships between things.

These were taught as separate topics often without any direct con-nection between them. Today, while these basics remain unaltered, teaching methods have undergone many changes. There are three main reasons why 'new' maths looks so different to adults who were taught by traditional methods. First the distinction between arith-metic, geometry and algebra has blurred with children being encour-aged to discover relationships between them. The next difference is one of emphasis. Teachers help children to understand the concepts behind maths rather than mechanical skills such as long division. Finally the focus is strongly on applications for maths, with problems rooted in practical problems.

Children are no longer expected to master maths through mechani-cal drills or by working their way down long lists of sums with little relevance to everyday experience. Just as the present day emphasis on reading is to learn words in context, so too are number problems pre-sented within real life situations. Let's start by looking at the mathe-matical skills your child will be expected to learn during the infant years, from five to around seven. If your child is older than this, you might want to skip directly to page 125. However, bear in mind that the ideas discussed below are fundamental to confident and proficient mathematical ability throughout your child's school career.

* Mathematics National Curriculum Working Group Report, 1988.

Your child and the National Curriculum

Under this scheme mathematics is divided into five attainment targets each covering important basic skills. There are different levels of attainment, within each key stage, which your child will be expected to satisfy. Although the majority of five to seven-year-olds will be working at Levels One and Two, some four-year-olds may have achieved Level One targets before starting school. At the top end of the scale some seven-year-olds will have progressed to Level Three while others are still working at Level One. At the age of seven your child is assessed and you will be told which level they have attained.

What your child has to know

Level One: using and applying mathematics

The skills to be mastered. Your child will be expected to know how to:
Use mathematics as an integral part of practical classroom tasks.
Talk about their own work and respond to questions.
Make predictions based on experience.

Example problem. Show your child a plastic and a metal spoon. Ask them to guess which is heavier and then check this by means of a balance.

Level One: numbers

The skills to be mastered. Your child will be expected to know how to:
Use numbers in the context of classroom and school. This means being able to count, read, write and order numbers up to at least ten.
Add and subtract using a small number of objects.

Level One: algebra

The skills to be mastered. Your child will be expected to know how to:
Devise repeating patterns.

Example problem. Ask your child to help you tidy their room. Start by placing two items of clothes side by side across the bed, for example pants, socks, pants, socks. Ask them to continue this pattern alone. Repeat the exercise using coloured shapes, such as stars, moons, triangles or squares placed on a sheet of plain card.

Level One: shape and space

The skills to be mastered. Your child will be expected to know how to:
Talk about models they have made.
Follow or give instructions related to movement and position.
Compare and order objects without measuring.

Example problem 1. Have a selection of objects, such as a box, pencils, counters and so on. Ask, 'Can you put the pencils inside the box?' 'Can you place the counters on top of the pencils?' 'Can you put the box under the table?' If your child has difficulty in following your instructions, demonstrate any words they don't understand.

Example problem 2. Play an I-Spy game in which your child finds objects which satisfy certain requirements, such as being small, round and red, or large, square and green etc.

Level One: handling data

The skills to be mastered. Your child will be expected to know how to:
Sort a set of objects describing criteria chosen.

Example problem. Ask your child to draw a picture of everyone in the family and write their names beneath. Now have your child draw different types of food, such as a loaf of bread, a bottle of milk, fish, fruit and so on. Ask if they can show which foods people in the family like best by drawing lines between that person and their favourite food. Can they answer questions such as 'What is Mummy's favourite food?' by looking at the diagram? Also ask how they like their eggs cooked, whether boiled, fried, scrambled etc, or potatoes served, whether mashed, as chips, roasted and so on. Questions like these help develop an understanding of the way different things can be sorted according to a set of criteria.

Level Two: using and applying mathematics

The skills to be mastered. Your child will be expected to know how to:
Select the materials and the mathematics to use for a practical task.
Talk about work or ask questions using appropriate mathematical language.
Respond appropriately to the question, 'What would happen if . . . ?'

Example problem. Ask your child how a bar of chocolate could be shared equally between three children. Do they understand it will have to be cut into three pieces? Can they solve the problem if you ask how a larger bar might be shared equally between more children?

Level Two: numbers

The skills to be mastered. Your child will be expected to know how to:
Demonstrate that they know and can use number facts, including addition and subtraction.
Solve whole number problems involving addition and subtraction.
Identify 'halves' and 'quarters'.
Recognize the need for standard units of measurement, eg metres, miles, pints, litres, seconds, minutes.

Example problems. Show your child two piles of bricks, one containing eight the other 12 bricks. Ask which has more and which less bricks. If that proves too difficult, tell them to make two towers of the same height, then ask which has more bricks.

Level Two: algebra

The skills to be mastered. Your child will be expected to know how to:
Explore number patterns.
Recognize the use of a symbol to stand for an unknown number.

Example problem. If one child has an apple, their friend brings a bag of apples, and they finish with four apples, how many were in the friend's bag?

Level Two: shape and space

The skills to be mastered. Your child will be expected to know how to:
Use mathematical terms to describe common 2-D and 3-D objects ie squares, circles, triangles, rectangles, hexagons, pentagons, cubes, cylinders, spheres, and rectangular boxes.
Recognize different types of movement.

Level Two: handling data

The skills to be mastered. Your child will be expected to know how to:
Interpret relevant data which have been collected.
Recognize that there is a degree of uncertainty about the outcome of some events but that others are certain or impossible.

Example problem. Think of different events which are either certain, uncertain or impossible. For example, 'It will get dark tonight' is certain, while 'It will rain tomorrow morning' is uncertain, and 'Tomorrow will be Monday' (if, for example, today is Tuesday) is impossible.

Level Three: using and applying mathematics

The skills to be mastered. Your child will be expected to know how to:
Find ways of overcoming difficulties when solving problems.
Use or interpret appropriate mathematical terms and mathematical aspects of everyday language in a precise way.
Present results in a clear and organized way.
Investigate general statements by trying out some examples.

Level Three: numbers

The skills to be mastered. Your child will be expected to know how to:
Read and order numbers up to 1000.
Demonstrate that they know and can use multiplication tables.
Solve problems involving multiplication or division.
Make estimates based on familiar units of measurement, checking results.
Interpret a range of numbers in the context of measurement or money.

Level Three: algebra

The skills to be mastered. Your child will be expected to know how to:
Use patterns in numbers when doing mental calculations.
Use inverse operations in a simple context.

Level Three: shape and space

The skills to be mastered. Your child will be expected to know how to:
Sort shapes using mathematical criteria and give reasons.
Recognize reflective symmetry.
Use the eight points of the compass to show direction.

Example Problem 1. Cut a potato in half and carve one surface into triangles. Dip it into paint and ask your child to produce a line of triangles along a sheet of paper.

Example Problem 2. Reflection – Draw half a butterfly, a house or a person and ask your child to complete the picture. If they find this too hard place a mirror along the centre line and show them the reflection.

Example Problem 3. Rotation – Cut a triangle from card and secure one corner using a paper-clip. Ask your child to draw around it. Move the triangle a short distance, then tell them to make another drawing. Continue in this way until the triangle has moved in a complete circle. Remove the paper-clip and let them see the pattern.

Level Three: handling data

The skills to be mastered. Your child will be expected to know how to:
   Access information in a simple database.
   Construct and interpret statistical diagrams.
   Use appropriate language to justify decisions when placing events
   in order of likelihood.
   To succeed at Level Three and beyond your child will have to learn
the following basic skills, all of which can be mastered far more easily
with your help.

Operations

This is a general term for addition, subtraction, multiplication and
division. After the age of nine most children have few problems with
addition. Some find subtraction harder since it can be looked at in two
ways. The first is 'taking away'. A child asked how many apples are
left after starting with six and eating two is performing a 'taking
away' operation. But subtraction can also be seen in terms of 'differences'. If John has six apples and Martin has two, what is the difference between them? Both sorts of subtraction are used in real life and
even when, as in the example, the answer is the same the mathematical thinking required is different.

Most children find multiplication harder than subtraction and division is often considered the most difficult operation of all. As with subtraction, there are two ways of looking at division. If your child has
nine apples to share among three friends how many will each one get?
Dividing by three provides the answer. But they might want to know
how many friends could be given three apples if they have nine to
hand out. Once again the answer is the same, but the mathematical
thinking different.

Helping your child master operations

Be on the look out for opportunities to practise addition, subtraction,
multiplication and division. For instance asking your child to add up
the price of shopping and subtract the total from the money in your
bag to make sure there is enough. Always offer a demonstration rather
than simply an explanation if your child fails to understand an operation. When Ben, aged eight, was baffled by division his mother did not
bother to explain on paper. Instead she offered him three pieces of

chocolate to divide equally with his brother. Without hesitation Ben broke the third piece in half. Then she gave him four pieces but asked for an equal share herself. Again Ben confidently handed out one piece each and broke the fourth into three. This simple exercise provided Ben with the insight needed to tackle division successfully.

Finding new ways of doing calculations also helps sustain interest and enhance confidence. One such method is:

Finger Maths

Children seldom have difficulty with their times tables up to five, but may get stuck with six and higher. This is where Finger Maths helps. It's a game most children enjoy and love showing off to their friends.

How to play **Finger Maths**: Your child places both hands in front of them, thumbs uppermost. The fingers are numbered as shown below:

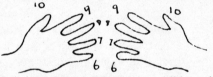

To multiply two numbers, say 7×9, your child touches the 7 finger on one hand to the 9 finger of the other.

Now they find the answer by counting the number of fingers *below and including* the touching fingers. In this example there are 6. This gives the tens portion of their answer. Next *multiply* the *above* fingers on one hand by those on the other to give the units. Here there are three above fingers on one hand and one on the other 3×1=3. Putting the two numbers together gives the answer: 63 which is, of course, correct.

There are just two conditions, when multiplying 6×6 and 7×6, which require a further calculation. After doing the multiplying you end up with either 16 or 12. Now you must *add* the '1' to the first (tens) number obtained. For example with 7×6 you'll get: fingers touching and below = 3. Fingers above: 3 on one hand and 4 on the other = 12 Adding the 1 from the 12 to first number gives 3+1=4. Finally put them together to arrive at 42.

With practice your child will find their built-in digital calculator is a fast, fun way of multiplying numbers from 6 to 10. You might like to pit the speed of finger maths against an electronic calculator. In most cases fingers are faster! This kind of game provides insights into the way numbers can be played with to produce correct answers.

Number Bonds

Are combinations of numbers used to form a particular number. For example the number bonds of 10 are: 1+9; 2+8; 3+7; 4+6; 5+5; 6+4; 7+3; 8+2; 9+1; 10+0.

Young children cannot work these out in their heads. You can often see their fingers moving as they seek to keep track of the calculation. This method is slow and prone to errors, since they may lose count and either come up with the wrong answer or have to start all over again. Once number bonds are fixed in their minds, however, children are able to recall them swiftly and accurately. If, for instance, you were asked what is 5+7, or 2×6 or even 36/3 the correct answer 12 should immediately spring to mind without any need for calculating it. Being able to recall number bonds quickly and easily therefore, is as important for your child's success in mathematics as knowing their times tables.

Helping your child master **Number Bonds**. Once under 10 number bonds (where one of the two numbers is less than 10) are mastered, extend this understanding to larger numbers. For example, if your child knows that 4+3=7 can they recognize a similarity with 14+3=17 and 14+13=27?

You can also start working with multiplication patterns:

$$2\times4 = 8 \qquad 20\times4 = 80$$
$$200\times4 = 800 \qquad 20\times40 = 800$$
$$200\times40 = 8000 \qquad 200\times400 = 80000$$

Here is an easily constructed toy, which makes learning number bonds faster, easier and more enjoyable.

Mr Maths Whiz Wheel

Construct the Wheel by following the instructions.

Constructing the Whiz Wheel. The Whiz Wheel is an easily constructed teaching machine that helps to transform learning into playing.

Materials needed. One piece of cardboard, 15cm × 20cm; two paper plates, one approximately 25cm in diameter, the other about 17cm in diameter; a packet of small gummed labels; sticky tape; a paper fastener.

How to build the Whiz Wheel

1. Paste Mr. Math's head, (illustration A) onto the piece of cardboard and cut out around the dotted lines.

2. Take the smaller of the two paper plates and cut along three sides of an opening about 2cm on each side, to produce a flap (illustration B).

3. Tape or glue Mr. Math's head to the back of the larger plate (illustration C).

4. Place 10 gummed labels around the edge of the larger plate. Now place the smaller plate on the larger and line up the opening with one of the labels.

   Raise the flap and make a pencil mark on the larger plate (illustration B) to indicate the position for a second row of ten gummed labels on the larger plate.

   Do this ten times then remove the plate, then attach the second row of labels on the larger plate.

5. Stick one label on the smaller plate, just above the opening. Attach the plates, smaller on top of the larger, using the paper fastener, so that you can rotate them (illustration C).

6. Decide which of the four operations, addition, subtraction, multiplication or division you want to begin with.

The results of the diagnostic interviews (*see page 138*) should have identified which of these arithmetic ailments is in most urgent need of treatment, if mistakes are being made on several under ten operations, start with the one which produced most errors on the assessment.

Now devise ten sums, using the operation (addition, subtraction, multiplication or division) you want to practise. Write the correct answer in the space beneath the window flap so that it can be seen when the two numbers in the sum are lined up.

*Using the **Whiz Wheel**.* Sit beside your child, holding the Wheel so you can both see it easily. Start by turning the inner disc around a few times, keeping the window flap closed. Stop when numbers on the inner disc line up. If constructed correctly the answer to the addition, subtraction, multiplication or division (depending on the operation chosen) will be beneath the window flap. Your child now tries to work

(a)

out as quickly as possible what the answer is, and then checks by lifting the flap.

Make a note of any problems which lead to uncertainty or produce the most errors. This will show you which of the under-ten number bonds are hardest for your child. You can then include more problems

(b)

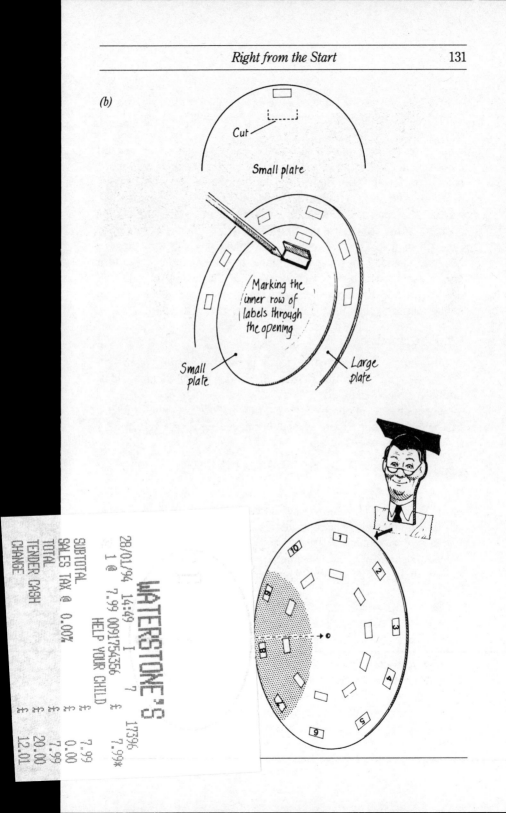

Cut

Small plate

Marking the inner row of labels through the opening

Small plate

Large plate

of this type in various number games (*see below*). But never concentrate exclusively on difficult sums or your child will soon become discouraged and lose interest.

As soon as they obtain consistently right answers over several games change the numbers on the smaller plate by sticking a gummed label with a fresh set of digits over the first. For a part of each Whiz Wheel session swap roles and let your child pose the questions. Give occasional wrong answers, then ask for help in finding the correct solution. In my experience most children greatly enjoy this 'teaching' role, which helps sustain motivation while fixing the right answer firmly in their memories. One warning, never allow the game to turn into a competition between children, since the less able child will quickly become discouraged. Provide plenty of encouragement and do not be concerned if, at first, your child makes many mistakes.

Hunt the Number

Another game which is useful to teaching Number Bonds is one where you have to find as many different combinations as possible to add or multiply to a chosen number.

Suppose the select number is 8. Answers include not only: 7+1; 6+2; 4+4 and so on, not forgetting 8+0; but also 4×2; 2×2×2; 16/2; 32/4 3+3+2; 2+2+4; 2+2+2+2, and so on.

Place Value

This is just a mathematical way of talking about hundreds, tens and units. While this may seem easy to you, children often become confused, especially where large values are involved. Yet it's impossible to understand any number larger than 9 without understanding place value. The number 777, for instance, consists entirely of 7s. Their *position* or place, tells us whether they represent 7 units, 7 tens or 7 hundreds.

Check your child's understanding by asking questions such as; 'How much is £4.99 to the nearest pound?' 'Add 1, 10 or 100 to a number?' 'What number comes after 9, 99, 109, 199, 999?'

Helping your child master **Place Value**. These problems are often easier, especially for 'implementing' or 'inventive' children, if demonstrated in a practical way. For instance using real money, with a £1 coin to represent the 1, nine 10p pieces for the 9 in the second column and nine 1p coins for the third column. Now ask how many pence there are on the table and what will happen if another 1p is added?

Gun Fight at the KO Corral

Here is a calculator game that helps your child understand place values. The level of complexity can be varied depending on your child's level of knowledge. For the simplest game key in a three digit number, say 456. Explain these are the 'baddies' who have to be knocked down one at a time by your child who is the Sheriff. This is done by subtracting numbers until none are left, eg: 456–6=450; 450–50=400; 400–400=0.

Make the game harder by adding the rule that the baddies must be knocked down in a particular order. Later you can increase the level of challenge by:

Using a four digit number.

Knocking down the baddies by addition rather than subtraction. In this version the game ends when the number totals 1000 or 10000 etc.

Using decimal numbers.

After your child has become expert with all the above see how well they can do when only numbers in the digits column can be shot down. This involves multiplying or dividing the displayed value by 10, 100, 1000 etc, in order to shift the required digit into the unit position each time.

Estimating Answers

One reason why mathematics scares so many people is the assumption that all answers have to be absolutely correct. Yet, in real life we seldom worry about pin-point accuracy. Approximate answers, when estimating the petrol needed for a journey, weighing ingredients for a cake, or calculating the amount of wood needed to build a rabbit hutch are usually perfectly adequate.

Some parents also believe that calculators and computers have done away with the need for an educated guess at the answer before carrying out a calculation. Why bother, they ask, when the correct solution is available at the press of a button? In fact using a calculator successfully depends on an estimate of the expected answer. Without an idea of what to expect, your child will have no idea whether the answer they come up with is spot on or wildly inaccurate.

*Helping your child master **Estimating**.* Estimating is another skill best taught using everyday opportunities. Give examples of 'rounding numbers' while counting up money. Adding 38 to 53, for example, is roughly the equivalent of adding 40+50 giving an estimate of 90. Encourage your child to practise estimating *time* for instance when walking to school, going swimming, tidying their room, preparing a meal; to estimate how much money will be needed when shopping; how many marbles are needed to fill a container; how many Lego bricks will be required to construct a model and so on.

Decimals

It's surprising that so many people, adults as well as children, grow pale when decimals are mentioned. Since we all have ten fingers (well, alright eight fingers and two thumbs), this is the most natural way for humans to count. Decimals are used when timing events: 'The new record time is 12.52 seconds,' says the television commentator excitedly; measuring using the metric system, 'You'll need a piece of string 25.25 centimetres long . . .' an instruction may tell us; and in buying things: 'The skipping rope costs £50.50p.'

Decimals are closely linked to the concept of place value, since the decimal point (.) is only a marker to indicate where whole numbers (units) and tenths start. So 5.5 is just another way of telling us there are 5 units and 5/10 of a unit. Now 5/10 is the equivalent of 1/2 or a half.

Using a calculator ask your child to find the decimal equivalents of 1/2; 5/10; and 2/4. They will discover that they are all different ways of expressing a half or 0.5. Check your child's understanding by asking them to add £3.41p and 40p on the calculator. If their answer is £43.41p they have not keyed in the 40p correctly, that is as 0.40p.

*Helping your child master **Decimals**.* Seek out opportunities to talk about decimal numbers in daily life, for instance when weighing and measuring, working with money or timing events to fractions of a second. Represent the decimal and fraction equivalent on a number line.

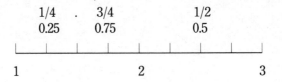

This helps your child to see they are the same.

Simple Fraction Equivalents

Imagine a cake shared equally between two children. Each person obviously gets half a cake. If two cakes are shared between four children, the result is the same. Each child has half a cake. When written as fractions this means in the first instance each child had 1/2 of the cake, in the second 2/4 portions of cake. Although different, 1/2 and 2/4 have the same value and so are described as *equivalent*.

Helping your child master **Fraction Equivalents.** Construct a set of twelve cards or 'decimal dominoes', with fractions on the top half and non-matching decimal equivalents of fractions, on the lower half. Here are some examples:

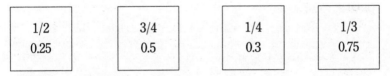

| 1/2 | 3/4 | 1/4 | 1/3 |
| 0.25 | 0.5 | 0.3 | 0.75 |

The cards are shared out and games of dominoes played by matching decimals to their correct fraction equivalents.

Logical Thinking

Children often need assistance in developing this vital mathematical skill.

Helping your child master **Logical Thinking.** This entertaining game helps do just that. You think of a number between 1 and 100 and tell your child to guess what it is by asking questions which can only be answered Yes or No. At first they are likely to pose random questions, such as, 'Is it 9?' or 'Is it 57?' If they persist in this unproductive strategy suggest you reverse roles and demonstrate how logical questions will find the chosen number far more rapidly.

For example: 'Is it less than 50?' 'Is it an odd number?' 'Is it greater than 25?' With this approach you identify the correct number after only seven or eight questions. When it's your child's turn again, you might find they ask 'Is it greater than 50?' then, if you answer no, demand: 'Is it less than 50?' If this happens, explain the second question is unnecessary.

Mathematical Thinking

This is in many ways the most crucial skill of all. There's no purpose in teaching your child to solve problems in a purely mechanical way with no understanding of *why* specific operations are carried out or what the answer actually means.

Helping your child master **Mathematical Thinking**. When your child is stuck on a problem suggest they adopt the 3-D approach. They start by *deciding* what sort of calculation is needed. Should they multiply or divide, add or subtract? When *doing* the calculation each step must be checked carefully. Needless mistakes undermine confidence and destroy motivation. Finally they *deliberate* on their answer. Does it look sensible or silly? This is important when using a calculator since it's easy to get the proportion wrong, saying for instance, that pocket money saved over a year will amount to £400 instead of £40.

Mental Arithmetic

After being rather neglected this skill is increasingly seen as important. You should use every opportunity to let your child practise carrying out calculations in their heads.

Helping your child master **Mental Arithmetic**. One way of doing this is a challenge to beat the calculator. A sum is written down, then either you or your child attempts to calculate the answer using mental arithmetic while the other uses a calculator. If number bonds have been well learned, your child should have no difficulty in coming up with the right answer far faster than the calculator can be operated. This gives a great boost to confidence and helps children to realize they do not always have to depend on their calculator when answering simple number questions.

Problem Solving

Encourage your child to master this skill using everyday activities involving mathematical thinking, like working out how long it will take to reach your destination when going on holiday, or working out what foreign currency is worth in sterling. Do not feel concerned that home lessons will conflict with anything your child learns in class. But you cannot go wrong by developing mastery of addition, subtraction, multiplication (a fast way of doing addition ie $3\times2=2+2+2=6$) and division . If in doubt about other lessons read the course text and talk over your approach with your child's teacher.

Calculator – friend or foe?

Although some people worry that calculators in class lead to dependency and mechanical reasoning, the evidence suggests just the opposite. Used properly the calculator can help your child develop a better feel for, and understanding of numbers.

Check out your child's calculator. Before you give your child a calculator, check the way it deals with a sum involving a number of different operations. Key in: 4+2×6=? If the answer is 36 the calculator works on numbers as they are keyed instead of following the rules of arithmetic which specify the order in which calculations must be performed. That is multiplication/division must always be done before addition/subtraction. If the answer is 18 the calculator follows those rules and is a superior tool for your child to use since the operation will seem more natural. To get the required answer in the first instance your child must key in the problem in as 2×6=4+4=? which could lead to confusion.

Assessing your child's maths progress

This can be tricky because much primary maths teaching involves practical projects, using scales, measuring blocks, working with calculators, packets of coins and so on. Because your child considers this play, they may give you the idea that little or no 'real' maths is done. And since much work is done verbally there are unlikely to be many written notes, perhaps adding to your fear that little progress is being made. If seriously concerned, take advantage of open evenings to see what teaching apparatus is available and ask how it is being used. Study completed projects and ask what others are being undertaken. But before making a fuss make certain your expectations are realistic.

Some parents feel they are being 'fobbed off' with an excuse if told that 'children vary in their rates of progress'. But this really is true and one reason why it is so unhelpful to compare your child with others in the same class. Furthermore each new skill involves mastering several steps. This means that a child who starts school knowing their numbers up to 30, but has no idea about counting objects must make up a great deal of groundwork before moving on to addition or subtraction. Children also experience learning 'spurts' when they shoot ahead followed by a period of consolidation during which progress may appear to slow or even stop.

All this means week by week monitoring is highly misleading. Far better to depend on month by month or even term by term improvements. You need only feel serious concern if your child makes either below average progress from one level to the next, or uneven progress from one term to the next, or a slower rate of progress in some aspects of maths than in others. If this happens talk to your child's teachers as soon as possible. Unless the next parents open evening is being held in the next week or so, make a special appointment.

Pin-pointing sources of error

If you to want help resolve misunderstandings and confusions it is essential to discover exactly where and why your child is going wrong. You can best do this in a relaxed session of diagnostic listening.

How to proceed. Give your child one problem, written on a single sheet of paper, at the start of a diagnostic session. The interview begins as soon as your child has completed or attempted to complete the sum, irrespective of whether that answer is right or wrong.

Start by asking a question along these lines, 'That's very interesting, can you tell me a little more about what you did there?' If this fails to produce a satisfactory answer continue with, 'I don't quite understand what you mean, could you explain how you did that in more detail?' If you are still unclear about the reasoning behind a particular number in the answer you should now inquire, 'Is there anything more which made you do that?' Should the child's reasoning remain in doubt you might try one further tactic before temporarily giving up your attempt to understand – at least for this session. Restate your child's last response and pause for a few seconds. This often encourages them to provide further information.

When diagnosing errors, keep these points in mind. Make a record of each interview. You may find it easier to tape an interview. This avoids the distractions of keeping a written note, guarantees the accuracy of the material extracted and ensures you obtain sufficient information to make an effective diagnosis. Question your child gently about their thinking behind each digit in the answer, working from right to left. If the answer was 567, for example, start with the 7, then the 6 and finally the 5.

Because children are not very good at explaining what was going on in their minds while working out a sum, you may use one or more of the probe questions listed above. Right as well as wrong answers must be investigated for three reasons. Firstly, focusing on wrong answers may only make your child anxious and defensive. This will render the diagnosis of difficulties harder and the interview less successful. Secondly, right answers may have been reached by an illogical route, a chain of reasoning which cannot be depended on to give the right answer every time. Unless you clearly establish the procedure used you could be overlooking an important source of future mistakes. Thirdly, to gain insights into faulty reasoning it is helpful to understand how your child thinks when getting answers right.

Five further ways to help

1. Identify any difficulties your child may be having using diagnostic listening.
2. Praise your child's efforts and let them know they are making progress.
3. Never feel disheartened by wrong answers. See them as learning steps along the road to a full understanding.
4. Never be too quick to provide the right answer. Remember what matters most is your child's understanding.
5. Ask How? and Why? questions as your child attempts a calculation. These are far more helpful than What? questions. Concentrate on understanding the thinking, not only the end results.

In this chapter it has only been possible for me to touch on some of the ways you can help your child become confident and proficient in the vital subject of mathematics. There are many good books which will provide fuller guidance together with excellent games. I suggest you read the maths books from the *Success* series published by MacMillam Education. These colourful and entertaining workbooks are graded for different ages. Another invaluable book is *Help Your Child With Maths*, by Alan T Graham, published by Fontana. This is not only highly informative but an enjoyable read with a host of interesting number games.

5

STAYING AHEAD – THE MIDDLE AND SECONDARY YEARS

Choosing the right school for your child

Selecting a primary school usually means finding one close to home, so travel is easy and your child has plenty of friends to play with. Choosing the right secondary school is usually a good deal trickier. Should you go for one with excellent exam results or a more relaxed atmosphere? Are slightly shabby premises and caring teachers better than superb facilities but a less dedicated staff? How can you be sure your child will fit in, feel happy and do well?

Under the 1980 Education Act you have the right to express a preference for a school of your choice, although the Local Education Authority (LEA) may overrule your preference. Should this happen, you can appeal to a tribunal. Your LEA is obliged to inform you of the necessary procedure. Many parents either never realize they have such a choice or meekly accept whatever is offered, complaining when things turn out badly and feeling thankful if child and school appear well suited. Because education is so vital it's important to choose a school which matches your child's needs – even if it makes you rather unpopular with local education officials.

For some parents the answer is to go private (*see The ABC of Learning*). But it's mistaken to assume this is always the best option. Many comprehensive schools offer an education which is every bit as good, and in some ways even superior to, the best private schools. Here's how you can make the best choice:

1. Start by noting your child's scholastic strengths and weaknesses together with their likes and dislikes. Do they favour highly structured work or do better work in less formal lessons? Do they have practical more than intellectual abilities? Are they outgoing or shy? Knowledge of your child, and past school reports are your surest

guides here. Having created this profile of your child, the next step is to try and find a school which matches it.

2. Ask friends and neighbours with children at local secondary schools for their views. But don't rely solely on these opinions since people's ideas and expectations about education differ widely and their comments may not be relevant to your child's needs. More reliable insights can often be gleaned from fourth and fifth formers at a particular school. Their liking for teachers and loyalty to the school will be apparent in spite of the usual grumbles and complaints. You'll also get a clear idea of how interested and enthusiastic they are about their studies. A positive attitude towards lessons is clear evidence of caring and imaginative teaching.

3. While the prospectus and open evenings for prospective parents will offer you a general idea of what's on offer, visiting the school during term time is usually much more informative. This can usually be arranged by phoning or writing for an appointment. When chatting to staff tactfully ask whether truancy is a problem and discover their views on discipline. Regret for the abolition of corporal punishment may betray a discipline problem or the belief that high standards demand strict discipline. Ask yourself how your child would respond to such a regime.

4. Observe how children behave towards one another in the playground. Does there seem to be excessive rowdiness or signs of bullying? Is the play area congested or can the children spread themselves and play freely?

5. Since exams are your child's passport to success and fulfilment any teacher who claims they are irrelevant should be viewed with suspicion. But an excellent exam record could indicate a school which only enters pupils who are certain to pass. This means many children will be denied the opportunity to study or be examined in subjects where, despite disappointing classroom performance, they might do well.

6. Assessing the attitude of teachers can be tricky. A head who comes over as amiable and understanding to parents may be a tyrant with children. Generally, however, one can sense the school's general approach and atmosphere. For most children the best choice is a school which encourages and supports all its pupils rather than rewarding only the high fliers.

Play your part

Having chosen the school it is essential to give them your full support throughout your child's career. This means attending open evenings, getting to know your child's teacher, and taking an active role in out-of-school activities. Many teachers complain about parents they describe as gate post grumblers. These are people who instead of voicing concerns or discussing any criticisms openly with the school prefer to grumble among themselves when collecting or leaving their children. I think one reason why this happens is that some adults find it difficult to talk to teachers. Not because the teachers are unapproachable or the parents shy, but due to subconscious feelings aroused by their own, less than happy, school-day memories. Later on I want to address some of these concerns, and suggest positive, practical ways of conducting a fruitful dialogue with your child's teacher. A dialogue which can prove of great benefit to you both.

Talking to your child's teachers

When Maureen went back to school to complain that a sarcastic teacher was making her eight-year-old's life a misery, she arrived back angry and left humbled. 'After just a few minutes with the headmistress I felt more like a naughty school girl than a grown woman with a legitimate grievance,' she recalls. Maureen, a career woman in her late twenties, is certainly not the only parent to feel that way. Talking to their child's teachers can make the most self-assured adult feel five years old and four foot tall.

As a result, instead of discussing difficulties or worries with teachers on equal terms, some revert to childish behaviour. Depending on their personality, they may become anxious and deferential or overcompensate by throwing their weight around. Not surprisingly, neither approach is helpful in creating those lines of open communication, between home and school, on which successful education depends. There are seven golden rules for ensuring that any talks you have with your child's teachers are positive, pleasant and productive:

1. Get to know teachers informally. Attend as many open days and Parent Teacher meetings as possible. It's always easier talking to a familiar face than a remote stranger.

2. Double check your facts before making any complaints. However truthful your child, try not to rely on their word alone. Without intending dishonesty, children easily misinterpret or misunderstand a situation.

   Jean was furious when her nine-year-old was punished for not completing a homework project on time. An assignment which, the girl insisted, was not due for another week. Jean's first reaction was to confront the teacher and demand an apology, but she was wise enough to check up first. Phone calls to other mothers revealed that her daughter was mistaken over the deadline. The teacher had been correct to reprimand her.

3. If upset or angry, always cool down before saying or doing anything. Instead of rushing over to the school, phone for an appointment. Explain briefly, and calmly, what you want to discuss and arrange a mutually convenient time.

4. Before meeting a teacher to register a complaint or obtain information, plan the questions you want to ask and the goals you hope to achieve. If uncertain about remembering the key facts of a complaint or problem, write them down and use the notes during the meeting. Never worry about being branded a 'trouble maker' or making life harder for your child in class. Provided you are courteous and constructive in your approach, good teachers welcome your involvement.

5. Be assertive, but never aggressive. State your position firmly and clearly, while avoiding personal attacks. Make your concern, or displeasure, clear and then work with the teacher to see what practical steps can be taken to overcome the problem.

6. Put yourself in the teacher's position. Ask what you would do in their place. This will help you negotiate an outcome that satisfies everyone.

7. Listen as well as speak. Don't be so eager to put over your views that you are deaf to what the teacher has to say. Not every conversation with your child's teacher is going to be about worries or complaints, of course. Often you'll just want to find out what progress is being made. Here careful listening becomes even more important. Don't be afraid to ask questions if you don't understand something, or request clarification for any comments which seem unreasonable. And if you disagree with what's been said then say so, and courteously explain why. Never be tempted to flatter, appease or politely

agree with a teacher just to stay on good terms. Fall into that trap and you really have gone back to school.

How well can you talk to teachers?

(Award two points for any statements with which you agree)

- I lose my temper very easily.
- I avoid things which upset me.
- I am impatient.
- I feel guilty without reason when talking to policemen.
- I do not suffer fools gladly.
- I have difficulty talking to strangers at a party.
- I am quick to complain about poor service.
- I am shy.
- I always return faulty goods.
- I dislike changes in routine.

How to score: Total your score for *odd* and *even* numbered statements separately. If you scored higher on *odd* numbered statements you respond with aggression when stressed. The higher your score the more aggressive you are likely to become. This means you try harder to stay cool in any discussions with your child's teachers.

If you scored higher on *even* numbered statements you are too easily brow beaten. The higher this score the harder it is for you to cope with a confrontation. Don't be afraid of asserting yourself where your child's future is concerned.

Equal scores mean you become aggressive in some situations and anxious in others. Try for a more balanced approach.

Reading your child's reports

The second line of communication are reports which the school prepares on your child's progress. Unfortunately these too sometimes generate more heat than light. Even mildly critical comments make some parents anxious and others angry, while children often become discouraged and depressed.

Most secondary schools send out reports, varying from a list of grades to lengthy assessments, either every term or once a year. Some arrange meetings where parents can discuss any criticisms with their child's teachers. More usually, however, families are left to make what sense they are able to from the report itself. It's a task which often proves difficult and upsetting. One problem is that, due to lack of space, teachers may resort to such platitudes as, 'A good term's work on the whole,' or shorthand comments which may sound more negative than intended. Coded phrases include, 'Must try harder . . . '; 'Has not applied himself sufficiently this term . . . '; 'Does not give the subject his full attention . . . '; 'Disappointing progress . . . '. Reading such comments some parents may conclude their child is lazy, lacks motivation or is unintelligent.

Never look on the report as a full and final judgment on your child's efforts and abilities. Instead consider it in the context of their school work as a whole. Compare reports across several terms to see whether specific difficulties can be identified. If you find any such learning problems ask the school whether additional coaching would be helpful.

1 If your first reaction to a bad report is anger or panic, give yourself time to cool off or calm down before discussing the criticisms with your child.

2. When doing so start by commenting on all the positive aspects of the report. Next deal with anything interesting which the teachers have said. Only then should you focus on alleged failings.

3. Take into account any stressful events during that term which might have undermined confidence or concentration. Problems at home, a change of school or simply moving to a new form can create emotional difficulties which lead to classroom set-backs.

4. On any subjects which give special cause for concern, discuss matters quietly and objectively in order to discover what is going wrong.

5. Never assume negative remarks are your child's fault for not trying hard enough. Take the phrase 'disappointing progress . . . '. This seems to imply your child has been idle in class, yet they might have worked very hard without being able to satisfy their teacher.

A youngster who starts off doing extremely well in a particular subject creates high expectations in the staff room. If they then do less well than anticipated, despite working diligently, the teacher's frustration may produce the criticism of idleness or insufficient effort. Not appreciating this an irritated parent tells their child angrily, 'You must work harder next term.' The youngster, hurt by this unjust criticism, may do less well from then on as confidence and motivation are undermined.

6. Review past work to find out whether your child's level of attainment has been consistently high, until very recently or whether it was always patchy. Children described as 'idle' in a report may be unable to make adequate progress because they have failed to understand basic points about the subject. Once these confusions are resolved they quickly catch up with their companions.

7. If your child's report contains inaccuracies or remarks you don't fully understand, take it up with the teacher concerned. This is important since, if left unchallenged, these mistakes remain on your child's record. Where you believe past reports have been unfair, ask whether you can see their file. At present about half of the Local Education Authorities allow parental access to their child's files. In addition the Data Protection Act gives you the right to see any information held on computer.

8. Finally, never pay too much attention to reports. One student, who consistently received the blackest of reports was assured by his form teacher, 'You are far too stupid ever to amount to anything.' And his name was Albert Einstein!

The Dos and Don'ts of reading reports

DON'T – fly off the handle, always stay calm.
DON'T – blame your child – it won't help.
DON'T – focus only on criticisms, instead take notice of positive comments too.

DO – read reports in the context of school work.
DO – identify and help resolve emotional barriers to achievement.
DO – discuss classroom difficulties objectively. Provide help where needed.

Giving your child confidence in class

Because Mike seldom put up his hand in class, some teachers considered him dull. But it was not lack of brains which kept the nine-year-old silent, it was merely a lack of confidence. Many children show the same reluctance to shine in school. Yet a readiness to answer – and ask – questions is essential for classroom success. For one thing unless your child is prepared to voice doubts when something is unclear, confusions may never be resolved. As they progress through school these misunderstandings and minor errors can make it impossible to master more complicated facts.

The way subjects are taught means that each piece of information is an essential building block. Unless the whole construction is soundly built and rests on sure foundations the topic will never be fully understood. As a result mistakes are going to multiply and your child's confidence will be further undermined. As self-esteem is eroded youngsters start to perceive themselves as classroom failures. And once that negative image has been formed intellectual achievement becomes increasingly unlikely.

A second reason is that children who raise their hands to ask sensible questions or provide correct answers are, not surprisingly, viewed as bright by teachers. This perception can profoundly influence the way they are taught. Research shows a teacher dealing with a child they regard as intelligent tend to be more patient, wait longer for an answer and give the child the benefit of the doubt if an answer is not entirely correct. When a child is viewed as less intelligent, however, many teachers are less patient, demand the answer more rapidly and show less tolerance for an ambiguous answer. There are three main reasons why clever and capable children are prevented from raising their hands during lessons. All are based on fear.

1. Fear of failure. If your child is driven by such anxiety they will be very reluctant to tackle new or unfamiliar activities. By sticking to what they know well the risk of failing is obviously reduced.
2. Fear of teasing. Many children would sooner be thought stupid than get labelled the teacher's pet.
3. Fear of criticism. Even when questions and answers are treated sympathetically, some children remain fearful of arousing adult displeasure. This is most likely if their parents are excessively critical.

Such fears are most likely to afflict children who lack the assurance to risk making mistakes, appearing different or feeling foolish. If your child is reluctant to speak up in class (*see box*) the best approach is to boost confidence at home. Here are six practical ways of helping:

1. Think of some activity your child would enjoy but which offers a genuine challenge. This need not have anything to do with school. It might involve swimming, running, playing chess, horse riding or amateur dramatics. Establish an overall goal. This should be neither so tough that your child has no hope of achieving it, nor so simple that success would have little meaning. A child able to swim the width of the pool might be set a challenge of three lengths. This overall target is next broken into a series of more easily accomplished goals. The pool challenge might consist of two widths, four widths, one length, two lengths and finally three lengths. Make a chart showing all the goals and hang it where the whole family can see. As each target is achieved tick it off. Be encouraging and supportive. Then, when the final goal is attained give your child a small reward, in addition to your congratulations. Achieving success when failure was a real possibility makes a child's self-confidence soar.

2. Help your child view mistakes not as a threat to self-esteem but more as a valuable learning experience. Allow some time, immediately after the disappointment, to vent anger and tears. Then start analyzing, calmly and objectively, what happened. Draw up two columns on a sheet of paper. Head one *What I did well* and the other *What I did wrong*. Help your child complete BOTH columns. At first they may find it far easier to think of all the blunders made. But with your help they should start to identify positive aspects of their performance.

3. Never imply you only love or respect your child so long as they satisfy your expectations. Avoid such comments as, 'You are a big disappointment to me . . .' or 'I always had such faith in you.'

4. Voice disapproval of your child's behaviour but never of your child. Commenting, 'I don't think you spent enough time revising for that exam . . . ' is legitimate criticism. Saying, 'You are just stupid . . . ' is damaging since, if repeated often enough, children come to see themselves as stupid and so no longer even try to act intelligently.

5. Always reward more than you punish. Studies suggest an appropriate ratio is five rewards for every punishment. Any less and there's

a risk of creating a fear of failure. If you are uncertain of the present balance, keep a written record for a couple of weeks, jotting down an 'R' for all rewards and a 'P' for any punishments. Rewards include praise, interest, attention and encouragement as well as extra treats, pocket money and so on. Punishments mean not just scolding or loss of treats, but sarcastic comments, your obvious disappointment, frowns, lack of interest and reprimands.

6. Expect a high standard but avoid being overly perfectionist. After 13-year-old Andrea delightedly told her father she had come third in class, he asked angrily, 'Why didn't you come first?' As a result she despaired of ever pleasing him and gave up trying. When commenting on your child's performance start by looking for all the *positive* things to say, then seek out everything *interesting* and only after these have been fully explored go on to consider any *negative* features. By taking these simple steps at home you can help transform your child's confidence in class.

Does your child raise their hand in class?

(Rate each statement below on a scale of 1– 5 where 1 = Not true at all and 5 = Very true.)

Your child . . .

- Is given a real say in family decisions.
- Enjoys team sports.
- Takes the lead when playing games.
- Likes meeting new people.
- Is seldom upset for long by set-backs.
- Asks for help when confused by homework.
- Is rarely tearful or moody.
- Does not mind spending the night away from home.

Score: 40 – 30: should have little difficulty. 29 – 20: may have problems now and then. 19 – 8: probably lacks confidence in class.

How you can help with the homework

In primary school your child is unlikely to have been given very much homework. With middle school, however, all this changes and working at home in the evenings and at weekends becomes an increasingly important part of your child's life. In many households it also marks the start of a difficult and often tempestuous challenge which can make life hell for the whole family.

For Alison it frequently meant tears and tantrums from her nine-year-old son Michael. He became by turn anxious, frustrated and angry if he didn't understand an assignment while she felt upset by her inability to help effectively. 'In some cases I just didn't understand the subject,' she admits, 'either because I had never learned it in school or the way it was taught seemed so very different. On other occasions I could have helped, but wasn't sure how helpful this would really be. Should I drop hints? Provide complete answers, or what? It seemed to me that if Mike didn't understand something it should be made clear in his answers, not covered up by my knowledge.' If you sometimes find yourself in the same position and wonder how best to help your child with their homework, here are some practical steps to take.

Start by recognizing that homework is more than just an irritating intrusion into your child's free time. Studies show that pupils who work well at home also do better in class and get higher marks in exams. To work efficiently your child needs peace, quiet and a suitable place in which to study. If lack of space makes this a problem, try getting together with parents who have a similar difficulty. Organize a rota system where one night other children do their homework at your house, along with your own child, but for the remainder your child goes to their homes. Allocate a set time for homework, this should be after your child has had a chance to relax on arriving home from school, but before eating their evening meal. If the body is busy digesting supper the brain will work less efficiently.

Watching television immediately before settling down to homework reduces alertness. A short period of brisk exercise, on the other hand, helps the brain perform more efficiently. After Alison encouraged Michael to enjoy fifteen minutes of energetic play before starting his homework both his attitude and marks improved. If your child has got into the habit of switching on the television as soon as they get home, there's bound to be resentment at first. Avoid this by suggesting an enjoyable game, such as hide and seek, playing with a ball, or going swimming. Start this new regime during the summer holiday, when they'll probably want to be outdoors anyhow, and never ban television completely. Start by reducing pre-homework viewing time by, say, ten minutes and using this period for active play.

If your child is rather disorganized, run a quick check (*see box*) on the homework scheduled for that evening as soon as they get home from school. That way if additional reference books or materials are required there should still be time to visit the library before it shuts or make necessary purchases.

If your child get's stuck and asks for help it's important to provide this in the most appropriate way. It is clearly pointless simply to answer questions for them. Apart from preventing learning this may lead teachers to assume they have a far greater knowledge of the subject than is actually the case. As a result confusions and errors in the early stages of learning a new subject may pass undetected, causing them to fall behind badly as the topic becomes more complex. Instead devise problems similar to the ones causing difficulty and use these to demonstrate the best way of finding answers.

Help break complex problems down into small, more easily understood, stages. Ensure your child understands each step along the way to finding an answer. Where facts have to be looked up in reference books, do not do this for them. Instead demonstrate how to use a wide variety of sources. Provide practice by asking similar questions and assisting in a search for answers. Knowing how to use reference books quickly and accurately is an essential skill every child should perfect early.

When demonstrating problem solving be certain you understand exactly how to approach the task before making any attempt. There is nothing so discouraging and confusing for a child than to watch an adult failing to find an answer. Young children especially are liable to assume that if *you* can't do it what chance do they have of ever succeeding! Check also that you are using the same methods for finding an answer that your child has been taught in class. Even if your approach is effective, the result could be to cause greater uncertainty.

John fell into this trap when he tried to help his 12-year-old daughter Jenny with her maths homework. Although good with numbers, the methods of calculation he had learned 30 years earlier were quite different to those his daughter was being taught. As a result Jenny became even more bewildered and her marks nose-dived. So always study your child's text and classroom exercise books carefully and, when unsure of yourself, practise privately before attempting any demonstrations. Provide opportunities to practise, under your guidance, and remain calm and patient, even when they may stumble over what you regard as simple procedures. By adopting this approach you can remove misunderstandings without doing the work for them. By assisting in this practical way you can help transform a frequently upsetting chore into a positive learning experience.

Avoid needless homework traumas by asking these six questions as soon as your child gets home.

- What subjects have you got to study?
- Have you got the school books you need?
- Are any additional reference books necessary?
- Will you need any special stationery such as graph or tracing paper?
- If needed have you your calculator?
- Are any craft materials, card, glue, paints etc, wanted?

Helping with questions and answers

How many times have you asked or answered your child's questions? If you are anything like the majority of parents, the answer will be thousands of times! Small children ask endless questions, often to the point of driving you to distraction and, as they get older, questions become more complicated but also less frequent. Increasingly the powerful curiosity of early years is blunted. Children tend to grow less inquisitive and more accepting. Things which would once have aroused intense interest start to be taken more and more for granted or seen as not worth finding out about. Which is a pity, because asking and answering questions can, when employed correctly, be one of the most potent means at your disposal for helping your child realize their true intellectual potential. Not only expanding knowledge but enhancing creativity, problem solving and decision making.

Asking questions

We'll start by looking at the right and wrong ways for adults to ask children questions. Studies have shown that three-quarters of classroom time is taken up by teachers asking questions. They use them to give directions, test knowledge, identify the cause of errors, misunderstandings or misconduct, and evaluate learning. But the same research also revealed that questions are least often asked with a view to stimulating the child's mind. This is because the kind of questions posed, and the way they are presented, makes only limited demands on thinking skills. Here's a typical school-type questions – 'When was the Battle of Hastings?' This is what we call a narrow question demanding only accurate recall of the required fact, a date, from long-term memory. The 'When . . .' part alerts children to the fact that they are going to be required to find a single, specific, 'correct' response. In this case the 'correct' answer, at least the one expected by the teacher is, of course, 1066. Although why this should be considered 'right' has always puzzled me. For one thing, the battle fought in 1066 took place not at Hastings but Senlac (now Battle) some seven miles north-west of Hastings. However in 1377 and again in 1380 the French directly attacked Hastings burning the ancient port to the ground. These dates seem therefore more appropriate, but would almost certainly lose marks to any child who gave such a response.

Narrow questions are also what are termed *convergent* in that they converge to a single, 'right' answer. Although, as we have seen, these may be 'correct' only in terms of educational conventions. Yet what is being tested here are memory and confidence instead of the more profound aspect of intellect. Which may explain why many truly great thinkers of our age, such as the English writer G K Chesterton, the American inventor Thomas Edison and the German physicist Albert Einstein did so poorly in school. So long as schools rely so heavily on testing retention and recall of information, it's obviously important that your child gains practice in responding efficiently to narrow questions. In the next chapter I shall be showing you ways of greatly enhancing this skill so that your child can remember all kinds of facts and figures far more easily and bring that information to mind rapidly and accurately, even when working under exam-room pressure. By asking *broad* questions which require *divergent* answers, rather than narrow ones demanding convergent solutions, you will stimulate a whole range of thinking skills.

How broad questions make bright children

Broad questions have many equally satisfactory answers instead of a single right response. They often start with 'What . . . ?' For instance, 'What would have happened if William had been defeated in 1066?' or 'What would happen if television were abolished?' or 'What would happen if dogs could talk?' Broad questions require *analytical* thinking in order to come up with an answer. Your child has to analyze the situation described, and then draw on a whole range of stored knowledge in order to come up with an answer. Ideas which might otherwise have never been connected may be brought together to come up with a reply.

Even broader questions may be asked which start with 'How . . . ?' For instance, 'How could you signal for help if stranded on a desert island?' or 'How can we amuse ourselves during the long car journey?' 'How might your homework be better organized?' Very broad 'How . . . ?' questions require *reflective* thinking. Your child must ponder on the various aspects of a situation in order to suggest possible solutions.

Analysis and reflection are key mental skills whose significance will grow as your child climbs the educational ladder. Yet they are only occasionally stimulated in normal lessons and remain untapped by the majority of questions asked in class.

Most young children love the freedom such questions give them. The majority of school children hate them for exactly the same reason, because they demand creative thinking rather than mechanical recall and they get worried and distressed by the fact that there is no, single, right answer. 'How do I know if I'm right,' one 12-year-old demanded irritably, 'if there isn't a right answer?'

Why having no obvious right answer should make some children feel so apprehensive is an important aspect of learning and one which I shall return to a little later. When asking either broad or narrow questions, there are three pitfalls to avoid.

1 – **Simplistic questions**. Such questions may be narrow, requiring only a well known fact – of the what is 2×2? variety. Or they could be broad questions but still pose such an obvious problem that your child's mind is not stretched to come up with a solution. By frequent use of this sort of question you can make your child mentally lazy as well as reducing motivation to learn.

2 – **Confusing questions**. These have so many elements to take into account that your child loses track of what's actually being asked.

3 – **Vague questions**. Are so general that no considered answer is possible. For instance, 'What do you think about cruelty to animals?'

When asking questions intended to enhance school success follow six golden rules and make certain that what you ask . . .

1. Is unambiguous. Your child must understand exactly what is being asked.
2. Relates to their level of knowledge and experience.
3. Stimulates thinking, especially analysis and reflection.
4. Is relevant to educational goals.
5. Captures their interest.
6. Is clearly stated.

Do not ask too many questions at any one time, or your child will either get bored or start feeling threatened.

Helping your child ask questions

Does your child raise their hand or lower their gaze when asked a question in class? If the teacher asks whether anyone has questions, do they remain silent even though confused on some points?

Every teacher knows how reluctant some youngsters are to pose a question despite wanting extra information or clarification of some inadequately understood point. Is your child one of them? If so then you should take practical steps to build confidence for it is a lack of self-assurance that lies at the heart of the problem. Successful learning requires that your child is prepared to answer questions, even when not certain of being right and without fear of being thought silly. For unless children are willing to do this, their teachers can never correct mistakes or be sure that lessons have been properly understood.

Children often remain silent in class out of a fear of failure in getting the answer wrong, this kind of anxiety quite often causes them to develop a special approach to classroom challenges known as the *minimax* strategy. It's purpose is to minimize any loss if things go badly and maximize possible gains should they go well.

Minimax in action

Here's how the minimax strategy could influence adult decision making. Imagine you are given three hot tips for a race meeting and decide to bet on the first horse tipped. This romps home at 100 to 1 giving you a good return on your stake. Since the first tip proved so accurate you place all your winnings on the second horse and this too comes in ahead of the field. How will you decide to treat the final tip? If you put all your winnings on the third horse you stand to gain the maximum amount if it wins, but forfeit everything if it loses. Equally if you don't bet any more money, you'll minimize your possible losses but may miss out on further winnings. The *minimax* approach would be to put some portion of your winnings, perhaps a half, on horse number three. That way you can maximize your gains should it come in first while minimizing your losses if it is not placed.

When questions are asked, a child using this strategy will reason like this: 'If I answer wrongly I shall feel silly (loss), be thought stupid by the teacher (loss) and probably get laughed at by the others (loss). If I am correct, I could still become unpopular (loss). If I say nothing but look like I know the answer I won't suffer any losses and I may still gain the teacher's approval if she believes I could have answered correctly had I made the attempt.'

After a while minimax thinking hardens into a habit, so that even when a child is confident of an answer silence is still preferable. The children most likely to adopt this strategy have ambitious parents who are constantly stressing the importance of school success and are only prepared to praise perfection.

Encourage your child to think about what they are being taught, and not to simply sit passively while the facts flow over them. As we shall see further on when I explain how to help your child to examination success, the key to effective learning is to have active involvement with the material. Because they fail to reflect on, or analyze, the information being learned, many children suffer from that most profound of all states of ignorance, not knowing what it is they don't know. Encourage your child to constantly question statements, answers, facts and figures by asking themselves broad questions demanding analysis and reflection – 'What might that fact imply . . . ?' 'How does this information relate to other knowledge I possess . . . ?' By self-testing their understanding as they go along, your child will help to organize and structure new knowledge, ironing out confusions before they cause any damage and correcting mistakes at the earliest possible moment.

Answering questions

Always give your child thinking time before providing answers to questions you have just asked. A study of American teachers found that they allowed sometimes as little as three seconds for a student to respond, before either giving them the solution or asking somebody else. So allow your child ample time to reflect on an answer. If they really are stuck, try phrasing the question slightly differently. It may well be that they actually know how to respond, but haven't quite grasped the point of your query. Check mentally that it is neither *vague* nor *confusing*. If there is still no response, offer a clue that should help point them in the right direction.

If you show them how to solve the problem then do not make the demonstration so rapidly and apparently effortless that they are both unable to see what steps have to be taken and become even more discouraged by their own failure. Many adults who are skilled at the activity being demonstrated present children with a mastery model. This was the main weakness of the approach adopted by a university mathematics lecturer who proved hopeless at teaching his 12-year-old son maths mainly because he knew the subject so well. When demonstrating how an answer was reached, his pen would speed across the page, spewing a rapid succession of figures, calculations and results which left his son's mind reeling. The boy simply didn't understand the logic behind his approach and felt discouraged that he couldn't work the problems out as swiftly or as accurately as his father. Which brings me back to a point I have already made several times in this book, but is so vital as to be worthwhile repeating here. Far more important than demonstrating mastery, which can only come with practice, is to teach determination and persistence when confronted by an unfamiliar problem.

Helping your child learn to learn

It's a curious fact that although your child is given hundreds of facts, figures, words, ideas and concepts to learn in school, he or she is never taught *how* to learn them. You will find no lessons in learning on the average timetable. No schools, that I am aware of, hold classes in effective remembering or seminars on reliable recall. As a result many children are seriously disadvantaged in class, not because they are incapable of learning but because they have never discovered how to make the best use of their brain. In this chapter you will discover how to help remedy that deficit by means of easily mastered, practical procedures which enable your child to acquire knowledge far more easily and enjoyably.

The anatomy of memory

Memory is often seen as having two parts. Short-term memory holds small amounts of information for a brief period, usually just a few seconds. For instance when you look up a telephone number and remember it only for the time it takes to dial. Long-term memory holds everything which we have permanently recorded. To transfer information from short- to long-term storage, it must be rehearsed.

One of the main reasons we fail to remember things is that we do not pay sufficient attention when given information. Many people find recalling names notoriously difficult for just this reason. When first introduced to somebody they may be so busy wondering what sort of an impression they are making, and thinking up something interesting to say that they fail to concentrate on the information. The stranger's name goes into short-term memory but, because it never enters the rehearsal buffer, it fails to be stored long-term. The way to avoid this is to listen carefully to the name, and repeat it as often as possible – either silently or aloud – during the first few minutes of the meeting. Likewise, when giving information or instructions to your child make certain they are attending sufficiently. This is especially important with very active or impulsive youngsters who may appear to be disobedient simply because they never store commands in their long-term memories.

The secret of successful learning

This may be summed up in just one word – *organization*. The more efficiently your child organizes information prior to learning, the more easily and accurately it will be retained and recalled. Unfortunately because children are never taught how to organize new knowledge correctly most learning is slow and ineffective.

Cast your mind back to your own studies. Did you find it easy to remember new material? Or was it a painful process of drumming facts and figures into an, apparently, reluctant memory? And after you had studied long and hard how much could you readily recall? When asked a question in class, or during an examination, did the answers spring to mind or was your memory blank? Blank that is until the teacher had asked another child, or the exam was finished? Then when it no longer mattered, all the information which had proved so frustratingly elusive only minutes before suddenly sprang to mind? These are all common learning experiences, and among the reasons why so many people moan about their appalling memories. Yet, the fact is nothing is wrong with the mechanisms of memory – rather the fault lies in how they have been put to work.

Stocking the memory warehouse

Imagine trying to stock a giant warehouse by flinging a vast variety of goods through the nearest available doors or windows. As the pile mounts ever higher, retrieving earlier items becomes increasingly difficult and time-consuming. Clearly that would be an absurd method for storing merchandise. Yet it is the way the majority of us store our memories. Now consider a warehouse carefully divided into sections. Within these sections, there are sub-sections, and then further subdivisions and finally carefully labelled filing cabinets with accurately identified boxes for each item. With such a methodical, highly organized system, finding an individual piece of merchandise becomes fast and simple. What's more, because of the elaborate cross-referencing system the information requested can be tracked down with a minimum of clues. The same applies when storing new knowledge in your mental warehouse.

The brain is sometimes compared to a computer, but its power far exceeds any man-made device likely to be developed in the foreseeable future. In terms of memory alone the potential of the 1,500 grams of grey matter in the human skull is prodigious. The most rapid expansion of knowledge occurs during the first five years of life when, it's been estimated, we learn half of everything we will ever know. By early adulthood, our brain has already stored a greater volume of information than could be contained in the more than nine million volumes in the British Museum Library. Fortunately memory can never be worn out by over-use. One estimate suggests it is capable of storing 11 new facts per second throughout life and still have ample reserves. But, like the muscles, it withers when neglected. As with fitness the motto is – use it or lose it.

Encourage remembering. Learning poetry or plays, memorizing speeches or quotations, playing games which exercise recall all help to give your child's memory a regular workout. The more your child tries to remember the faster remembering will become. The more your child learns, the easier learning becomes. The human brain is the only container in the world which gets larger the more it holds. But memory can easily be impaired by negative beliefs. Discourage your child from making comments like, 'I've got a terrible memory . . . ' or 'I can't remember history . . . ' or 'I'm hopeless when it comes to recalling figures.' While such statements are false, they can create a self-fulfilling prophecy of failure if said often enough and believed strongly.

How facts are filed

Normally we have no need to think about the headings and sub-headings our memory uses to categorize information. This is achieved automatically as part of previously mastered strategies. Before reading further try this quick test, and ask your child to do the same.

List 1

Name a weapon starting with	s	_____
Name a bird	p	_____
Name a flower	d	_____
Name a vegetable	c	_____
Name an animal	h	_____
Name a fruit	b	_____
Name a musical instrument	f	_____
Name a man's name	M	_____
Name a jewel	d	_____
Name a country	N	_____

Time taken _____

List 2

Name a weapon ending with	r	_____
Name a bird	k	_____
Name a flower	p	_____
Name a vegetable	t	_____

Name an animal	e	_____
Name a fruit	m	_____
Name a musical instrument	n	_____
Name a man's name	d	_____
Name a jewel	y	_____
Name a country	o	_____

Time taken _____

Most people complete list 1 faster than list 2. Why? Because the brain stores names under their first letter, so that access is rapid and fairly easy. Searching under the last letter is possible to do, but takes longer and is harder. By organizing new information efficiently, facts can be recovered rapidly and reliably from a variety of clues.

The knowledge network

Have you ever remembered an answer by forgetting the question? You want to bring to mind a name, phone number or favourite quotation but the fact remains tantalizingly elusive. You can almost, but not quite, recall it. It's on the tip of your tongue, but can't be put into words. So you abandon the frustrating task and go on about your normal routine. Then, unasked and unexpectedly, that missing answer pops into your mind. Often it happens first thing the following day. You go to sleep on a problem and wake up knowing the solution.

When this happens, and it's a common occurrence, you have just experienced the power of your brain's knowledge network in action. You see every fact, every single item of knowledge which has ever been filed away in memory – or more accurately in *memories* since, as we shall see in a moment, your brain has many different kinds of storage and is linked to everything else. Sometimes the pathways between them are short and simple, at other times long and complex. The shorter the route the faster the access.

Twenty years ago, two American psychologists, Collins and Quillian, proposed that our memory for words, the so-called semantic memory, might be organized as an interconnected network. Each word in this network is stored with a set of pointers to other words. As an example, information about birds, such as the fact they have wings, lay eggs, are covered with feathers and so on would all be stored at one level in the network. You can get a feel for your own semantic network in action, by answering yes or no, as rapidly as possible to whether the following are animals: dog, hoof, sofa, lion, car, amoeba, pencil, lobster, giraffe.

Although this is a crude experiment, and your speed of response is influenced by both the order in which words were presented and any previous experience you might have had of this kind of task, you may have noticed it took slightly longer to say yes to 'amoeba' and 'lobster' (assuming you did answer yes) than to 'lion' and 'dog'. According to the 'network' theory this could be because, for most people, amoebas and lobsters, not being prototypical animals, are stored at a different level. This suggests recalling information would be faster and more reliable if related facts were stored close together on the network. In other words:

Short Links = Rapid, Accurate Recall

Imagine two motorists setting out to drive from London to Glasgow. One heads straight down the motorway directly to Glasgow. The other takes a long, meandering route, heading first south, then west, then north and east and finally north again. Both arrive at their destinations. But motorist number one completes the journey in a minimum amount of time and with the least risk of getting lost, confused or finishing up at the wrong destination. Driver number two not only takes far longer but also makes many mistakes, motors in circles, heads up dead-end streets and is never entirely confident of reaching the goal.

It's the same with your child's memory. Consider three children about to sit an examination. The first has organized their learning so that all the information relevant to that task is tightly organized with short, clear links between each item. When asked a question they can head straight to their goal with a minimum waste of time and maximum confidence. The second child has a reasonably well organized memory, except that many of the links between key facts are longer and less direct than they should be. As a result accessing the knowledge needed to answer exam questions takes longer than necessary and is more prone to error. Like the motorist, they stand more chance of taking a wrong turning. What is more, the additional anxiety caused by having less confidence in their memory impairs performance still further. Because of this they are unable to answer all the questions, fail to retrieve important facts and come up with incorrect information. Finally we have a child whose learning has been chaotic.

They have worked hard and the facts needed to pass that exam are all in their memory but, because of its disorganized state they cannot be located in time. They can answer only a few questions, discover many apparent gaps in their knowledge and make many mistakes.

My experience of teaching the method described below to hundreds of students, of all ages, suggests that whatever the theoretical basis, this is a very practical approach to more effective studying. You and your child should now attempt the memory test (*see box.*)

Memory test

Your child reads the list once then sees how many nouns can be recalled – IN THE RIGHT ORDER.
Rabbit. Ship. Cracker. Rickshaw. Herring. Book. Fire Engine. Bird Bath. Stop Watch. Saddle. Elf. Banana. Policeman. Telephone. Airliner. Kitten. Jelly. Harmonium. Turtle. Raft.

Scores
17 – 20: Excellent. Now try the list backwards!
12 – 16: Good. Could you go *backwards*?
 6 – 11: Average. The first and last words were probably recalled most easily.
 0 – 5: Low. But don't worry. By using the method described in Memory Magic (*see page 164*) you'll find it easy to remember all those words, in any order, after just one reading.

How did you get on? You probably found it easiest to recall the words at the start and end of the list. This is quite usual and is known in memory research as the *primacy* and *recency* effect. In other words we recall most easily and accurately what we hear first and last. It's those awkward words in the middle that get muddled. The main problem about recalling the list is that all the nouns are already stored in your memory. They are common English words which you learned years ago. But there are no specific links between them. It is as if each one is stored in its own filing cabinet and these are located in different rooms of a large house. This means that when you remember 'rabbit' or 'turtle' the words offer no clue as to the next item on the list.

Looking in the file marked ship, for example, you find a vast amount of information about vessels and the sea – notice how many associations spring to mind when you think about that noun for a few moments – but the word 'cracker' is almost certainly not one of them. That would be stored in a file marked 'Christmas' or 'birthday', and perhaps another marked 'biscuit'. When your child fails to make links between new knowledge, recalling one item is not that much help in bringing to mind the other facts needed.

Memory Magic

Now I am going to show you how much more powerfully your memory operates when you do two things:

1. Make the links between each item to be remembered short and specific.
2. Switch from using your word (or semantic) memory to one of the many others kinds of memories you possess. In this case your visual memory.

Here's what you do: first ask your child to create a mental image of each word. This should be vivid and bizarre. Then, link those images together to create a Movie in the Mind. Let's look at a mind movie based on that memory test. Ask your child to read that list again and, this time, to conjure up the images I describe.

The Mind Movie in Action

Rabbit. Imagine a huge rabbit wearing a captain's cap at the helm of a . . . **Ship.** Make this a very unusual vessel, maybe an old Mississippi paddle steamer with tall, black smoke stacks belching into the sky. But the ship turns out to be so small that it tumbles from a . . . **Cracker**, with brilliant red, green and gold colouring. Picture that same cracker seated in a . . . **Rickshaw**, being pulled through narrow, cobbled, streets. Imagine crowds staring in amazement at the sight. Even more remarkably, the rickshaw is being pulled by a . . . **Herring**, who is flipping along the congested streets and bumping into things because it is also reading a . . . **Book**. See a huge, musty tome with curling yellow pages filled with mystical symbols. The cover is made of deep brown velum, with the title printed on it in golden letters. Because the herring's attention is distracted it crashes headlong into a . . . **Fire Engine**. See a red monster of a machine with a long turntable ladder and brass helmeted firemen clinging to the side. The fire engine is racing along, alarm bell clanging noisily, to fill a . . . **Bird bath**. Imagine one as tall as the Empire State Building and made from marble. In it is a . . . **Stop watch**. Create an image of this watch in the shape of a weird bird, with a long, pointed, yellow beak and thin, black match-stick legs. This watch bird is taking a drink from the bird bath while, strapped to its back is a . . . **Saddle**, a large, ornate, cowboy saddle with silver fittings and hand-tooled leather. The sort of saddle on which John Wayne might have won the West. Only now, instead of a cowboy sitting in the saddle there is an . . . **Elf**. See his sharp features, pointed ears, bright green eyes and a green tunic. He is enjoying a . . . **Banana**, a huge, bright yellow fruit. Just then a . . . **Policeman** hurries up. Imagine a fat, jolly, ineffective Keystone cop, constantly falling over his feet and holding a . . . **Telephone**, one of those old-fashioned, black candlestick phones with a large dial. On the other end of the phone is an . . . **Airliner**. The aircraft is holding the phone by curling one wing around to form a hand. It has a mouth just beneath the flight deck and is balanced on its tail. The airliner is talking to a . . . **Kitten**, a fluffy, black and white kitten with a pink bow holding the phone in one paw and listening to the airliner while sticking a spoon into a huge, red . . . **Jelly**, quivering on a silver platter, it wobbles every time the kitten sticks in his spoon. The jelly is shaped like a . . . **Harmonium**. Imagine an old musical instrument which gives out clouds of dust as it is played by a . . . **Turtle**. See the miserable-looking creature, tears streaming down a scaly face as he clumsily hits the keys with two huge flippers, while sitting on a . . . **Raft**. Conjure up an image of a cartoon raft, constructed from scraps of driftwood with a pair of ragged trousers flying at a mast which is made from an old oar. The raft is drifting towards a speck on the ocean. As it gets closer I can see a huge, white rabbit wearing a captain's hat standing at the helm of a . . . **Ship**. Which brings us back to the start.

Crazy? It probably reads like that. But try the technique for yourself and you'll be amazed at how easily your child can remember that list. And not only from first to last, but starting at the end and working backwards. Or, indeed, beginning anywhere you care to and moving in either direction. Use the images I have suggested, or let your child invent their own bizarre images when creating their own memory movie. Suggest everyone in the family who completed the first test tries again, this time using Mind Movies. Note the number of words remembered, in sequence, and note the score down here. You may like to write your original scores down again too, for comparison.

Name	_____	Score (1) =	Score (2) =
Name	_____	Score (1) =	Score (2) =
Name	_____	Score (1) =	Score (2) =
Name	_____	Score (1) =	Score (2) =

How did you get on this time? Almost certainly a great deal better than on your first attempt. Now try running the loop backwards. Start with 'raft' and work through each image until you get to 'rabbit'. Test yourself by starting anywhere in the loop and moving either forwards or backwards. You'll find the words just pop into your mind easily and effortlessly. With a little practice 20 or more words can be imaged and remembered in little more time than it takes to read carefully through the list.

The technique as I've described it here is mainly a fairly impressive party piece. By using it your child can astonish their friends with their powers or memory. This is no bad thing, since it builds confidence and the more they trust their memory the more impressively it is going to function. But as a practical strategy for school learning, this approach has a several drawbacks. For one thing, while it is fairly easy to form images of single nouns, creating pictures of more complicated ideas and concepts is a lot harder and less satisfactory. My purpose of introducing it here is to provide you with first hand experience of two points central to successful learning. The first is that we have several ways of remembering ideas other than by using words (*see below*). Images are a powerful alternative, which greatly assist retention and recall. Secondly, I wanted to provide a practical demonstration of the value of developing links between separate items of information. We shall be exploiting both these strategies in the more practical procedures described below.

Giving your child a mistake proof memory

I am going to describe two ways of doing this, one for older and the other for younger children. I suggest that you let your child try both, to see which is preferred. It is important that they feel comfortable with the approach adopted. What you are going to do is help them to organize knowledge in such a way that each item to be learned is linked to its neighbours, rather along the lines we followed with the list of nouns. This method works well with such subjects as history, geography, English literature, biology, and certain parts of chemistry and physics. In fact any subject where there is a lot of textual information to learn. It is not an effective way of remembering foreign languages or formulae in mathematics, or most physics and chemistry. I shall be providing different ways of memorizing these successfully later in the chapter.

Creating a Knowledge Wheel

Step 1: The facts to be remembered are first transferred from books and texts to small cards. Plain 3" × 5" index cards are ideal. The amount of information on each should be limited to no more than 25 words. These notes are kept brief by putting down only the essential facts, using abbreviations, and small illustrations if appropriate. It is helpful to use different colours when creating the notes, for instance *red* for any numbers – such as dates in history or export figures in geography. *Blue* might be used for names of people and places. *Green* for actions or functions and so on.

Cards relating to a particular subject, and the topics within that subject area, should always be stored together. They can be added to, or modified, as further knowledge is acquired. For instance biology cards might include such topics as: heart function, digestion, the nervous system, muscles, skeleton and so on. Transferring information from texts to cards not only helps your child remember the facts more readily, by storing them in their visual, semantic (word) and muscle memories but also organizes them clearly.

Step 2: A number of cards relating to a particular topic are selected for learning. This number should normally be between 15 and 25 depending on your child's age, current level of learning ability and the amount of confidence they have in their memory. Experience has shown that using less than 15 cards slows learning unnecessarily while more than 25 can make the task too complex – at least when first used. Encourage your child to start modestly and build slowly as the skill of learning from knowledge networks becomes more practised.

Step 3: Any of the cards can be chosen to start the Knowledge Wheel. This is placed face up on the table. Now a second card, containing a fact your child thinks is logically connected to the first, is selected and placed either above or below the first. A third card is picked, which contains information relating to facts on the second card, and this too is placed face up on the table. This process continues until *all* the cards are lying, face up, on the table in the form of a circle. The Knowledge Wheel is now complete.

Step 4: Your child next reads *aloud* each fact in the Knowledge Wheel two or three times. While reading, they should also make an effort to create mental images of the facts.

It is helpful, where possible to try and find ways of linking images of neighbouring cards, as we did when learning the list of 20 nouns previously.

Step 5: All the cards, except one, are turned face down. Your child reads the information on the remaining upturned card *aloud* and then attempts to recall facts on the cards either above or below it in the Knowledge Wheel.

It doesn't matter, at first, whether they travel around the Wheel clockwise or anticlockwise. Although, once started in a particular direction they have to continue going that way. If the fact is remembered, then the card is turned face up and the information checked for accuracy. If the information cannot be recalled, the card is simply turned over and read *aloud* a couple of times.

Step 6: Several trips should be taken around the Wheel, starting at a different card each time. Sometimes your child should proceed clockwise, sometimes anticlockwise. After four or five trips around the Knowledge Wheel, all the information it contains will be recalled easily and accurately.

Step 7: When the learning session is over, the cards should be carefully filed away for further use. A good way of doing this is to use a suitable size box, or buy a specially made index card container. This should be divided into subjects and then subdivided into topics. Alternatively, your child may prefer to keep a separate storage box for each subject. Use coloured cards to separate subjects and topics. Encourage your child to develop their own filling system, since the more personally meaningful it is the better. Return to each Knowledge Wheel from time to time to ensure that memory remains fresh, and use them when revising for exams.

Knowledge Wheels in action. Not all topics will be covered in just 25 cards of course. Some may require many more. Although the actual number of *facts* on each specific topic your child needs to remember for most school subjects is surprisingly small. For instance a child who could recall 25 key facts about each of the main topics being examined should do fairly well in many exams. However, if many cards are used to cover a topic, or an entire subject, they should be learned at no more than 25 per session. When organizing the sequence in which topics are learned, your child's individual learning style must also be taken into account. I shall explain what this is and how it influences learning later on. When learning, work for no more than around 20 minutes and then take a break since longer study sessions are self-defeating.

Why Knowledge Wheels are so helpful. Learning in this way enhances your child's memory in FIVE important ways.

1. It involves active learning. Your child starts remembering from the moment information is extracted from school texts and written on the cards.

2. It stores knowledge in several different memory locations. Your child reads the information aloud (sound memory), writes it down (word or semantic memory) and creates images (visual memory).

3. Because the links between important facts are short and direct, recalling the contents of an entire Knowledge Network is rapid and precise.

4. The facts are closely linked so remembering one allows the others to be recalled.

5. Logical connections between facts are easier to see than when working from text books or class notes. Do not be surprised if, at first, your child seems reluctant to use this approach because, while efficient, it is unfamiliar.

The Space Pilot memory machine

Illustrated on page 170 is a simple way of making the network learning method more interesting and appealing to younger children.

Take the illustration to your local copy shop and ask for it to be enlarged to A4 size.

The principle is exactly the same as when using the Knowledge Wheel but this device turns the task into an enjoyable game. Here's how to use it.

Step 1: Explain to your child that the Space Pilot makes exploring and learning facts and figures faster and more fun. The copied illustration should be pasted onto stiff card. Use a sharp knife to cut out the visor, the reversed key-hole shape underneath and around three sides of the flap. Young children will need help with this task.

Step 2: Place a large sheet 15" × 12" (30 × 38 cm) of plain paper on

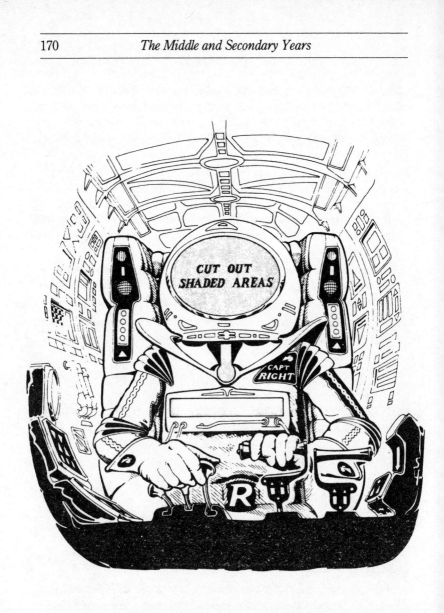

a firm surface and, using the visor as a template draw 15 to 25 ovals on the paper, so that they form an approximate circle.

Step 3: Your child heads the sheet with the subject and topic area being studied. For instance: History – Civil War. Using textbooks and classroom notes, they copy brief, key, facts into each of the ovals. As you will realize, these are the equivalent of the index cards in a Knowledge Wheel. Once again note down only essential information. Encourage abbreviations, drawings and different coloured inks to identify various sorts of information, names, dates, battles and so on.

Step 4: When all the notes have been completed, your child draws straight lines linking the ovals. Each oval is connected to its immediate neighbour to complete the network.

Step 5: Your child places the space pilot over one of the ovals so the notes can be read through the helmet visor. These are read *aloud*. The pilot is moved to the next oval and the procedure repeated. This continues until all the notes have been read and is repeated two or three times.

Step 6: The space pilot is now placed *anywhere* on the network in such a way that the facts in just one oval can be read through the visor. As before, your child reads these aloud and then tries to remember facts from an adjoining oval. The initial direction is unimportant, they can move around the network either clockwise or anticlockwise, but having started going one particular way must continue doing so. The reserved key-hole allows lines connecting the ovals to be seen, so keeping the space pilot accurately positioned on the network. If your child get's stuck, they lift the equipment flap uncovering some of the words in the next oval. This is often sufficient to jog their memory and allow all the information in that oval to be recalled.

Step 7: Your child now moves the space pilot so that the visor is over the next oval and checks their recollection of that note. If incorrectly recalled they read it aloud again to refresh their memory.

Step 8: Your child continues around the network in this way, until all the notes have been either remembered accurately or read again. Several trips should be taken, starting at a different place on the network each time and varying the direction of travel.

The value of the Space Pilot.

1. It helps make learning more fun. Most children, especially boys, enjoy using the space pilot.

2. By making remembering more interesting, it increases the motivation to learn.

3. Children who have had difficulty remembering and recalling facts in the past often do so well when using the Pilot that their confidence receives a welcome boost.

4. Jogging the memory by providing a hint, through the equipment

flap encourages active involvement with the material which significantly enhances learning.

Your action plan for successful learning

Do not be surprised if, at first, your child seems reluctant to use the Knowledge Wheel or Space Pilot. This method of learning, although far more efficient than your child's present approach, will obviously seem strange and unfamiliar. However, after experiencing its ability to make learning faster and more effective, your child should become motivated to use the procedure again. Start with a subject your child finds fairly easy, since this will reduce any anxiety about attempting a new way of learning.

Knowledge Wheels and the Space Pilot are potent ways of improving memory. But they are not the only ones. Here are seven practical techniques your child should find helpful. I call them Memory Magnifiers.

Memory Magnifier 1 – Chunking. In 1956 an American psychologist called George Miller published an intriguing paper entitled *The Magical Number Seven Plus or Minus Two*. In it he suggested that the capacity of short-term memory was limited to around seven items of information. For instance, if I were to read a series of numbers over to you, the chances are very good that you could recall seven of them. Some might remember up to nine others only five – hence one part of the title. But why magical?

Well, as Dr Miller pointed out, the number '7' has many mystical associations; the seven names of God in the Hebrew tradition, the seven gods of good luck in Japanese folklore, the seventh son of a seventh son being said to possess magical powers.

So far as improving your child's memory is concerned retention and recall can be aided if lengthy information is chunked, that is broken into around seven segments. Here's an example. First try and remember these digits after reading them a couple of times:

324654876554243091

Because there are 18 letters you would have normally found this an impossible task – unless, of course, you used some additional strategy for memorizing it. Now try the same task again, this time chunking the figure into sets of three digits:

324   654   876   554   243   091

Although still tricky, I think you'll agree the task is at least possible. Words too can often be chunked to advantage when remembering how to spell them. The spelling of Mississippi, for instance, becomes far easier to learn if the word is chunked into MIS-SIS-SIPPI.

Memory Magnifier 2 – Creative day dreaming. We have already seen how helpful images can be when trying to remember information such as a list of nouns and in the Knowledge Wheel. Creative day dreaming takes this idea a stage further to enable imagery to be used for all kinds of learning. First get your child to relax physically and mentally using the procedures described on page 195. Next encourage them to picture the information to be learned as a series of mental images. Younger children will find it helpful if you guide this imagery by taking them through the scenes.

Suppose, for instance, your child is studying geography and has to learn the exports from a particular country. This can be a fairly dull and daunting task, when sitting before a list of products and trying to remember what goes where and in how great a quantity. Instead, your child relaxes and then pictures themselves down at the docks. The scene should be conjured as vividly as possible, so that it is a full-colour 'sound movie'. As they walk around the jetties they picture great ocean liners being loaded with cargoes. Each is marked with the country of destination in bold, red, letters on the side and stern. And the exports being craned aboard also have key information printed on them in red. There are motorcars, for instance, each printed – again in red – with the total number (or cash value) of cars exported each year. As grain pours from chutes into the holds of another ship, the total tonnage or monetary value involved is seen written, once more in brilliant red paint, on the chutes. Why red? Well, studies have shown that it sticks in the mind better than any other colour.

To take another example. Imagine your child has to learn about the Battle of Marston Moor which took place during the Civil War, in 1644. Rather than try and cram places, dates, troop numbers and the names of commanders into their memory as a dull list of facts, they should be encouraged to step back in time and produce a Mind Movie of the famous battle. They must see themselves on that fateful July 2nd, standing watching the troops assemble on Marston Field. To the right are the Roundheads, Cromwell's cavalry some 1500 strong, and beyond them the rest of the Parliamentary forces under Crawford, Baillie and Fairfax. To the left the Royalists under the command of

Prince Rupert, with the cavalry of the impetuous Byron facing Cromwell. They should picture themselves wandering among the troops and horsemen, hearing the sounds of weapons being loaded, the clink of stirrups and tramping men. Each set of troops carries a large banner, on which bold letters and numbers (in red of course) identify them and give the total present.

In their movie, they can then follow the course of the battle. Rupert, deciding that it was too late in the afternoon to fight so that his men could rest and eat. The Round Heads under Lord Leven starting the battle by firing a cannon and advancing steadily to engage the enemy. The fatal charge by Byron who, in defiance of his leader's orders, launches an assault on Cromwell's cavalry and so costs the King his crown. While doing some creative day dreaming your child may find it helpful to tape record the key facts and then play the tape back while lying mentally and physically relaxed.

Creative day dreaming is a skill which must be practised. All children have the ability to create such powerful images, although it comes more easily to some than to others.

Memory Magnifier 3 – Plug into many memories. If you are asked how to spell a slightly unfamiliar word what would you do? Probably say the different syllables over to yourself, testing out different sequences of sound. You may also want to write the word down. Looking at it you might realize that something was not quite right, and try another version. Here you are attempting to tap into three of your brain's memories.

1. The sound, or auditory, store. You know how different sounds are spelled so this may give you a clue.

2. The visual store. Comparing the word you've just written down with your memory of how it should look.

3. The movement, or kinaesthetic, store. Your brain stores up the commands which are sent to muscles in the arm, wrist, hand and fingers whenever a word is written. By writing out the word you are not sure of, your brain is able to check the movements made against those used on previous occasions.

This list by no means exhausts your memory stores. You also have a memory for taste and smell. In fact our smell memory is among the most potent we possess. Professor Trygg Engen, of Brown University, has discovered that people are able to distinguish between odours smelled 30 days earlier with 70% accuracy. This compares with a recall rate of only around 10% for visual or sound memories after the same period. Of course such memory decay only occurs when the sights or sounds are not mentally reviewed and rehearsed during the intervening period.

The more memory stores your child uses the higher the chances of recovering that knowledge at a later date. As well as reading the information, they should listen to it, and, where appropriate, plug facts into muscle memory as well. By making a tape recording of important facts, and then playing this over again at odd moments your child will find recall far easier. A personal cassette player allows them to listen to the cassette while travelling to school or going for a walk. Tapes should be preserved together with related written information and used when revising for examinations (*see page 223*).

Memory Magnifier 4 – Use memory joggers. Ranging from tying a knot in your handkerchief to remembering a birthday, to jingles like 'Thirty days hath September, April, June and November . . . ' memory joggers, or mnemonics, are the best known of all techniques for remembering things more easily. Probably the most frequent users of mnemonics are medical students struggling with the complexities of human anatomy. The ten cranial nerves, for instance, are more easily remembered by the eccentric slogan: 'On Old Olympia's Towering Top A Finn and German Vault And Hop' than as the olfactory, optic, oculomotor, trochlear, trigeminal, abducens, facial, auditory, glossopharyngeal, vagus, accessory and hypoglossal nerves! Perhaps the most remarkable user of mnemonics was a Russian journalist named Shereshevskii who could commit virtually anything to memory, from lists of numbers hundreds of digits long, to poetry in foreign languages and elaborate scientific formulae.

At a more mundane level, it's probably easier to remember the colours of the rainbow by means of the mnemonic 'Richard of York Gains Battles In Vain' than as a list of Red, Orange, Yellow, Green, Blue, Indigo, Violet. The problem with using too many mnemonics is that your child may remember the jogger but forget what it actually stands for. However, when used in moderation, and only for facts which are not easy to remember in any other way, they can be helpful. So encourage your child to develop their own memory joggers, which should be as eccentric as possible to ensure they stick in the mind. If they are in verse so much the better, since rhythms are usually easier to recall.

Memory Magnifier 5 – The Method of Loci. This technique was developed by a Greek poet named Simonides of Ceos around 500 BC. He had been hired to entertain guests at a banquet by reciting a lyric poem in praise of their host, the nobleman Scopas of Thessaly. Soon after the feast ended, Simonides was summoned from the hall to meet two men waiting outside. While he was away, the roof of the building collapsed killing all the guests. The corpses were so crushed that relatives could not identify them. But Simonides was able to name all the victims by bringing to mind where they had been sitting in the room. Later he developed this idea into a memory technique known as the *Method of Loci*. Adopted by orators it allowed them to deliver long speeches from memory with perfect accuracy. The method can still be used to good effect today and it remains the basis for many of the 'Instate SuperCharged Memory' courses you often see advertized in newspapers and magazines.

To employ Simonides' technique your child brings to mind some very familiar location, such as their house or school, and then wanders around it in their mind's eye placing the objects to be remembered at different locations. To recall the list at a later date they have to walk back through the house and 'retrieve' each item placed there. For instance, suppose you have asked your child to go shopping and bring back: two herrings, a box of chocolates, a pound of apples, six bananas, a tin tray, six dozen pegs, a newspaper, a screwdriver, dog biscuits and a pair of gloves. Instead of making a list, they imagine opening the front door and looking at the hall table, on which they mentally place two herrings. Going into the kitchen, they picture a large box of chocolates on the draining board. On the fridge they see a pound of apples, and on the cooker six bananas. Walking through into the living room, they imagine a tin tray on the television, six dozen eggs on the sofa and a newspaper on the mantlepiece. Finally, going upstairs, they see a screwdriver on the landing, dog biscuits on their bed and a pair of gloves in the bathroom. To recall the list, they only have to walk back through the house and 'retrieve' each item placed there. Try this for yourself and see how well it works

When well practised the Method of Loci is remarkably powerful. Your child can use it for a whole range of school subjects, including remembering formulae in mathematics, physics or chemistry. These should be imagined written up, in bright red ink, on the walls or even the ceilings of different rooms, or else jotted down on clean white sheets of paper which are left at familiar locations around the house.

Memory Magnifier 6 – Spot messages. This is an excellent way of painlessly committing foreign language vocabulary and formulae to memory. The words, or equations, are written (use *red* ink) on slips of paper and stuck up around the house. (The 'Stick It' note pads, which will attach to virtually any surface without doing any damage, are ideal.) Words in a foreign language can be stuck onto relevant items, for example (French), (German) or (Spanish) might be fixed to a chair. Every time your child glances at a spot message the fact will become more deeply fixed in their memory.

Memory Magnigifier 7 – Picking the right roment. Research has shown that the body is regulated by daily, or circadian, rhythms. These govern a whole range of natural functions, including whether we feel alert or sleepy. They also have an effect on how well we can remember things. At Sussex University, Simon Folkard and his colleagues gave schoolchildren a story either in the morning or late afternoon. They were then tested either immediately afterwards or several days later. Those tested right away did best when they had learned in the morning. But delayed testing favoured children presented with the story in the afternoon.

By studying in the afternoon more than in the morning your child may well find that long-term remembering gets a boost. But because people vary considerably in their biorhythms it's a good idea for your child to experiment by learning at different times of the day. Some of us really do seem to be early birds, best able to study and remember first thing in the day while others are night owls, whose brain appears to function most efficiently after dark. Learning just before going to sleep has the advantage of not introducing anything else to interfere with what has been memorized. However, cramming late into the night is a bad idea since it not only makes falling asleep harder but can also prevent your child from enjoying a good night's rest. Ideally there should be a gap of at least one hour before the last piece of serious learning and going to bed. During this time non-intellectually demanding activities, such as watching TV, listening to music, reading an entertaining, light, book or going for a stroll help consolidate what has just been studied.

Memory Magnifier 8 – Building a learning ladder. This is constructed from a sheet of stiff card, or cork covered board, about 30" x 36" (76 × 91 cm). The rungs can either be drawn directly onto the card or created by stretching ribbons to form the uprights and rungs. This has the advantage of allowing the shape of the ladder to be adjusted depending on the amount of information being displayed. Facts and figures about the subject, written on small index cards, are attached to the board by coloured pins. At the top of the ladder go cards containing very general information, below them cards which deal with the topic in greater detail. The further down the ladder one progresses the more specific the facts become. Additional notes, and any relevant postcards, photographs, illustrations, plans or sketches are placed around the side of the ladder with coloured ribbons being used to link them with key facts within the ladder.

A learning ladder 'Dealing with the American Civil War', for instance, might have at the top cards giving the dates it started and finished, who the opposing sides were and who led them. Within the next rung are cards listing key battles with dates, locations and numbers of troops involved. As one proceeds to the lower rungs, information about the personal habits and commanding styles of the generals and civilians involved would be included.

The ladder is placed in a prominent position and looked at now and again. Even a casual glance in passing is enough to help impress facts into your child's memory. After being in place for a while it is dismantled, the cards carefully filed away, and a new subject displayed. While it is on display, new information can be added as required and old cards revised or replaced. The learning ladder aids study in two important ways. First, by encouraging your child to organize information which has to be learned. Second by jogging the memory briefly but frequently.

How does your child learn best?

So far we have looked at ways in which information can be organized to enhance retention and recall. But effective presentation also depends, to a large extent, on your child's personal style of learning. By identifying their individual style you can help organize material in the most effective way. Start by asking your child to complete the questionnaire below – make it clear there are no right or wrong answers. You may like to assess yourself as well, since knowing your particular learning style will make any studying you do far more effective.

How to complete the assessment. Just tick whichever statement best describes your normal approach to learning a new subject or your attitude towards studying in general.

1. When learning something new I:
   (a) Like to gather information from many different sources.
   (b) Would rather study from one or two books.

2. I would sooner:
   (a) Know a little about a great many things.
   (b) Know a great deal about just one or two things.

3. When reading a book, I normally:
   (a) Skip from one chapter to another, often glancing ahead at sections of special interest.
   (b) Read methodically from the first to the last chapter, making sure I have understood one section before attempting anything new.

4. I am best at remembering:
   (a) General ideas.
   (b) Specific facts.

5. Of the subjects below I prefer:
   (a) Art and English to maths or science.
   (b) Maths or science to art and English.

6. My idea of an ideal holiday is to:
   (a) Spend a short time in several different places.
   (b) Stay in just one place and explore it thoroughly.

7. When in a library, I:
   (a) Browse around many departments.
   (b) Spend most of my time in just one department.

8. The teachers I like best:
   (a) Have lots of different stories to tell about their subject.
   (b) Stick to one topic and explain it very carefully.

9. If carrying out a task, I like to:
   (a) Think of many aspects of the subject.
   (b) Only consider the main topic.

10. When revising for exams I:
    (a) Have no general study plan.
    (b) Carefully organize my studies.

11. If I see a picture hanging slightly crooked, I:

    (a)   Feel no desire to straighten it.
    (b)   Want to go and straighten it.

Add up all your (a) and (b) scores.
Total number of (a)s =   (b)s =

What the scores reveal. If your child scored more (a)s than (b)s their learning style is what we term *Top Down*. A higher score on (b) statements indicates that the preferred learning style is *Basement Up*. Scores within 2 of each other ie 6 (a)s and 5 (b)s show that either learning style can be used with equal ease.

How Top Down learning works

Suppose you wanted to learn all about London. One way would be to get aerial photographs and study the overall layout of the city. You would see how Brixton, which lies south of the river Thames was situated in relation to Hampstead which is to the north. You could identify Greenwich to the east and Ealing to the west. This would give you a general feeling for the subject so that, when you later started to acquire more and more information about Brixton, Hampstead, Greenwich and Ealing, these facts could be slotted into an overall view of the city. This is the kind of learning which children with the Top Down style most prefer. They like to see where they are going before embarking on their journey. If studying human biology, for instance, it would be a tremendous help to Top Down learners to be given a short conducted tour of the whole topic before starting to explore its different systems, such as the heart and lungs, digestion, and so on.

The benefits of Top Down learning. The child has a good overall grasp of the subject and can see where new information fits into the pattern of previously acquired knowledge. Mistakes tend not to discourage Top Down learners as much as they do those following the Basement Up style. They are seen as valuable learning experiences which stimulate a desire for further knowledge and understanding.

The problems with Top Down learning. Most school lessons and text books are constructed along Basement Up lines. This means that Top Down learners never get a chance for the overview needed. They may also be accused of having butterfly minds, of never concentrating for long enough on any single topic to master it thoroughly.

Furthermore in subjects where depth rather than breadth of knowledge is demanded, they may do less well than Basement Up learners.

Finally because it often takes many weeks of study before the overall shape of a course, and the relevance of much which has been taught, becomes clear, Top Down learners may become discouraged.

How Basement Up learning works

Let's go back to the idea of learning about London. Top Down learners would find it best to start with an overview. Basement Up learners would probably find this approach very confusing. They learn best when able to construct their knowledge carefully and methodically, never moving onto a new fact until they are sure of having understood an earlier one. Their approach to London, would be through first taking a particular topic, such as transport, and finding out all they could about that, before moving onto the next.

The benefits of Basement Up learning. Most school courses and text books are designed to suit this style of learning. On day one in the class, your child is taught some specific facts. On day two, new facts are added and this continues until the topic has been covered to the depth demanded by the school syllabus. All this favours the Basement Up learner. They are also good at acquiring knowledge in depth, and so tend to do better at subjects such as maths or science which demand this type of approach.

The problems of Basement Up learning. There is a tendency not to see the wood for the trees. The child is so concerned with gathering facts that they are unable to relate them to larger issues. One often finds, for instance, that a child possesses the specific items of knowledge needed to solve a novel problem but is unable to generalize from those items in order to come up with a solution. Mistakes prove a great source of discouragement to the Basement Up learner. Like an expert bricklayer constructing a house, they need to be sure that each new layer in their structure is sound before adding another.

Mastering both learning styles

If your child scored an almost equal number of (a)s and (b)s on the assessment it suggests that he or she is capable of using both these styles according to the demands of a particular learning task. Where there is a clear preference for either Top Down or Basement Up learning, help your child acquire a greater mastery in the less well developed style. Here's how to do it:

Top Down to Basement Up. Encourage your child to continue taking an overview of subjects being learned. Help make available a wide range of information on each topic. But, at the same time, encourage them to explore key topics in greater depth. They'll find this much easier to do using the system below. This allows fresh information to be added quickly and easily, so that their knowledge can be expanded slowly but surely and with an overall goal constantly kept in view.

Basement Up to Top Down. Encourage your child to take a more general view of new subjects. Help to create an overview of a topic by making use of the Learning Ladder (*see page 177*). At the same time reassure your child about mistakes. These must come to be seen not as threats to learning, but as essential stepping stones to greater achievement. Do this by defusing any anxiety that may arise and enhancing self-confidence.

Learning styles and studying

In order to learn, or revise, a subject most efficiently, your child should structure the information according to their particular learning style. This is done as follows:

1. The material to be learned is divided into main subject areas. This is normally very easy to do since it only means following the headings in your child's textbook or lesson notes.
2. Subject areas are further divided into key topics. Again this seldom presents any difficulties since this is the way textbooks and lesson notes are organized.
3. Topics are placed in groups of *four*. These should, whenever possible, be related to one another in some way.
4. The topics are learned in an order decided by your child's favoured learning style. For revision purposes the same procedure is adopted.

To illustrate how this system works, let's look at photography since this is a subject with which most people have some familiarity.

Main subject headings: Cameras. Taking Pictures. Processing Films. Printing Negatives.

From this partial list, we will consider Taking Pictures in more detail to see what topics would be included:

Taking Pictures: Exposure readings. Shutter speeds. Film – black and white/colour. Film speeds. Focusing. Filters.

These topics are then grouped into fours, for example:

Topic 1 – Focusing lenses. *Topic 2* – How shutters operate. *Topic 3* – Exposure readings. *Topic 4* – Film speeds. These are then learned as follows. If your child favours Top Down learning follow Plan 1. If your child favours Basement Up learning follow Plan 2.

Plan 1 – for Top Down learners

Start by learning Topic 1 – Focusing lenses. Take a short break. Next learn Topic 2 – How shutters operate. Take a short break. Revise both Topics together. Take a short break. Add the third topic by learning about – Exposure readings. Take a short break. Revise *all three* Topics together. Take a short break. Learn Topic 4 – Film speeds. Take a short break. Finally revise *all four* Topics.

Read around the subject. At the same time Top Down learners should be encouraged to find out as much as possible about the subject to gain an overview. Continuing to use photography as an example, your child should be encouraged to dip into a variety of photographic books and magazines, on sports and fashion, press and advertising, medical and industrial photography. Although much of what is read may not be fully understood at their current level of knowledge, this will motivate them to learn more rather than discouraging them from further studying.

Plan 2 – for Basement Up learners

This demonstrates the most effective way of organizing knowledge if your child's favoured learning style is Basement Up.

Start by learning Topic 1 – Focusing lenses. Take a short break. Next learn Topic 2 – How shutters operate. Take a short break. Then revise both these topics together. Take a short break. Add the third topic by learning about – Exposure readings. Take a short break. As you will have noticed, up to this point the two plans are identical. Now they diverge to take account of the Basement Up learner's desire to build new knowledge slowly and methodically. Learn Topic 4 – Film speeds.

Chart summarizing Top Down learning plan:

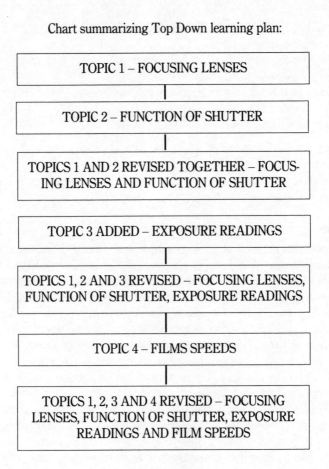

Take a short break. Revise Topics 1 and 2. Take a short break. Revise Topics 3 and 4. Take a short break. Revise *all four* Topics together.

Avoid mistakes whenever possible. These tend to discourage Basement Up learners far more than Top Down learners and should be avoided whenever possible. This can be achieved by adopting a very methodical, step-by-step approach to acquiring new knowledge. Your child should only proceed to a new topic once the previous facts have been understood.

Chart summarizing Basement Up learning plan:

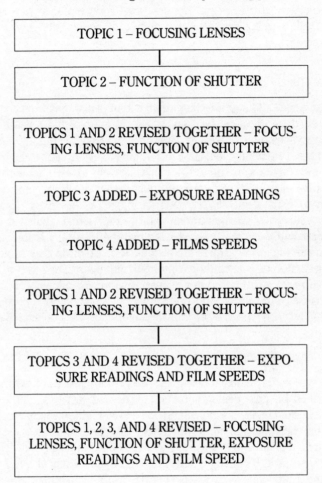

TOPIC 1 – FOCUSING LENSES

TOPIC 2 – FUNCTION OF SHUTTER

TOPICS 1 AND 2 REVISED TOGETHER – FOCUSING LENSES, FUNCTION OF SHUTTER

TOPIC 3 ADDED – EXPOSURE READINGS

TOPIC 4 ADDED – FILMS SPEEDS

TOPICS 1 AND 2 REVISED TOGETHER – FOCUSING LENSES, FUNCTION OF SHUTTER

TOPICS 3 AND 4 REVISED TOGETHER – EXPOSURE READINGS AND FILM SPEEDS

TOPICS 1, 2, 3, AND 4 REVISED – FOCUSING LENSES, FUNCTION OF SHUTTER, EXPOSURE READINGS AND FILM SPEED

Helping your child overcome anxiety

Excessive anxiety is one of the most common causes of underachievement in class. It affects every aspect of your child's school performance, from making friends to studying and playing sports to exam success. No matter what your child is attempting, high anxiety

ensures they will do it less effectively. In this chapter I shall explain
the causes of excessive anxiety, describe the unhelpful ways it is usually dealt with and provide practical procedures for helping your child
overcome it.

How anxiety arises

When your child starts feeling anxious they will suffer from some, or
all, of these disagreeable sensations: rapidly beating heart; fast,
uneven, breathing; increased sweating; dry mouth; queasy tummy;
giddiness; trembling; blushing or turning pale; feeling sick; muscle
cramps. At the same time their mind is likely to be filled with such
negative ideas as: 'I can't cope,' 'I must get away,' 'I am going to lose
control,' 'I shall faint,' 'Everyone is staring at me.' As anxiety rises further your child's concentration lapses, intellectual ability declines
sharply and even well learned facts may be forgotten. If they suffer
from chronic anxiety, there are also likely to be difficulties in getting
to sleep, despite constantly feeling tired, nightmares, bed-wetting, loss
of appetite, apathy or an increase in minor ailments such as
headaches, sore throat and upset tummy. What possible purpose is
served by such a distressing and apparently purposeless response?

Fighting or fleeing

The symptoms of anxiety form part of a primitive survival mechanism
which enabled our distant ancestors to respond swiftly and efficiently
to physical danger. It is sometimes called the Fight or Flight response,
since, when life and limb are threatened, these are often the only
options available. We can fight to overcome the enemy or flee and
hope to escape. It is this Fight or Flight mechanism, technically known
as the Autonomic Nervous System (ANS), which brings about the
physical and mental changes in your child whenever anxiety arises.

To see how the ANS aids survival let's take a trip back in time, and
imagine one of our prehistoric ancestors foraging for food. Suddenly
hearing a noise from the nearby forest he becomes tense and alert.
Was it the breeze rustling the branches or a man-eating animal about
to attack? Even while turning over these possibilities in his mind, our
ancestor's ANS instantly moves into overdrive. To either fight or flee
successfully important physical changes must take place. Arm and leg

muscles must be provided with extra food and oxygen to ensure maximum strength and stamina. This food, in the form of glycogen from the liver, and air from the lungs, is delivered to muscle cells by the blood. Vigorous action produces heat and carbon dioxide, dangerous by-products which must also be rapidly removed by the blood. Heart rate increases to satisfy this demand, so too does breathing, to draw more oxygen into the body and expel a greater volume of carbon dioxide. To ensure sufficient blood is available for the muscles and brain, some is diverted away from the digestive system, and from the tiny capillaries directly beneath the skin. As a result the stomach may suddenly feel queasy, while the person grows pale. To disperse the excess heat generated by vigorous action, sweating increases and cools the body as it evaporates from the skin.

Fight and Flight in the modern world

Even today there are occasions when, faced with a physical threat to survival, this primitive mechanism makes the difference between life and death. An elderly woman beats off a mugger, a mother lifts a heavy tree from her crushed car to rescue a trapped child, a poor swimmer manages to swim through heavy seas to safety. Afterwards they find it hard to understand where their newly found strength and stamina came from. The answer is from the high levels of arousal triggered by their Fight/Flight response.

Unfortunately most of the threats we face are psychological rather than physical. Your child, for example, will be challenged by an irate teacher, baffling exam questions, or the ending of a friendship far more often than objective danger. In these, and a host of similar situations, neither fighting or fleeing are possible and the high level of arousal is more a handicap than a help. So why can't we just tell ourselves not to be so silly and somehow make it clear to the ANS that there is no physical, danger and would it please stop making life so difficult? The trouble is our ANS regulates bodily functions in much the same way that a computerized pilot flies an aircraft – automatically. It controls all those routine, but essential, functions such as digesting food, pumping blood, and breathing. Which is just as well. Imagine trying to order your heart to beat once a second, your lungs to inflate 17 times a minute, your stomach and intestines to process lunch and so on.

The ANS makes life possible by liberating the 'thinking' brain from these essential, but routine, chores. There is, however, a price to pay for such independence. Because our ANS normally operates without instructions from the 'thinking' part of the brain, we are unable to give it direct commands. We are in the same position as a pilot who, seeing his aircraft about to fly into the side of a mountain politely asks the autopilot to gain altitude or change course. It is impossible, for instance, to instruct your heart to beat faster or slower or to prevent your lunch from being digested just by thinking about it. This means that when the ANS switches your child's body onto emergency running their 'thinking' brain is incapable of countering that command. Even when they fully realize there is no need to become anxious, the body continues to respond as if their very life was under threat. Telling themselves or being told, to keep calm and stay cool has no soothing effect on the ANS. In fact quite the opposite is likely to happen. Knowing there is no real danger, but still finding themselves anxious, children believe control is slipping out of reach. This increases anxiety still further, since there are few more frightening sensations than loss of control.

The changes which have been brought about by the ANS, increased heart rate, rapid breathing, more sweating and so on, can only be corrected and the body returned to normal running by the same mechanism which speeded them up in the first place, that is the autonomic nervous system. Such a reduction in anxiety is made possible by the fact that the ANS has two branches, one for *stepping up* arousal and the other for *bringing it down again*. These are technically called the sympathetic and parasympathetic branches of the ANS. Under normal conditions these work together to maintain a level of arousal suited to the activity being tackled.

As your child sits watching a relaxing TV show, for instance, the slow-down branch of their ANS exerts most influence. Their heart rate is slow and breathing steady. Then a horror film starts. They feel afraid, and although not in any real danger, their ANS treats the situation as if life was threatened. The step-up *sympathetic* branch of the ANS takes over and prepares the body for Fight or Flight. Heart rate, breathing, sweating and muscular tension all increase as your child becomes more alert. These changes are triggered by chemical messengers called hormones, which carry ANS instructions to all parts of the body. Adrenaline, the best known of these hormones, is sometimes dubbed 'jungle juice' because of its key role in this primitive response.

That sudden lurch in the pit of your stomach when you have been startled, is caused by a the release of adrenaline.

Imagine a child sitting an important exam. What is under threat here is intellectual and emotional survival. Perhaps they are strongly motivated by a desire to avoid failure (*see page 203*) which turns the prospect of a failing grade into a terrifying prospect. Maybe long cherished ambitions hang on the outcome of that exam. As the moment when they must start answering questions draws closer, doubts creep in. 'Can I really cope with this challenge?' 'Suppose I fail?' 'I am bound to do badly . . .' The Fight or Flight mechanism responds to these negative ideas with increased physical arousal. Noting that the heart is beating faster, the stomach is churning, and the mouth has gone dry, the child becomes even more concerned and doubtful of their ability. These worries strengthen the step-up mechanism still further and the body becomes even more aroused.

But because part of the brain recognizes that the fears are groundless, the slow-down branch also struggles to return the system to normal functioning. As a result the body becomes a battlefield, the sympathetic branch orders the heart to beat faster and the lungs to work more rapidly while the parasympathetic instructs both to slow down. Blood is removed from just beneath the skin and sent to the muscles, making the child turn pale. It is returned by the slow-down branch and so causes blushing. Additional blood, rich in oxygen and glucose, reaches the brain making the child light headed. Then it is diverted away again leaving them giddy. The muscles tense and relax until they feel like jelly. The inevitable result is confusion, uncertainty and a total inability to recall facts and figures that have been revised carefully and were known perfectly until the anxiety attack began.

Later on I shall explain how to help your child bring these distressing symptoms under control, or prevent them from occurring. But, for the moment, let's consider some of the ways in which your child may try to cope with anxiety.

How we handle anxiety

The most widely used defence is avoidance. This may be direct and physical. Your child has a maths test on Monday which they dread. So, come Monday morning they complain of a headache or tummy upset, sufficiently bad to avoiding going to school. If this doesn't work, and anxiety is sufficiently strong, they may decide to truant.

Anxiety and truancy. School phobia is an anxiety so intense that some children cannot bring themselves to attend class at all. This powerful fear is not always caused by things which happen in class, however. Sometimes a child may be fearful about what is happening at home while, they are away. If there are frequent family rows, for instance, or one of the parents is ill, a child may want to stay behind and keep and eye on what's happening. There is no point in punishing truancy caused by a phobia, since this only makes the child more frightened than ever. Instead try and discover the cause of the fears using *diagnostic listening* (*see page 218*) and take whatever practical steps are open to you to make your child's life easier. This might involve making changes at the school, for instance by talking to them about an overly critical or sarcastic teacher.

Anxiety, impulsivity and day dreaming. Avoidance can also take the form of impulsive behaviour or day dreaming. By acting impulsively your child reduces the amount of time which has to be spent confronting the feared activity. A child who is terrified of sums, for example, is likely to rush through them to get the distressing task over and done with as rapidly as possible. This, not surprisingly, leads to careless errors and avoidable mistakes. Impulsive children also say things without thinking and tend to be physically clumsy.

Day dreaming allows your child to slip away from the anxiety arousing situation into a peaceful world of their own. Unfortunately, of course, it also prevents them from learning important lessons in class. By improving their skills with any subjects currently causing difficulty, using the methods described in this book, you should help reduce excessive anxiety and day dreaming to a significant extent.

Anxiety and denial. Another widely used defence is denial of reality. A child failing in class may deny that school success is important. They could become rebellious or apathetic, indifferent to criticism and unresponsive to encouragement. Instead of becoming angry or despairing over this negative, unrealistic, attitude see such a response for what it really is – an anxiety reducing strategy. I shall be explaining how to improve the lack of motivation which often underlies such an attitude later on.

Anxiety and projection. Children who feel anxious and incompetent in lessons may project their sense of failure onto others. Unsuccessful students, for example, often blame their parents for sending them to a bad school, their teachers for being idle or incompetent, other students for disrupting classes and making serious studying impossible, and so on. While there is sometimes truth in these allegations, projecting personal failings onto other people is also a strategy for reducing anxiety.

If your child seems to be adopting this form of defence, start by finding out how whether there are reasonable grounds for such accusations. Talk to other parents and students. Find out whether the school has a reputation for poor teaching or a lack of classroom discipline. If there are reasonable grounds for complaint, take what practical steps you can to improve matters. At the same time try to discover the underlying causes of your child's anxieties.

What makes children anxious

1. Meeting adult expectations. This is most likely when parents, or teachers, are overly perfectionist or convey the impression, however unintentionally, that love and high regard depend on constant achievement. But such anxieties can also arise even in the absence of pressure to succeed. The desire to do as well as an older sibling or compete with a high achieving friend can make your child live in dread of failure.

2. Social anxieties. These are aroused by meeting new people, making friends, getting along with others. I have discussed some of the ways in which you can deal with bullying and help your child develop friendships earlier in the book.

3. Novelty anxieties. These focus on unfamiliar tasks where your child has no clear idea what to do or how to proceed. Often this is linked to a strong fear of failure. Practical ways of tackling this source of anxiety will be described later on.

4. Study anxieties. Areas of concern here include coping with intellectual demands, worries for the future, fears about things going wrong. By teaching your child to learn more easily and think more effectively, many of these anxieties can be greatly reduced. Enhancing motivation and self-esteem, using the procedures described later on will also help make your child feel far less anxious.

5. Sexual anxieties. While these are, occasionally, due to an assault, or attempted assault, by an adult or older child, they are more frequently caused by sex scenes on TV or videos, sexual horseplay between older children, blue jokes, the boasts of more physically mature companions or a misunderstanding of sex education lessons.

Compulsory showers and changing rooms also cause anxiety for modest or shy children. This problem is usually greatest around puberty – the onset of sexual maturity. Puberty tends to produce an exaggerated awareness of bodily imperfections, a spotty back, fat legs or flat chest. Being obliged to display these to their companions can be enough to plunge some teenagers into the depths of despair.

A second cause of distress is the different rate at which children mature. Puberty in boys usually occurs around the age of 13, but may start as early as seven or as late as 19. Girls reach puberty, on average, slightly early than boys but again the age range is very wide. Being of similar age youngsters may in fact be markedly different in their physical maturity. The teasing which often occurs in changing rooms only makes the less developed child feel inadequate, inferior and anxious.

But probably the source of anxiety which is hardest for some parents to accept, is an adolescent's sexual ambivalence. During this stage of emotional growth many teenagers find themselves erotically attracted to members of their own sex. This may take the form of hero worship between boys, or crushes on an older girl or teacher. Even when this attraction involves sexual fantasies, or even experimentation, such attraction certainly does not mean your child is going to grow up gay. It is a normal stage in sexual development. Not realizing this, an adolescent who finds same sex nudity in showers or locker rooms arousing can experience intense guilt, depression and anxiety. Here are some practical Do's and Don'ts for helping:

- Don't write to the school asking that your child be excused from showers. The likely outcome of this is to get them branded as 'different' and so make teasing more likely.

- Do respect your child's desire for privacy. His or her bedroom should be off-limits to everybody without their express permission.

- Don't barge into the bathroom while he or she is in there.

- Do accept your child's desire for modesty. If you've brought your child up to feel no shame about nudity, their sudden desire to cover everything up may be difficult to understand. But, you must accept this as an important, and perfectly justifiable, right.

- Don't shun your responsibility to provide factual information where ignorance is a cause of anxiety. If you are not sure of the facts, then get a good, basic, sex education text.

• Do offer reassurance when asked for it. Take your child's anxieties in this area seriously, not as a joke or an embarrassment.

Discovering your child's secret fears

Having some idea of why anxieties can arise, and the ways in which your child may seek to defend him- or herself against them, will make it easier to identify the cause of their specific fears. The first essential is to master the art of diagnostic listening (*see page 218*). Pay close attention to what is being said, smile and nod to encourage your child to talk, but refrain from commenting until you have extracted all the information possible. For instance your child may start to explain that they are frightened by violence on TV. Rather than immediately offering reassurance, get them to discuss these feelings more fully. Maybe the real focus of their dread is violence at school, from a master or older boy. Your child's paintings and drawings can provide you with valuable insights into fears which they are unable to put into words. Be on the look out for recurring themes in pictures, such as violence or a sense of alienation. When your child has a full choice of colours to choose from, yet favours red or purple even when inappropriate, the choice can be a sign of bottled up anger (red) or misery. Notice too how your child depicts him- or herself in drawings, especially when these show school or family scenes. Are they drawn as large as others or as an insignificant little figure in the background?

Helping an anxious child

Play acting. Acting out fears in improvised dramas, can encourage a fearful child to become more confident about potentially stressful encounters. You and your child take on different roles, such as a teacher and pupil or husband and wife and play out a scene which focuses on a suspected anxiety. Experiment with different ways of responding to one another: aggressive, defensive, passive or assertive. Let your child experience different emotions and try out various social skills within the safety of a 'game'. By swapping roles, you can help them appreciate both sides of an argument and, by helping to express fears openly you'll make it far easier for your child to come to terms with them.

Provide accurate information. If anxiety is caused by ignorance, offering clear, factual, information, appropriate for your child's level of knowledge can be extremely helpful. The unknown or imperfectly understood is usually far more frightening than calmly presented facts. You'll find it easier to explain things which you may find rather embarrassing if you overcome your own anxieties about them. Learn to relax yourself, using the procedure described for older children, and then imagine discussing the subject, calmly and rationally, with your child.

Relaxation and guided fantasy. These are powerful antidotes to anxiety. By teaching your child to relax physically and mentally, by means of physical exercises and guided fantasy, you will be giving them skills whose value extends far beyond childhood. As an adult they will be able to use the same procedures for controlling stress and coping with anxiety provoking challenges. To understand how relaxation works, it will be useful to review what we know about the way anxiety arises.

As we saw earlier, the ANS, our Fight or Flight mechanism, produces important changes in bodily functions. These occur very rapidly and are not normally capable of being controlled by the thinking brain. I say not normally capable, because there are ways of regulating the ANS and so preventing anxiety symptoms from arising. To see how this may be done, compare the two branches of the ANS with the reins of a horse and imagine that the animal has been pulled to the right by pressure on the right-hand rein. To return the horse to a straight line the rider must now apply pressure to the left rein. Similarly when the speed-up branch of the ANS has taken charge, it is possible to restore the system to normal running by stimulating the slow-down branch.

This can be done in two main ways. The first is by eating. You may have noticed that a good meal will calm your child down, indeed one reason why some people have a weight problem is because they munch a chocolate bar or reach for a cream cake when feeling anxious. The second, and more practical way, is to master the art of relaxation. By strengthening the power of the slow-down branch, relaxation brings your child's anxiety quickly, and naturally, back under control.

Teaching relaxation

I am going to describe two relaxation procedures. The first is for younger children, up to the age of about nine. This you can read aloud as you guide your child through the exercise. The second is for older children who can read instructions and go through the procedures for themselves, with older children you may meet a certain amount of resistance, especially from boys who sometimes think of relaxation as sissy or a waste of time. If this happens, point out that the procedures can be useful not just for controlling anxiety in class, but also on the sports fields. Similar methods are now used by leading professional sports persons, including tennis players, skiers, runners, and footballers. Why not make relaxation training a family affair and go through it together? Everybody can benefit by mastering these simple procedures.

Relaxation 1 – for younger children. Choose a time when you can spend an uninterrupted 15 minutes together in a quiet room. There should be no spectators, especially in the form of older brothers or sisters. Either a child joins in or stays out of the room. Find some lively music, marching bands or a rock group, to which your child can jump about or march around the room. Now explain you are going to play a version of musical chairs. Only when the music stops your child must flop down into a comfortable chair just like a puppet whose strings have suddenly been cut. Play the music for a while, and encourage your child to be very active, moving both arms and legs as they dance around the room. Stop the music suddenly and tell your child to drop down and flop out. Pick up an arm or leg to see how relaxed it is, congratulate your child when relaxed, encourage them to notice and relax muscles which still feel tense. Young children are usually far less tense than older ones and seldom have any difficulty in achieving this. Repeat three or four times.

On the fifth occasion, after your child has flopped down in the chair, ask them to close their eyes lightly and remain quite still. Legs should be uncrossed and hands lying either in their lap or by their sides. Give instructions along these lines. There is no need to follow the script exactly, far better if you put it into your own words while ensuring the general procedure is followed. 'Lie still and let your muscles go all loose and floppy. Feel yourself sinking deeper and deeper into the chair. Breathe lightly and, each time you breathe out, feel your body growing limp and heavy. I want you to imagine yourself playing in a beautiful garden. See and smell the beautiful flowers, feel the warmth of the sun on your face, listen to birds singing in the trees. Imagine lying down on the grass to have a rest after playing. There is a little stream nearby and you can hear the water gently bubbling along. As you lie there you feel very happy, peaceful and calm.'

Help your child to develop these images as vividly as possible. At first they may have some difficulty in concentrating on it for more than a few moments. But, with a little practice, it should be possible to sustain the scene for several minutes without too much difficulty. If your child finds it hard to conjure up the garden scene, then try some other surroundings. Any images which bring about a sense of happiness, peace, and security are suitable. They might, for instance, prefer to imagine themselves stretched out on a sandy beach, listening to the sea gently uncurling, or to picture themselves snuggled up in a comfortable arm chair in front of a fire on a winter's night. Discuss the sort of scene which makes your child feel most relaxed and content, then work with them to develop the image.

If they are made anxious by some activity or situation, use the relaxation session to help them overcome those fears by imagining themselves confronting them calmly and confidently. Let's suppose your child feels shy about talking to other children. Here's how you could help reduce those unhelpful anxieties during a relaxation session.

Start with the lively movement to music and the instructions to flop out and unwind. Take them into the imaginary garden and let them spend a few moments enjoying the peaceful atmosphere. Then say something like this: 'Now I want you to picture yourself in the play-ground at school. There is a child in your form you've always wanted to go and talk with but have never managed to speak to. See that child standing by himself (herself) in one corner of the playground. Go over and say hello. Imagine yourself walking across the playground. Notice the other children playing, what sort of weather it is, how crowded the playground is, what the buildings surrounding it look like. You've reached the other child and he's (she's) looking towards you. Picture yourself smiling and saying "hello". You feel calm and relaxed. He's (she's) smiling back. Now imagine talking to him (her) about the lessons you've got today . . . '

Encourage your child to develop this clear and detailed scene which make use of all the senses, so that they not only see the surroundings but also hear the sounds associated with them, as well as experiencing any other relevant sensations – such as smell, taste and touch. This variation of creative day dreaming (*see page 173*) may be used for all sorts of activities, from playing sports to taking tests and examinations.

Relaxation – for older children. These instructions can either be read to the child, read by the child or tape recorded and played back during the session. Choose a time when you can be uninterrupted for 15 minutes. You'll need a quiet room and a comfortable bed or chair. Take off your shoes and remove any tight clothing, such as a belt or tie. You are going to learn how to relax very quickly and deeply by doing just the opposite, that is deliberately tensing all your muscles at the same time. Read through the instructions below several times until you know which muscles to tense, and how to put them under tension, without referring to the book.

Sit or lie and tense the main muscle groups:

1. Clench your fists.
2. Try and touch the back of your wrists to your shoulders.
3. Hunch your shoulders.
4. Press your head back against the bed or chair.
5. Clench your teeth and frown hard.
6. Take a deep breath and hold it.
7. Flatten your stomach.
8. Stretch your legs and point your toes.

I suggest you practise by tensing each of these eight muscle groups in turn. Hold the tension for a slow count to five and feel it building up and up. Let go completely. Unclench your fists and allow your fingers to rest lightly on the bed or chair. Drop your shoulders and relax your jaw. Unfurrow your brow and smooth it out. Keep your eyes lightly closed. Breath quietly and evenly, let your stomach relax and your legs go floppy. Each time you breathe out feel yourself becoming more deeply relaxed.

Imagine that you are standing under a stream of clear, warm, water. See the water flowing down from the top of your head, through your muscles. Flowing down your shoulders, forearms, wrists and hands and then out of the tips of your fingers to disappear into the room. Feel it pouring down your spine and chest, down your thighs, calves, ankles, feet and finally emerging from the toes, before disappearing into the room. As the fluid pours through, your muscles then become warmer and warmer, heavier and heavier. Every time you breathe out feel yourself sinking more and more deeply into the bed or chair. Imagine you are resting on a small, white, cloud which is drifting silently across the sky and carrying you with it. The cloud is very soft, like a giant feather bed. Notice the sunlit countryside speeding beneath you. The blue sea appears, and a long, golden beach. Your cloud descends slowly until it is resting on the beach. See yourself stepping off onto the warm sand. You lie down on the beach. It is a very peaceful, safe place. Your very own magic island to which you can return any time you start feeling tense or anxious. It is quiet, beautiful and belongs entirely to you. Feel how good it is just to lie on the sand, listening to small waves breaking gently on the beach, smelling the scent of tropical flowers, feeling the gentle, warm breeze on your face. Lick your lips and taste the slight tang from the salt.

Conjure up this image as vividly as you can. See, hear, taste and touch your surroundings. Keep your breathing light and steady. Do not be surprised, or concerned, if at first it's a little difficult to hold the image. Distracting thoughts may come into your mind. When this happens, simply notice the thought has occurred and then dismiss it from your mind. If it proves hard to shift, imagine writing the thought on the sand with a stick. Then picture the sea coming in and washing away those words. Alternatively, see the thought placed on a cloud and sent drifting away into space so that it can no longer trouble you. Practise three or four times a week for the first three weeks, then a couple of times each week to stay in practice. Just before going to sleep is ideal because it ensures a good night's rest.

Once you are able to hold the relaxing image for a while, you practise using other images for reducing any anxieties which you experience in different situations. For instance if you become anxious just before playing a sport, picture yourself in the changing room, about to go onto the sports field. Imagine feeling excited and eager to play, but confident rather than anxious. If conjuring up that scene causes any anxiety, switch back to the island and spend a few moments relaxing again on the beach before returning to the activity. After a while the anxiety will disappear from the fantasy scenes. While this won't also mean that it vanishes in real life as well, you should find managing your anxieties far easier when facing the actual situation. You can use this approach for dealing with any situations which make you stressed and tense, such as: taking tests or examinations, answering questions in class, making a presentation to other students, acting in the school play or taking part in any kind of entertainment, standing up for yourself in an argument, responding to criticisms from a teacher, or talking to strangers at a party.

Create the scenes as vividly as possible, and try out different approaches. For instance when imagining standing up for yourself in an argument, test various ways of responding and picture the way others would react to each approach. You might imagine losing your temper. How does the other person react to that? And how do you feel, both during the confrontation and afterwards? Now see how it feels not to lose your temper, even though the other person has lost theirs. Imagine standing your ground while asserting yourself so that your views or feelings are clearly understood. How did that approach feel, both during and after the fantasy encounter? Again, while such guided fantasy is not going to make confrontations completely anxiety free, you should find yourself dealing with them far more confidently, and successfully than before.

Enhancing your child's motivation

Motivation is essential to all types of school achievement. When correctly motivated your child will have the enthusiasm and confidence needed to overcome virtually any obstacle to learning. Without motivation even the brightest child is unlikely to enjoy much classroom success. In this section I shall be explaining how motivation arises, why too much is as unhelpful as too little, considering the effects of rewards and punishments and describing the differences needed for achievement and fear of failure.

Motivation – praise and punishment

The traditional method of motivating children is the carrot and stick approach. Attainment is rewarded, with praise, good grades or prizes and failure is punished by criticism, scolding or ridicule. While this may produce the desired results in the short term, it is an insensitive and unreliable way of attempting to regulate a subtle and complex process. Rewards, for instance, generate neither a personal interest in the subject being studied nor sustain the degree of motivation essential for enduring success. Indeed by over rewarding an activity, you can actually diminish a child's interest. In one experiment, two groups of children drew pictures. One was told they would be awarded an impressive certificate complete with red ribbon and a large gold seal. The others had no reward other than sheer enjoyment in the task. Later it was noticed that the children who won a certificate showed less interest in drawing than those who received no additional reward. The difference was simple. The first group regarded the drawing as work, the second as play. As Mark Twain wisely remarked, 'Work consists of whatever a body is obliged to do and . . . play consists of whatever a body is not obliged to do.'

A similar problem occurs when punishments are used to prevent children from doing something. If, for instance, a child obeys a mild request not to play with an attractive toy they will come to see that toy as less attractive. But when the mild request is replaced by a strong command, backed up with the threat of punishment, the child continues to regard the forbidden toy as highly attractive. In other words they feel that the only reason they are not playing with that lovely toy is from fear of being punished. Because of this temptation, they are likely to play with the toy again whenever possible. This makes misbehaviour more, and not less, likely.

Effective motivation stems from a desire to achieve goals regarded as *personally* relevant and important. Do not over reward your child for doing something which they already find pleasurable since doing so could replace satisfaction with a desire to earn a prize or your approval. In the long term this is a far less satisfactory form of motivation. At the same time it will be useful to introduce a series of rewards for tasks which are necessary but not seen as involving. Much of school work falls into this category.

Never use frequent punishments as a means of regulating your child's behaviour. Not only are these ineffective in changing attitudes and conduct, but undermine self-confidence, diminish self-esteem, inhibit creativity and can lead to long-term emotional problems.

Success and motivation levels

Common sense might suggest the more highly motivated your child is the better. In fact the opposite holds true. Excessive motivation can prove just as handicapping as having insufficient desire for achievement. You probably recall occasions in your life, perhaps when going to an important job interview or on a first date, when you tried so hard to succeed you ended up failing miserably. In this case your level of motivation was too high. At other times when you regarded some activity as dull and irrelevant, your performance was poor because you had so little interest in the task. Here you failed through a lack of motivation. Finally, there were occasions when you succeeded magnificently without trying especially hard. From the start you felt confident of achieving all your goals. In such cases your level of motivation was just right. So let's consider what happened in the first two situations that made failure more likely than success.

Motivation and thinking

From the vast array of potential information available to our brain during every waking moment we pay attention to only a tiny amount. More than a million items bombard the brain each second. Less than half a dozen are chosen for consideration. Much of this onslaught is filtered out at low levels in the brain. Other information is noted subconsciously but not attended to unless it suddenly achieves a higher priority. While reading these words, for instance, you are oblivious – until I direct your attention to them – of such sensations as the weight of your body on the chair, sounds from other rooms or the street and so on. Yet part of your brain is still aware of your surroundings. If you had left a saucepan on the stove and suddenly smelt burning, for example, this high priority message would immediately reach your 'thinking' brain and call for prompt action.

Our ability to focus attention is well illustrated by what is called the cocktail party phenomenon. In a crowded room, buzzing with dozens of different conversations, you have no difficulty in filtering out all except the person talking to you. In fact one part of your brain is still monitoring other conversations and, if anything of personal interest is mentioned – such as your name – you tend to hear this and switch attention.

In class your child too is surrounded by a torrent of information. What they attend to depends on their level of motivation. If bored by the lesson, their span of attention is likely to be very wide. They may look at children in the playground, listen to sounds from the corridor, study graffiti on the desk top, watch other pupils, and even occasionally tune in to what the teacher is saying. Sometimes they may be brought back with a shock by being accused of not paying attention. In part such a charge is justified, they were certainly not attending exclusively to the teacher. But they were, of course, paying attention to a great many other things.

Now imagine that class are told they must take a test at the end of their lesson. Any child who fails will be punished. At once they all become highly attentive. Too attentive in fact, because they now focus very narrowly and miss important facts.

Since successful problem solving or decision making involves selecting out relevant facts from the mass of available information, excessive motivation impedes clear thinking. Here's a problem that demonstrates the need to be selective in which information you attend to. As a guide, I have also provided the IQ indicated by the time you take to come up with an answer:

6 seconds or less	– Highly intelligent
7 – 10 seconds	– Average IQ
10 – 15 seconds	– Low IQ
More than 15 seconds	– Extremely low IQ

The bee and bike problem. Two cyclists, one American and one British, are on the same straight road but 20 miles apart. At the same instant they begin pedalling towards one another at a constant 10mph. There is a bee on the handlebars of the American's bike. The moment he starts to move the bee takes off and flies to the handlebar of the oncoming British bike. Then immediately returns to the American's bicycle. He continues doing this, covering the ever decreasing distance between the two cycles at a steady 15mph air speed.

Assuming no time is lost in turning around at the end of each flight, what distance will the bee have covered by the time the two cycles meet? Start timing yourself now. Did you solve the problem and, if so, what was your IQ rating?

The only *relevant* information in that problem, was the distance and the speeds. Being 20 miles apart and cycling at 10mph the cyclists will meet after 1 hour. We know the bee flies at 15mph. Therefore in one hour it must have flown 15 miles.

Take no notice of those times and IQ ratings. They are completely fictitious and put there only to increase your motivation to a point where it got in the way of solving the problem. This ability to filter out all but the relevant information from our surroundings is what we mean by concentration. Professor John Easterbrook, an American psychologist, has established a clear link between the right level of motivation and selective attention. Here is how it works.

In all problems or learning tasks, there are certain essential *cues* which tell your child how to proceed. When identified and used correctly they act as sign posts pointing to the correct solution. Children are taught which *cues* are important in any particular task and how to make use of them once identified. But it is up to the child to spot which they are and to take no notice of irrelevant facts. Or, to use the terms discussed earlier, to identify the *Givens, Operations* and *Goals*. Suppose your child is asked to solve the equation:

$$\text{Find x when } 2x + 3 = 5x - 3$$

To find the answer, they must bring all the 'x' terms to the same side of the = sign. This requires an ability to filter out, or temporarily ignore, any number not accompanied by an 'x'. Without doing this the problem cannot be solved.

Professor Easterbrook likens motivation to a telescope, which magnifies some details but excludes others by narrowing our field of view. Up to a point this enables us to concentrate on essentials, but when taken too far, significant information will be lost.

Efficient learning depends on achieving the right level of motivation. This varies from one child to another and from one subject to the next. But even when there is a below average level of overall motivation, it is still possible they will be satisfactorily motivated in some subjects or activities. These are easily identified by the fact that they enjoy doing them and may do well at them. Similarly, even when excessively motivated overall, it may be that for certain activities your child's level is still satisfactory. High levels of motivation are characterized by anxiety, stress, obsessive concern with not making mistakes and worry about the consequences of failure.

The need for achievement and the fear of failure

Infants have little or no concept of success or failure. They simply behave, attempt to do things and, if they don't turn out as expected try again. As they grow older, a desire to avoid failing can come to dominate their approach to challenges. They desire achievement not just because this feels good, but because failure makes them feel so bad.

Students motivated by a strong need for achievement and a powerful fear of failure may do equally well in class. But there will be important intellectual and emotional differences between them. Let's consider the intellectual ones first. You may have noticed how some children dislike novelty and change. Their preference for the familiar task and routine activity is often caused by a fear of failure. If nothing has changed they can be fairly sure that an approach which proved effective in the past will do so again. Students driven by a fear of failure are conservative in their outlook. They resent different teaching methods, new topics, unusual ideas or novel approaches. They prefer *convergent problems* (*see page 83*) to which there is a single, correct, answer to *divergent* questions where there are many possible solutions. Often they hate having to think for themselves, to take a chance, make a guess, use hunches and rely on intuition. Everything needs to be cut and dried. Their confidence is built upon the certainty that comes from what is known.

Occasionally, however, a child driven by this form of motivation will attempt something which is quite beyond their capabilities. They will embark on a challenge where failing is a virtual certainty. This seemingly contradictory behaviour is easily understood when you realize that if you attempt the almost impossible and fail, then the difficulty of the challenge – rather than any personal inadequacy – will be blamed. Imagine, for instance, that an indifferent swimmer decides to do a sponsored swim across the Channel, a challenge quite clearly beyond their ability. As they sink gently beneath the waves a mile or so off shore, their unsuccessful attempt still wins them praise. It's only natural to admire courage and determination, however misplaced. Hauled spluttering into the rescue boat they have little sense of failure.

But now suppose they had decided to swim six lengths of the local pool. Because this is a task on which even a poor swimmer might be expected to make a fair showing, their lack of success cannot be attributed to the toughness of the challenge. If they have to give up after only a few lengths, they will know that they have failed and feel extremely humiliated.

Both a desire to stay with what is known, and the occasional attempts at tackling the impossibly difficult, undermine a child's classroom performance. And this becomes especially true later in their school career, when increasing emphasis is placed on independent, creative, thinking. On the emotional side, a fear of failure is usually associated with above average levels of anxiety – perhaps you have noticed this in your own child. As we saw in the previous section, chronic anxiety undermines a child's physical health as well as confidence and self-esteem.

Your role in motivation

Before reading further answer the questions below: When pleased
with the way my child has behaved I . . .

1. Kiss and hug him/her.
   Frequently   Occasionally   Seldom   Never
2. Praise him/her and say how pleased I am.
   Frequently   Occasionally   Seldom   Never
3. Provide a special reward or treat.
   Frequently   Occasionally   Seldom   Never
4. Do nothing to make their achievement seem special.
   Frequently   Occasionally   Seldom   Never
5. Say that their achievement was no more than I expected.
   Frequently   Occasionally   Seldom   Never
6. Point out their mistakes and show how it could be better.
   Frequently   Occasionally   Seldom   Never

When displeased with the way my child has behaved I . . .

7. Scold or punish him/her physically.
   Frequently   Occasionally   Seldom   Never
8. Say how disappointed I am at their behaviour.
   Frequently   Occasionally   Seldom   Never
9. Withhold a privilege or treat.
   Frequently   Occasionally   Seldom   Never
10. Do nothing to show my feelings.
    Frequently   Occasionally   Seldom   Never
11. Explain how their behaviour could and should have been different.
    Frequently   Occasionally   Seldom   Never
12. Wait for their behaviour to improve naturally.
    Frequently   Occasionally   Seldom   Never

How to score
For answers 1 – 3 award points as follows:
Frequently +5, Occasionally +3, Seldom +1, Never 0
For answers 4 – 9 award points as follows:
Frequently –5, Occasionally –3, Seldom –1, Never 0
For answers 10 – 12 award points as follows:
Frequently +3, Occasionally +2, Seldom +1, Never 0

Add the positive and negative scores separately and subtract the negative from the positive total. For example: (+16) and (–12) = +4 total score.

What your score reveals:

Your score	Your influence on motivation
+ 15 to + 8	HIGH
+ 7 to + 3	OPTIMAL
+ 2 to any negative score	LOW

Use this result, together with your subjective impression of your child's overall motivation in class, to direct you to the most appropriate procedures for helping develop a healthy level of motivation in your child.

If your child is: fearful of making mistakes, worried about set-backs, overly anxious before a test, constantly seeking approval, then it is possible that their level of motivation is too *high*.

If your child is: able to take set-backs and mistakes in their stride, recover from failure, approach unfamiliar tasks confidently and enthusiastically, and generally copes well with novel challenges, it is likely that their level of motivation is *optimal*.

If your child is: bored by school, lacks energy and enthusiasm for most lessons, never seems particulary concerned whether they succeed or fail, it is likely that the level of motivation is too *low*.

1. Your influence high/your child's motivation high. If there is a fear of failure, they may be more concerned about doing well to earn your praise than out of interest in the task itself. Use procedures 1 and 3 (*below*) to reduce excessive need for achievement and banish the fear of failure.

2. Your influence optimal/your child's motivation high. This combination of scores suggests that although you are making a positive contribution to your child's motivation, it remains somewhat too high. This could be due to the fact that they are emotionally dependent on adult approval. In this case even fairly neutral comments such as 'I'm pleased you did that . . . ' or 'What a pity you didn't do that . . . ' could be sufficient to make them strive overly hard for success. It may also be that while your child is too highly motivated in some subjects, they lack sufficient interest in others. In such cases you should reduce their motivation in the former and work to enhance it in the latter activities. Procedures 1 and 2 (*below*) will prove helpful.

3. Your influence low/your child's motivation high. This is a rather unusual combination of scores. Although your approach seems more likely to reduce motivation, your child's motivation is still excessive. It is likely that your critical attitude has created a desire to avoid failing at any cost. It is important to start rewarding achievements more frequently, while dealing with set-backs and failures in a more neutral manner.

4. Your influence high/your child's motivation optimal. If a fear of failure is suggested by their behaviour use procedure 3 to help transform this into a positive need for achievement. At the same time work to improve motivation in any subject where your child seems to lack interest and involvement using procedure 2.

5. Your influence optimal/your child's motivation optimal. This is the most favourable combination. It suggests that your child's motivation is ideal while your actions help sustain this positive need for achievement. If any fear of failure is present use procedure 3 to help eliminate it.

6. Your influence low/your child's motivation optimal. Your child's level of motivation seems perfectly satisfactory although your own contribution does not appear especially helpful in maintaining this desirable state of affairs. If any fear of failure is present use procedure 3 to help reduce it. At the same time try and be more positive towards your child's achievements. Offer praise and encouragement more frequently than criticism.

7. Your influence high/your child's motivation low. This suggests you are more interested in achievement than your child is. If a fear of failure is present use procedure 3 for reducing this fear and enhancing motivation. Use procedure 2 for building motivation, especially in subjects where your child is currently doing poorly and shows insufficient interest. Consider the extent to which your expectations are influencing this somewhat negative attitude. Sometimes an over emphasis on the importance of school attainment can make a child feel so anxious that they use avoidance to reduce these unpleasant feelings. Failure may then become a habit. If there is an older, more successful and highly motivated child in the family then this too could be contributing to their present lack of motivation. They may have abandoned hope of ever enjoying the same degree of success.

8. Your influence optimal/your child's motivation low. Although your actions in sustaining motivation seem satisfactory, it appears that your child's performance may still be driven by a fear of failure. This could be due to the unhelpful influence of one or more teachers at school. Did your child become less interested in, and enthusiastic about, school work shortly after moving to a new school or a higher form? If this does seem a likely answer, then you should take the matter up with the school.

9. Your influence low/your child's motivation low. Your child seems insufficiently motivated to achieve success at school, and your assessment score suggests that you could be partly responsible. You will find procedures 2 and 3 helpful in enhancing motivation and reducing the fear of failure. But it is also important to change your own attitudes towards success and failure. Be on the look out for, and praise, achievements. At present you may take them too much for granted. At the same time, become less critical of failures or set-backs. Although you may believe pointing out mistakes helps your child learn from them, a more effective solution is to reduce motivation and undermine self-confidence. The procedures described below will help you to reduce a need for achievement when too high, and enhance it if too low as well as remove the fear of failure. None of them is, however, a cook book recipe that can be applied to all children. You will need to approach them thoughtfully with your child's unique, personal, problems in mind and adapt as necessary to meet their individual needs.

Procedure 1 – reducing excessive need for achievement. For use only if you have noticed your child often tries *too* hard to succeed. With the level of motivation reduced you should find that, while they are no less successful, school challenges are approached in a more relaxed manner. They should also gain greater enjoyment from activities which are currently causing some anxiety.

Read through the 15 activities listed below and tick any where you *actively* encourage your child to . . .

1. Tackle new challenges with enthusiasm.
2. Be independent instead of running to adults for help.
3. Learn dancing.
4. Achieve high marks in school work.
5. Learn to speak confidently in front of others.
6. Stand up for himself/herself.
7. Take pride in everything he/she does.

8. Make decisions on personal matters, such as what leisure clothes to wear, how to spend pocket money etc.
9. Earn his/her own money by doing a part-time job.
10. Take part in competitive events and sports.
11. Do household chores.
12. Excel at games.
13. Develop interesting hobbies.
14. Be self-disciplined.
15. Take care of others.

Now note down any additional activities on which active encouragement is currently provided.

_____   _____

_____   _____

From the statements ticked, select *two* which you regard as among the most important. Continue to reward your child, with praise and encouragement, for meeting these expectations but stop providing rewards for any of the remaining statements ticked. This does not mean you must ignore, or even worse, become critical of other attainments. Continue noticing and commenting on successes in these areas. But, from now on, try and do so in a neutral manner. Instead of saying, for instance, 'That was very good indeed, I am proud of you . . . ' you might simply comment, 'Now you've finished that, why not try this?' You need not worry that this change will cause your child to abandon any tasks which, because they are fun and interesting to do, provide a powerful intrinsic reward. They may, however, start showing less interest in those which provide no genuine satisfaction or enjoyment and were only undertaken to gain your approval. This approach will allow your child to feel more relaxed when confronting new challenges and more willing to persist in the face of set-backs.

Procedure 2 – enhancing low need for achievement. This should be used if your child's behaviour suggests too low a level of motivation. As need for achievement increases you should find your child becoming more enthusiastic and confident when tackling difficult tasks. Start by selecting one or two goals in subjects where your child seems to have too little need for achievement. Those chosen must satisfy three essential conditions. They must be viewed, by your child, as achievable, believable, and desirable. In other words they must feel that they lie within their grasp and are worth striving for. If they appear too difficult to accomplish, motivation could be reduced still further. At the same time it is essential to avoid making them so trivial that their attainment will be meaningless.

Achievable goals. Suppose, for example, you wanted to improve your child's marks on a maths test. In the past they have received an average of 20 per cent. Your eventual goal is to raise this to 90 per cent. But if this is set as the immediate goal, your child may consider it so beyond their ability that no serious attempt is made to reach it. By pitching the initial goal at a more modest 40 per cent, you could well be setting a goal your child does regard as achievable. Later, of course, you will move from 40 to 50 per cent, and then up to 60 per cent and so on until your desired goal is achieved. At first you will need to help your child decide what goals should be set, but it is important to hand over responsibility for this task as soon as possible in order to ensure that need for achievement is sustained when not closely monitored by you.

Believable goals. The second qualification for the goals set is that they appear believable. This is a very important consideration, since some parents set their children goals which, although realistic to an adult, seem unbelievable to the child. There is no point in insisting, 'But you could do this if you'd only try harder' when your child firmly believes what you are asking is impossible.

When motivation is low, self-confidence is also poor, and perceptions of abilities and difficulties are distorted. Remember it is the child's view of their own capabilities which matters. Work from their baseline, even when it strikes you as being far below their true level of expertise and knowledge. Never allow your child to feel that you consider their goals trivial or worthless.

Desirable goals. The final qualification for a successful goal is that it is seen as desirable by your child. Hopefully there will be rewards arising from mastery of that goal, since this provides the most effective form of motivation. Where this is not so, and much of school learning lacks such intrinsic rewards for many children, then find out how your child would like to be rewarded for achieving that goal. Possible rewards would be extra treats and privileges, a present or a token – such as a plastic counter or stars to stick on a wall chart – which can be saved up and exchanged for a larger reward.

Set sub-goals. Once you and your child have established a goal which is achievable, believable and desirable, the next step is to work out the sub-goals by which it can be reached. These can be compared to a series of stepping stones leading from where your child's is now, in terms of knowledge or skills, to the new level of attainment. To make the process of working towards an overall goal more exciting, play the game of Treasure Trove.

To do this ask your child to paint a large picture showing an ocean dotted with many small islands plus one larger one containing a treasure chest. Next draw and cut out a galleon from stiff card. Then write an overall goal on a small card and attach it to the treasure chest using a paper fastener or piece of Blue Tak. Work out a series of sub-goals by which that main goal might be achieved. Write these on cards, and place one on each of the islands. Your child can plot a variety of routes from the starting point to Treasure Island, each involving a different number of islands, or sub-goals. If better progress is made than was originally anticipated, the course can be changed and the number of subgoals reduced. Where original sub-goals proved too far apart, more should be added and a greater number of islands visited en route to Treasure Island.

Suppose your agreed overall goal is to increase the number of sums solved correctly in a weekly test. These sub-goals are planned after maths skills have been improved using the procedures earlier. Instead of saying, 'Now you know how to do them I shall expect full marks on the next test . . . ' (an anxiety-arousing instruction) your child is asked how many they think they might now get correct. Let's say they get 8 out of 20, this becomes the first sub-goal. They are also prepared to believe they might, eventually, get 18 out of 20 right so this is the overall goal placed in the Treasure Chest. Other sub-goals, all of which the child regarded as achievable and believable, could be 10, 12, 14, and 16.

The reward for attaining each sub-goal could be a crayon or simply recognition and a little praise, while landing on Treasure Island itself will earn an attractively decorated box to keep the crayons in. With the sub-goals and final target written out your child works towards the first sub-goal. When this has been attained, the agreed reward is provided and the galleon travels to the first island. Indeed, a reason often given by teenagers for disliking school is that classroom lessons seem so far removed from their everyday lives, problems and interests. The only way to change this attitude is to demonstrate the practical relevance of school learning. A child who enjoys a hobby such as model-making, electronics, photography, carpentry and so on – but can see no good reason for doing maths – might be encouraged to recognize the importance of sums in their favourite leisure activity. For precise measuring, calculating the values of resistors when building electrical circuits, mixing chemicals and estimating the amount of timber needed for a construction. This is especially helpful for children with Inventive and Implementing thinking styles (*see page 76*).

Similarly, a child fascinated by science but bored with history might find the topic more worthwhile if they were to study the historical background to scientific discoveries, relating them to the social conditions and beliefs of the age. With a little imagination and thought it is usually possible to develop a link between your child's special interests and almost any subject on the school timetable.

Procedure 3 – banishing the fear of failure. Before you can use this procedure for reducing your child's fear of failure, they will need to have mastered the relaxation skills described previously. Start by identifying an activity which currently causes your child problems and which may be avoided because of the risk of failing. After a relaxation session, help your child to develop a creative day dream (*see page 173*) in which they see themselves tackling the feared activity with confidence and success. Ask them to imagine doing this as vividly as possible, helping to create a fantasy film which starts with your child setting out to do the task, and ends with its accomplishment. Keep each session short, five minutes is usually sufficient. When your child feels capable of tackling the activity in their imagination, the time has come for real-life practice. If possible do this under conditions where some control can be maintained. For instance a child afraid of examinations, might find it helpful to sit at a desk in the room where the exam will take place and practise the relaxation methods described earlier. At the same time you should praise successes far more than you criticize set-backs and failures. Never be tempted to turn Treasure Trove into a contest between two children. Each should be competing only against themselves, otherwise motivation may decline in the child who is starting to fall behind.

This practical procedure must be accompanied by a gradual changing of attitudes towards work and achievement. It may be that your child believes they should only attempt tasks that can be done perfectly. Encourage the view that if a job's worth doing it's worth doing badly! This may sound like poor advice, since we usually encourage children to try their very best at all they do. But, at first, everybody performs any unfamiliar activity with far less skill than will be possessed after practice. The great thing is to make a start, to take the plunge and have a go. Don't allow your child to consider mistakes as things to be feared and avoided at all costs. Rather, they should be viewed for what they are – valuable contributions to learning. Wrong answers can help you understand how and why difficulties are occurring more effectively than right ones since these only demonstrate the sort of problems your child can already solve.

Make school subjects relevant. Not every child is going to find every subject on the timetable equally relevant and rewarding.

The power of positive listening

Do you sometimes listen to your child without really hearing what's said? Every parent is guilty of such inattention from time to time. In fact recent research suggests we pay attention to less than a quarter of what children tell us. Whether or not this matters depends, of course, on what is being said. But when it comes to encouraging classroom attainment, positive listening is an essential ingredient of success. The best way of explaining what positive listening involves, is to consider the different ways in which we listen to what adults or children want to tell us.

The first distinction to make is between *hearing* and *listening*. Because most people consider them one and the same they tend to regard *listening* as an instinctive ability rather than a learned skill that must be practised and perfected. The result, says Madelyn Burley-Allen in her book *Listening: The Forgotten Skill* is that, 'We make little effort to learn or develop listening skills and knowingly neglect a vital communication function, thereby denying ourselves educational development and increasing self-awareness.' Yet listening represents 40 per cent of all communications, which means that a large proportion of the knowledge, ideas and beliefs your children acquire, result from listening.

Psychologists have found that we spend around three quarters of the time in verbal communication yet studies have also shown that the average parent or teacher, listens with an efficiency of only about 25 per cent. Which means that 75 per cent of the things which are said to them are either never heard, or simply disregarded. American psychologist Dr Anthony Alessandra has identified three levels of listening. At level three, we pay attention with only half an ear to what's said. We may fake interest and attention, but really have no clear idea of what the conversation is all about. Level three listening is usually fairly obvious to the speaker who quickly realizes that they are failing to hold their audience's attention. It is at this level that *negative listening* occurs.

During level two, or *neutral* listening, close attention is given to the words used but their deeper meaning is ignored. This is a far harder type of listening for the speaker to detect, since his audience appears to be giving him undivided attention. When only an exchange of facts is involved level two listening is perfectly satisfactory and appropriate. But if the message is a more subtle and complicated one, involving feelings as well as factual information, the result can be confusion and misunderstanding. Because the facts were attended to but the hidden message or tone of voice or accompanying body language disregarded, a different meaning from that intended may be conveyed. 'I'm not worried by the examination tomorrow,' says a child, who is, in fact, terrified by the prospect and longs to talk about their fears. 'That's good,' is the mother's cheerful response. The woman has heard only the surface meaning while missing the deeper message. Had she paid attention to the uncertain voice tone, or noticed the sad expression and tense posture which accompanied those words a very different impression might have been gained.

Level one involves active or *positive* listening. This is the type of listening essential to your child's educational success. Here attention is paid both to the content of the message and the manner in which it is presented. Listening in this way makes it easier to discover what's going wrong in your child's studies. You can also help ease worries and problems by persuading your child to talk openly and honestly about them. Let's start by exploring four major negative ways of listening. Understanding what these are and how they arise should make it easier for you to avoid using them in the future.

Inattentive listening

This stems from an adult's mistaken belief that it is possible to do two things at once. For instance, you are busy cooking lunch when your child hurries in with something to tell you. When this happens do not fall into the trap of listening distractedly and with only half an ear. Instead make a swift decision on priorities. Is the meal more important than what your child has to say, or should you finish cooking before listening?

If cooking takes precedent, explain politely but firmly that you are not able to pay attention at that particular moment. Arrange a time when you will be free to offer your child your undivided attention. At first they may be slightly upset by this apparent rebuff. But provided you keep your promise to spend time listening – and this is essential – they quickly learn that you are interested in their ideas and worries. Then, far from being offended they'll be flattered that you take them seriously. When you sense that the message is a crucial one, and cannot be delayed, stop whatever you are doing, sit down and listen quietly and attentively to what's being said.

Children too are frequently guilty of inattentive listening, both at home and in school, which is why they so often fail to take any notice of instructions or are unable to recall lessons. So far as retention of lessons is concerned, one problem is that many teaching sessions go on far too long. Studies have shown the average span of human attention is only around 20 minutes. After this time, concentration falters and we become increasingly distracted and inattentive. The younger the child the briefer their span of attention, and with infants it can be less than 5 minutes. The way to hold attention is to break down formal instruction into short, easily assimilated chunks. Then give the child a chance to put what has just been learned into practice. You should bear this in mind when designing any home training programme.

If you need to convey important instructions or commands to a young and/or easily distracted child, make quite certain your message has got through. What seems to be disobedience is frequently simply the result of inattentive listening. Your child fails to carry out an order not through naughtiness but merely because that message never penetrated the *inattention* barrier to get through to the brain in the first place. If you find yourself in this position, here's what to do:

1. Kneel down to the child's level so that you can have easy eye contact.
2. Gently place your hands on each cheek to hold the head steady. This obliges them to return your gaze and helps keep them still long enough to listen attentively.
3. Give your order or instruction clearly while maintaining eye contact. Then ask your child to repeat back what has just been said.
4. If correct, then state it a second time slowly and clearly. If your child's version was wrong then say it again and have them repeat it

back. Continue until they have been able to tell you accurately what
your instruction or command was.

Emotional listening

Never attempt to listen while feeling a strong emotion, such as anxiety
or anger. Strong emotions act as filters, screening out all but a small
proportion of what is being said and making you deaf to anything you
would sooner not hear. There is a tendency to pay attention to anything which confirms our views while disregarding any evidence that
contradicts it.

When nine-year-old Peter brought home a bad school report, his
father was furious. He believed, quite wrongly, that the boy had been
lazy. In fact Peter's difficulties were largely due to a new, inexperi-
enced and extremely sarcastic form teacher who had made his life miserable throughout the term. It was the anxiety and damage to his
self-esteem caused by this master, rather than a lack of effort, which
had led to the poor report. But when Peter hesitantly attempted to
explain what had gone wrong, his words fell on deaf ears. As a result
his father not only failed to discover what had gone wrong that term,
but made his son extremely reluctant to talk about his fears in the
future. Always allow yourself a cooling off period of at least 10 minutes. Calm down and assess the situation as objectively as possible
before attempting to listen.

Dismissive listening

This happens when you have already made up your mind what to
think about your child's performance or behaviour. Adults listening
dismissively often give the game away by interjecting such comments
as, 'What nonsense . . . don't be so silly . . . you're far too young to
understand.'

A little while ago I overheard the following conversation between
ten-year-old Jane, and her mother. The girl begged to have the hall
light left on while she went to sleep. Her mother, who considered this
babyish, retorted that she walked home from school on dark winter
evenings without seeming afraid. 'But darkness always looks more
scary indoors,' Jane told her mother gravely. This was an intriguing

comment, which probably betrayed a hidden host of anxieties. It was an invitation to discuss those fears. But instead of listening positively, and picking up the significance of her daughter's remark, the mother simply said, 'Don't be silly . . . ' and clicked out the light. Because she had already made up her mind that Jane was behaving like a baby, she dismissed the child's comment without thought.

It's not only adults who are guilty of this type of negative listening of course. Children do the same when told anything they would sooner not hear. 'You must work harder . . . ' a mother tells her son. 'OK, OK,' responds the boy dismissively, having already made up his mind that hard work is a waste of time. Anxiety and dismissive listening often go hand in hand. By refusing to pay attention to the child's comments adults can protect themselves from feeling anxious in two ways. The first is by avoidance. As I explained earlier this is a very common defence mechanism in the face of anxiety. If you don't pay attention to what you are told, the fear-arousing idea behind it can also be ignored.

During a counselling session a teenager who badly wanted to drop out of school told his father, 'I hate still being treated as a child . . . ' 'But you are still a child,' his father retorted dismissively. Instead of looking further at what this might have meant to his son, and how those feelings of painful inferiority could have been eased, the man chose to dismiss them as irrelevant. As a result the boy did eventually leave school without taking the examinations he could have passed with ease.

Dismissive listening also prevents anxiety arising by denying the reality of a situation. A child doing badly in class was trying to explain to her mother why she had such difficulty in following the lessons. Instead of attending to what her daughter was saying the woman, who was intensely ambitious, said brusquely, 'You just have to do better. That's all there is to it.' By refusing to acknowledge her daughter's difficulties and failures this woman reduced the anxieties aroused by the prospect of her daughter failing to fulfil her lofty dreams, but she also ruled out any possibility of understanding the girl's problems and helping her overcome them. If your child seems indifferent towards their difficulties and disinterested in constructive offers of assistance, then recognize these as instances of dismissive listening. Instead of becoming angry or anxious yourself, use the positive listening procedures described below to explore the self-doubts, fears and uncertainties which lie beneath that apparently uncaring attitude.

Judgemental listening

Here the purpose of listening is to pass judgement on the child's abilities or attitude. For instance a parent who has judged their son to be careless, may only listen to the boy's explanations about his low marks to find an excuse for saying what a slipshod and slovenly worker he is.

Neutral listening

This level two type of listening is adopted either during a casual exchange of views or when being given factual information. In neither case would it be appropriate to probe for any deeper meanings. Children should develop the skill of neutral listening as early a possible, since it is an important way of acquiring information. I shall be explaining how to enhance your child's level two listening ability later on.

Positive listening

As I mentioned earlier, this level one type of listening involves paying attention both to what is being said and to what is left unspoken. It means listening with your eyes as well as ears, observing the way expressions, gestures, eye movements and posture accompany the words. There are two main types of positive listening – *diagnostic* and *empathic*. Both have a vital role to play in enhancing your child's intellectual and emotional development.

Diagnostic listening. Here diagnosis is used in the medical sense for pinpointing the cause of your child's difficulties and problems in school. Choose a time when you are not going to be interrupted or impatient to complete another task. Open the conversation with a friendly but neutral comment, such as, 'You seem a bit upset today. Would you like to talk about it?' Be careful to keep your tone as neutral as possible, avoiding any hint of anxiety or criticism – either of which are likely to make your child clam up. Even when asked correctly, your child's immediate response to this friendly overture may be an insistence that everything is alright. This is especially likely if you have got out of the habit of talking openly about your feelings or if, in the past, you have tended to be somewhat critical.

Do not be misled, or put off by such a dismissive rebuff. If your child has been moody or miserable recently then it's a fair bet that something really has gone wrong despite protests to the contrary. Be patient but be persistent. Say something along the lines of, 'Well, I've noticed that you seem miserable and I'd like to help. Do try and tell me what's happened?' Ask at least three times before acknowledging, temporary, defeat and letting the matter drop. But keep a careful eye on events and, when a suitable opportunity arises, return to your theme.

Once your child has starting talking, say as little as possible yourself. Encourage them, by nodding, smiling and showing obvious interest. Even if you get upset or irritated by what is being said, be sure to keep those feelings to yourself. Your expression should remain friendly, your tone calm and your comments warm, sympathetic and encouraging. The appropriate time to express your sadness or anger is after the diagnostic session is completed, once you've listened long and carefully enough to understand what's precisely gone wrong. Any interruptions before then, especially critical comments, only inhibit self-disclosures and may make it impossible for you to get to the root cause of a problem.

Imagine, for instance, how a patient would respond if, after admitting to being a heavy smoker, the doctor had retorted, 'Well, if you are such a fool as to smoke you've only yourself to blame!' Faced with such an attack they would be extremely reluctant to make further admissions. Yet without knowledge of other bad habits an accurate diagnosis could prove impossible. So be careful to avoid listening either judgementally or dismissively. As well as attending to what's being said, pay special attention to the following:

1. Your child's tone of voice. Is there are conflict between what they are saying and the way in which it is being said? Do they for instance, sound sad when giving you what seems to be good news, such as promotion to a higher form, or appear strangely unmoved when recounting an apparently upsetting experience. Such conflicts offer clues to powerful emotions simmering just beneath the surface.

2. Which words are emphasized. If your child were to say, for example, 'Honestly, it's *nothing*,' then you could be fairly certain that what had happen was really important to them.

3. Be on the alert for jokes, especially self-mocking comments. Humour is often used to convey ideas or describe feelings which arouse great anxiety or embarrassment.

4. Watch your child's expression, gestures and posture (*see box*). Notice too any pauses, hesitations or repetitions which often betray anxiety or some other strong emotion.

Key body language signs

- *Blocking*. Child crosses arms or legs. Avoids eye contact. Leans away, which reveal embarrassment, anger, discomfort or anxiety.
- *Fidgets*. Scuffing shoes, playing with fingers or pencil, fiddling with clothes, which reveal anxiety and fear.
- *Picking or pulling*. At skin, hair, clothes or, especially in small boys, genitals, which reveal anxiety but also aggression turned inward. The child is angry but feels, or is, unable to vent their rage against anybody else.
- *Head grooming*. A smoothing movement made by drawing the palm down across the back of the head. Seen mostly in older children which reveals ambivalence. Your child is unsure whether to attack or retreat. Seen when uncertain what to do for the best.
- *Illustrators*. Are rhythmic hand and arm gestures used to accompany words and emphasize points. The number employed also varies from child to child. These reveal confidence and assurance. Watch for the moment when these decline and, especially, if they are replaced by *blocking* movements or *fidgets* since this reveals increasing anxiety and uncertainty.
- *Eye contact*. When your child's gaze meets yours. This is a very subtle signal. Excessive eye contact usually indicates aggressive feelings, but can also reveal deception. Your child is carefully monitoring your expression to see just how much you believe. Avoiding eye contact implies embarrassment, anxiety or deceit depending on the circumstances. Strong aversion to gaze in a very young child is often found in autism.

Never worry about long silences. Most people dread them to such an extent that they feel compelled to say something, anything, to break the silence. This is something professional interviewers often use to their advantage, since it often leads to disclosures people never intended to make. Allowing your child quiet thinking time, undistracted by not having to listen to your comments, makes it easier for them to find the words needed to describe painful ideas or complicated feelings. During the silence remain alert and attentive, smile reassuringly and continue to give eye contact but say nothing.

When using *diagnostic* listening to pinpoint errors in reasoning or understanding, avoid correcting mistakes as they are identified. If you do, the whole flow of your child's explanation will be inhibited. Furthermore they may be unwilling to admit to any other misunderstandings. So just note that something is not properly understood and continue gently probing for further errors. Say something like, 'That's very interesting, can you tell me a little more about it?' In this way you are able to dig deeper and deeper through the layers of reasoning, perhaps uncovering a fundamental misconception or item of misinformation buried deep in their knowledge structure. Only when you are satisfied that all the mistakes have been identified, can you go back and correct them.

Diagnostic listening is not easy. It takes time and practice to perfect. At first you'll find yourself breaking the child's flow by offering a reassuring comment or criticizing an irritating admission. Yet, however well intentioned, such interruptions only make it harder to find out what's really going wrong. Talk and listen in a ratio of around one to ten. In other words, for every one minute spent talking to your child, ten should be devoted to positive listening. By adopting this powerful procedure you'll be encouraging your child to reveal a great deal about their feelings, attitudes, ideas, opinions, beliefs and thinking processes. Never betray this trust by exploiting their confessions or using them to ridicule, belittle or criticize at a later date.

Earlier I compared diagnostic listening for educational purposes to the process of making a medical diagnosis. Just like a physician you must regard all your child's self-disclosures as privileged information and never betray their confidence. It must not be disclosed to anybody else, without their knowledge and permission, or used for any purpose other than that of helping them become happier, more successful and more fulfilled.

Empathic listening

This is used not to identify the cause of difficulties but to help your child come to terms with powerful emotions. You are not so much concerned to find out why something has gone wrong as to provide an attentive ear. A sounding board for distressing feelings which will become easier to handle once they have been expressed in words.

Occasionally reflect back any comment which seems particularly important or relevant by repeating it in a slightly paraphrased form. For instance, if your child has been explaining how miserable they were over the way a friend had treated them, you might reflect their remark back by saying, 'I see you are really hurt by not being inviting to the party.' This serves three purposes. Firstly, by demonstrating that you have really been paying attention it encourages your child to explore their feelings more deeply. There is nothing like a sympathetic and attentive audience for stimulating self-disclosure. Secondly, it ensures you have properly understood what your child has been saying. For instance, given the comment above, your child might reply; 'No, it's not just that. It's really because he/she didn't invite me but did invite someone else.' Finally, reflecting back a comment allows your child to hear an idea which is causing distress expressed by another person. This tends to reduce its power to cause pain and make difficult feelings easier to manage.

Do not be afraid to help your child confront unhappiness directly. A constant stream of well intentioned, Pollyana comments along the lines of, 'It doesn't matter . . . It's all going to be alright . . . stop being sad . . . ' is very unhelpful. For one thing, however unintentionally, you are patronizing your child's feelings by saying, in effect, 'Your distress is neither significant nor meaningful.' At the same time you are inviting the child to avoid experiencing emotions, by implying that such feelings are bad and wrong. This leads to conflict and confusion. On the one hand the child is all too painfully conscious of their unhappiness, anger or anxiety. Yet, at the same time, a grown-up whom they love and admire is demanding that they smile and be happy.

Emotions which are constantly blocked and denied expression build up beneath the surface, finally making their presence felt by stress related difficulties or psychosomatic illness. By listening to your child in the ways I have described you not only have a better understanding of their hopes and fears while gaining insight into problems but you will also enable them to cope more easily with intellectual set-backs and emotional upsets.

Helping your child to exam success

It is a mistake to believe that hard work alone can guarantee your child good exam results. No less important than a sound knowledge of the subject being examined is proficiency in four specific exam taking skills. These are:

1. Knowing how to make the best use of limited time, both while revising and when sitting exams.
2. The ability to recall information rapidly and accurately even under exam room pressure.
3. Being able to construct answers which meet the examiner's requirements.
4. Understanding how to control exam nerves and to prevent performance being undermined by needless anxiety. Although rarely taught in schools, these four skills are crucial to examination success. In this section I shall explain how you can help your child to master them.

1. Getting time on your side – while revising

The earlier your child starts revising the better. Six weeks prior to the first exam is about right, but certainly serious revision should begin no less than one month before the first examination. An early start avoids the frantic, last minute, panic revising which is both ineffective and anxiety arousing. By allowing plenty of time, studying can be done in brief but regular sessions.

This, research suggests, is the most effective way of learning. Concentration and motivation are sustained more easily, retention of information is enhanced and recall is significantly improved. I advise revision sessions lasting 20 minutes, with 10 minute breaks between them. Although your child will need to spend more time on subjects which are especially difficult, make sure they do not fall into the trap of neglecting those they find easy. Such misplaced confidence has caused many promising students to do unexpectedly poorly in exams where high grades were predicted by both candidate and teachers.

It is equally unwise to ignore subjects that they consider impossibly difficult on the pessimistic assumption that, since failure is inevitable, there's no point in wasting time revising. By thinking hard and study-ing diligently, topics which seemed incomprehensible often start mak-ing sense. Such persistence is, of course, especially necessary with subjects essential for acceptance by the university, college or course on which your child has set his or her heart.

Many children, especially those who have never got into the habit of unsupervised studying, find the self-discipline needed for successful revision hard to maintain. By providing the practical assistance described in this section, taking an interest and offering encourage-ment you can help overcome this hurdle.

Creating a revision timetable. In addition, your child may find it helpful to chart their progress on a revision timetable. This helps sus-tain motivation and gives your child a sense of continued achieve-ment. The chart also ensures that every subject being examined is allocated study time, so preventing an unpopular subject from being neglected or an enjoyable one given excessive revision time. Your child's revision timetable should be marked out on a large sheet of paper and pinned up prominently in their workroom. Subjects being studied are listed down the left column, and the days available for revision along the top.

The first decision to make is how many days a week and hours per day can be set aside for revising. This will depend not only on your child's enthusiasm for studying, but also on the amount of other work to be done. Usually there is less time available for revision at the start of the period, when there will still be homework demands, than closer to the exam itself. So your child will have to be flexible and realistic in allocating time. I suggest revising for only six days per week, setting aside one whole day for relaxation and enjoyment.

Suppose your child decides that it will be possible to fit in two hours revision on every week day and four hours on Saturdays. This gives 14 hours revision per six day week. If they follow my suggestion of revising for only 20 minutes at a time, with a break of ten minutes between sessions, they will be able to complete two study sessions per hour, or 28 in a week.

Their next task is to decide how many revision sessions should be allocated to each subject. The easiest way is, of course, to divide the total number of subjects being revised into the sessions available. With seven subjects to study and 28 periods per week, four sessions of 20 minutes each could, in theory, be set aside for each one. In practice, however, your child will probably want to spend more time on some subjects than others. They might feel that biology and maths, on which they had fallen behind, require seven sessions a week each, leaving 14 sessions to be divided among the remaining five subjects. As they become more confident in biology and maths, however, they might allocate more to other subjects. As they complete each revision session, the appropriate box on the chart is blocked in. Using a different colour for each subject will allow them to check progress at a glance, and make sure all subjects are being sufficiently revised.

The revision timetable in action. To see how such a revision schedule could work in practice, let's imagine your child starts work at 6 o'clock in the evening and has set aside four sessions, or two hours, for revising. Their first session lasts from 5 o'clock to 5.20, when they take a ten minute break. The timing should be fairly accurate, so as not to overrun on the allocated revision period. A kitchen pinger, or alarm clock, helps ensure good time-keeping. If they intend to start another subject during the second study period, part of the rest break will be spent clearing away one set of revision material and setting out the next. That done, your child should leave their desk, walk around the room, listen to some music, get a breath of fresh air, and generally wind down from the study period. This short break will ensure that the newly stored knowledge is consolidated into memory and prevent it becoming muddled up with the next set of facts to be studied. When the rest period is finished, your child must return to their revision straight away. Developing the habit of self-discipline while revising is very important to eventual success.

They now work from 5.30 to 5.50 when the second ten minute break is taken. Once again they should get up from the desk, stretch, walk around and distract the mind from what has just been studied. The second hour is a repeat of the first, with the fourth and final session coming to an end at 6.50. The last ten minutes are used for putting away study notes and preparing for the next day's revision.

If your child wants to work for longer than two hours, then the time available should still be split into blocks of 120 minutes with a ten minute break between them. For example four hours of revision starting at 5 o'clock, would be divided into eight sessions as follows:

Session 1   5.00 – 5.20
Break 1   5.20 – 5.30
Session 2   5.30 – 5.50

Break 2	5.50 – 6.00
Session 3	6.00 – 6.20
Break 3	6.20 – 6.30
Session 4	6.30 – 6.50
Long Break	6.50 – 7.10
Session 5	7.10 – 7.30
Break 5	7.30 – 7.40
Session 6	7.40 – 8.00
Break 6	8.00 – 8.10
Session 7	8.10 – 8.30
Break 7	8.30 – 8.50
Session 8	8.50 – 9.10

Although it may appear that your child is wasting precious time by taking so many breaks, they actually study with far greater efficiency by adopting this, more relaxed, approach. The student who burns the midnight oil, kept awake with cups of black coffee, is demonstrating not great industry but considerable ignorance and incompetence. They may look like a hard working youngster, but they are actually a student with no understanding of how their brain works best.

Getting time on your side – while taking the exam. Few students make any serious attempt to manage their time during an examination. They simply start answering questions and hope to be able to finish. As a result many fail to do so, their final answer being either scanty and rushed or missing entirely. The student who gloomily remarked that the shortest time in the world is the last five minutes of an exam, summed up the feelings of many. Yet the panic stricken race to finish can easily be avoided by planning and discipline. Using past examination papers, or information supplied by teachers, your child should work out how much time to allow for each answer. If, for example, they must produce four essays in two hours how long should they spend writing each? The obvious answer would be 30 minutes per essay. But this is not correct, since it fails to take account of the time needed to read the paper and select which questions to answer. Yet it is on the choice of questions (*see below*) that success or failure can often depend.

Reading time is occasionally allowed in addition to the the actual exam, but when it is included in the total time available, your child must allow for it when planning how to allocate the time. Additional time must also be set aside for reading and checking each answer (*see below*).

Let us assume that reading exam questions and checking the answers takes a total of 20 minutes. On a two hour paper with four questions to answer, this will leave 100 minutes for writing the essays, or 25 minutes for each.

Your child should have an easy-to-read watch and keep a close eye on the time. They must also stick to their timetable, even when tempted to write a far fuller answer to a question where their knowledge is greatest.

2. Recalling information under exam pressure

If your child has been learning by means of the procedures I described earlier then recalling information, even when anxious, should prove far easier. While revising, encourage your child to place knowledge in as many memory stores as possible. For example:

1. By making notes – even when these are thrown away at the end of the study period.
2. Tape recording facts and playing them back.
3. Creating visual images or making drawings.
4. Actively working with the material being studied. Rather than try and rote learn facts, interact with them by constantly asking questions about the topic.

   What are the key points or issues? How did certain things occur? Where, when and why did they happen? Who was present? Once your child is able to answer such basic questions without reference to notes, they will have a sound grasp of the topic.
5. Never attempt to learn anything your child doesn't understand. Some students naively believe if they accurately regurgitate a passage which makes no sense to them an examiner will be taken in, however this is rarely the case. Furthermore learning incomprehensible information is extremely tedious and time consuming.

   Encourage your child to try and identify the point at which their understanding gives way to confusion. Perhaps they have failed to grasp a vital concept at an earlier stage in studying and this gap in their knowledge is making it impossible to make sense of subsequent information. Suggest they reread notes and references and asks teachers for guidance and further explanation.

   Teach your child to break down complex ideas or problems into smaller units. This is a process called Progressive Fragmentation or *Profragging* for short. It works like this: your child fails to understand a concept, argument, problem or worked answer. So they split that passage into two parts. Now they asks themselves whether the two parts are more comprehensible? If they are not each is then split twice more. Do they make sense now? Often they do – if not they split each pair twice more. At some point under-standing will suddenly dawn.

6. If your child finds it hard to remember complicated formulae in maths or science suggest they make a note of them on cards and reads them *immediately* before going into the exam room – they must make sure to leave them outside the door of course to avoid a charge of cheating. As soon as they are allowed to start writing, the formulae are jotted down on scrap paper for future reference.

Using the knowledge network. During the exam your child can easily recreate the knowledge networks developed when studying and revising. This should be done on a sheet of scrap paper. Here's how they go about it: after reading the question carefully, they note down anything at all they can recall about the topic.

They must not worry if the mind seems blank at first, but simply remain calm and freely associate any ideas linked to key words in the question. They might also find it helpful to imagine themselves back at home, setting out the fact cards for that subject or operating the Space Pilot (*see page 169*).

Thanks to the organized way in which they acquired knowledge, recalling just one fact from a relevant network will enable them to bring all the rest to mind. As facts are recalled they are quickly written down. Once they have remembered all the information available on the subject, the notes are transformed into a blueprint from which to pre-pare the answer. They do this by choosing a fact or idea with which to start the answer, then circling and numbering it (1). Next they identify a fact, or idea, which follows logically from the first, circle it and num-ber it (2). They continue in this way until all the relevant facts have been given a number. The few minutes spent creating this blueprint is time well invested, since it allows a well organized, logically structured, essay to be written far more quickly and easily. Since all the key facts have been written down beforehand there is far less chance of any being left out. The clear presentation will impress the examiner, espe-cially if they have just marked a dozen or more poorly structured, hap-hazardly organized answer papers, and so win extra marks.

Effective presentation, provides evidence that your child has applied *divergent* thinking to the task instead of simply setting down a list of ill considered facts. Your child may sometimes gain an important additional bonus from this approach. If they are allowed, or required, to hand in all rough work with completed paper, tell them to be sure to include these essay blueprints, having first clearly crossed them out to make it clear they are rough notes and not part of the final answers. The advantage of doing this is that, if there are some good points or important facts in the blueprint notes which somehow got left out of the finished answer, they may gain credit for them. However any mistakes on these rough notes cannot lose them any marks. This could prove especially significant if your child has a borderline paper, with may be only a single mark between one grade and the next. Under these circumstances, examiners tend to go back over the paper to see if there is any way of awarding that additional mark, and so promoting the examinee to a higher grade. A good point on the working notes might just tip the balance.

3. Creating effective answers

There are seven golden rules for answering exam questions successfully, and your child should be familiar with each of them. Suggest they read at least this section of the book and perhaps discuss their reactions to my suggestions with you.

1. Choose your questions with care. This is vital. Teachers are often amazed at their students' choice of questions, since they frequently ignore those on which they could do well and, instead, attempt far harder and more complicated ones.

2. Answer the easiest question first. This will help you settle down and gain extra confidence. Any initial anxiety will decline and your brain will start working more efficiently. Then tackle the next easiest question, and so on leaving the toughest one to last. When doing short answer or multiple choice questions, skip any you can't answer right away and return to them later if time allows. Research has shown that long pauses for thought is not only a waste of time, it also undermines confidence and increases nervousness. Study the question carefully and work out a possible answer, before looking at those provided. Does your provisional answer correspond with any of the choices? If it does then you are very probably correct. Frequently an apparently correct – but actually wrong – answer, a distracter, is placed close to the top of the list. Take care to avoid this trap. If you can identify the wrong answer(s) and the distracter(s) then whatever remains must be correct.

3. Understand what is being asked. Make certain that you understand what was in the examiner's mind when setting the question. There are certain key instructions which appear over and over again on essay questions. These are frequently misunderstood by candidates, so leading to lost marks.

Discuss – Here you are being told to describe several sides of a topic as clearly as possible. It is not enough just to present one viewpoint or argument.

Compare – You are being asked to look for similarities and differences between different things. This is not the same as discussing them.

Analyse – Complicated topics must be broken down into their individual elements and relationships between different topics identified and described.

Evaluate – You are being asked to make a judgement on the issue, but this is not an invitation to wild surmise and woolly thinking. Judgements must be soundly argued and supported by evidence.

4. Make certain an answer is relevant. Candidates often fail or under-achieve because they produce answers which are either partly or completely irrelevant. This can happen for a variety of reasons. Perhaps they misunderstand the question. Study past papers and, if doubtful about what certain questions mean ask your teacher, discuss it with a friend or check with your parents to make certain you are on the right lines. Perhaps they twist the question to fit an answer of which they feel more confident. A classic example is the student who was convinced there would be a question on the Egyptian pharaohs in his history exam. So he devoted much revision time to them. But when he read the paper, he saw with dismay that the only question on monarchy concerned the British Royal Family. 'The most important thing about the British Royal Family,' he wrote in desperation, 'is that they are nothing like the pharaohs of ancient Egypt. These people . . . ' and he then wrote an essay on the only subject he had bothered to revise. Needless to say he failed.

You can help your child avoid this, by making sure that as they explain what past questions are all about, they are sticking firmly to the point.

Candidates also disregard the question asked and answer one of their own choosing. For instance a student asked to write an essay on 'What it means to be a European' ended up by describing the history of the Common Market. Never be tempted to ask your own questions in exams, even if you can answer them more fully and factually. You can only earn marks on those parts of your answer which are relevant to the examiner's questions.

Another cause of lost marks is when the answer is partially relevant. It either starts wide of the mark and wastes a lot of time before finally getting to the point, or it begins on target but quickly becomes confused as the candidate gets side tracked by irrelevant issues. Try preparing sample answers to essay questions, set them aside for a while and then come back and read them again. This is also excellent practice in structuring answers correctly and completing them in the time available. Was all of your answer relevant, or were you tempted to demonstrate your knowledge by including interesting but irrelevant facts?

5. Create logical answers. When writing an essay, follow this plan to ensure that your ideas are presented logically. Start by answering the question very briefly. This 'nutshell' introduction summarizes the points you will be discussing. Starting off like this helps ensure that your answer will be relevant and offers the examiner an overview of the approach you intend to take. Deal with not many more than three topics. In the average length essay there is simply not enough time to discuss many more successfully. Conclude by restating the answer in summary form, this time taking into account the points made in the essay. Write as legibly as you can. Bad handwriting can cost you marks. Do not overlook the value of diagrams, charts and graphs. These can often convey quickly, clearly and attractively what might take scores of words to explain.

6. Answer every question. Many students fail, or under-achieve, because they do not realize the vital importance of answering all the required questions. They mistakenly believe that excellent answers to some of the questions will earn them a good grade. A glance at the way marks are allocated will show why this cannot be the case. Suppose there are four essay questions to be answered in an hour, and equal marks are awarded for each. This means that if your child answers two questions very well, but runs out of time for the remainder they cannot hope to get more than 50 per cent. In fact since examiners rarely award full marks for any answer, a more likely result would be 40 per cent or less.

Depending on the Board this would rate from a failing grade to a low pass. At A level it might merit an E grade. But suppose your child made a fair attempt at all four answers and received marks of 17, 18, 16 and 15 on them. This gives a total of 66 per cent, which is a clear pass on all Boards, and a B grade with most of them.

7. Check your answers. Having finished the question, there's a natural desire to race on to the next one. But it is essential to spend a few minutes checking through what has been written. This is just as important as careful reading of the question, since marks are frequently thrown away through mistakes that would easily have been noticed had the answer been checked.

4. Coping with exam nerves

Your child's chief antidote to examination anxiety is the relaxation procedure which I described on pages 195–99. This should be practised and perfected well in advance of the examination.

Use creative day dreaming to enhance confidence. Your child can use this method (*see page 173*) not only for enhancing learning but also as a powerful means for reducing anxiety and enhancing self-confidence. Here's how to do it.

After relaxing and calming the mind your child creates a day dream in which they picture themselves, at school, on the day of the first exam. They imagine going into the examination hall, sitting down behind the desk and preparing to start. They see themselves turning over the paper, and reading through the questions. Encourage them to create a vivid Mind Movie (*see page 164*) that includes sounds as well as pictures. They must try and hear the scraping of chairs as everybody sits down, the rustle as exam papers are turned over, the ticking of the wall clock. If this starts making your child feel anxious, they should immediately switch off the exam scene and return to the soothing image which was taught as part of the relaxation method. They repeat the word CALM each time they exhale and feel the tension slipping away from them. Then they return to the exam room. Your child imagines feeling calm, confident and able to answer all the questions. They must avoid making overly optimistic predictions such as, 'I am not going to have any difficulty at all with this paper.' Instead they should acknowledge that there may be difficulties, unforseen problems, or set-backs, but then see themselves handling them confidently and effectively.

A positive coping statement might be, 'I know this is going to be a challenge, but I have worked hard, understand how to remember information quickly and accurately, know how to remain calm and relaxed. All this makes it far easier for me to succeed.' When waking up on the day of the exam, a short relaxation session while still in bed can settle butterflies and improve confidence. If your child gets the chance to relax immediately before going into the examination room, so much the better. When sitting in the exam room, they should remain relaxed and calm while waiting to begin. Their breathing should remain quiet and steady. Each time they exhale they should silently repeat the word CALM.

Warn your child that, on first reading the question paper they may believe that all the questions are beyond them. This can trigger feelings of despair and panic. Reassure them that such a response is perfectly normal, and that they should simply read them quietly and calmly a couple of times. On second reading, they will almost certainly seem less daunting. After choosing the first question, they should remain relaxed and allow ideas triggered by key words to flow into the mind. They should never strain to remember, since attempts and forcing memory to work slow down recall and increase the risk of inaccuracy.

Count down to the big day

Now let's consider the things your child should be doing during the last few days before the first exam.

1. Check revision is on schedule. Remember the importance of revising actively, by asking questions, making notes and using visual imagery to enhance recall. Use past papers to test what has been revised. Practise developing knowledge networks from memory and using them as a blueprint for writing answers within the time allowed. Help your child by reading these answers and checking they are relevant. But make certain your comments help sustain motivation and confidence instead of undermining them.

2. When there are only two days left for revision, your child should concentrate on just the first two exams. All related fact cards should be read at least once.

3. Make sure your child takes plenty of exercise in the fresh air. They should eat fresh food including fruit and vegetables, and stay away from junk food. They should also avoid drinking too much tea or coffee while studying since this could impair memory during the exam.

4. Is your child sleeping soundly? If not a walk in the fresh air and a relaxation session last thing at night may help. Discourage them from studying right up to bedtime. Ideally there should be a gap of at least an hour between the final revision session and going to bed. Fill this time with something enjoyable and distracting, such as watching a favourite TV programme. Sound sleep, a sensible diet and regular exercise are as essential to exam success as disciplined studying.

5. Help prepare a check list of all the things your child will need for the exam, do they have a spare pen, are the batteries in their calculator fresh?

6. With one day to go there is no reason, if your child has revised methodically, why they should not take the day off from studying.

7. Before they go to bed the night before the exam, help – or encourage – them to prepare everything needed for the following day. This will prevent a last minute panic that can undermine concentration and impair performance.

   Encourage your child to eat a good breakfast, since this ensures ample reserves of energy as well as making it easier to control exam nerves. An egg, fish or meat should be included, in addition to bread or cereals, because protein helps the food to be digested more efficiently and maintains high levels of energy until lunch. They should be discouraged from drinking too much coffee or tea since caffeine increases the risk of anxiety.

8. Make sure they set off in plenty of time, so that a cancelled bus or delayed train is not going to send anxiety levels rocketing.

9. Last minute revision is not a good idea, neither are anxious discussions with fellow candidates. These simply confuse and mislead. Far better to spend any free time calmly collecting ones thoughts, and perhaps retiring to a quite place – the lavatory is a possible

sanctuary – for a few moments of mental and physical relaxation. If your child feels that reading through their notes immediately before taking the exam will help, then encourage the use of a few summary cards which detail the key issues. But, it is far better to trust in the methodical revision of the past weeks.

10. After the exam, advise them to steer clear of those post mortems as everybody talks about their answers and kicks themselves for not remembering important facts. This is not a helpful way of passing the time, since its most likely effect is to reduce confidence and increase anxiety. Instead they should come home to relax, unwind and start revising for the next exam.

By following these easily mastered procedures, planning revision methodically and being self-disciplined in their studies, your child should be able to meet the challenge of exams more confidently and successfully than ever before.

THE ABC OF LEARNING

This is a rapid reference guide to key ideas and facts in education.

Alternative education. Education is compulsory. Schooling is not. Some 70,000 parents teach their children at home. You must satisfy your Local Education Authority (LEA) that you can provide an 'efficient' full-time education 'suitable' for your child's age, aptitude and ability. Children attending a State school must be deregistered, by writing to the head teacher and LEA. Contact Education Otherwise for further information (*see Useful Addresses*).

Anxiety. When appropriate it helps keep your child safe. If inappropriate or excessive, it damages **self-esteem** and impairs performance. Usually, produces such bodily symptoms as a rapidly beating heart, dry mouth and upset tummy. The mind may be filled with panic-stricken thoughts. Problems linked to chronic anxiety include bed wetting, disturbed sleep, poor appetite and increased risk of physical illness. .

Apathy. In usually active and enthusiastic children may be due to the onset of a physical illness. Poor diet, an allergy, or insufficient exercise could also be to blame. Often stems from anxiety, perhaps caused by an inability to cope with school work. Equally, bright children, finding lessons all too easy become bored and frustrated. Around puberty hormonal changes produce high stress levels which sap the energy and create negative attitudes.

Autism. Characterized by an inability, or unwillingness, to communicate with others – including parents. Symptoms include social withdrawal and a liking for rhythmical movements; rocking, whirling, jumping. Autistic children are often educationally retarded even when of above average intelligence.

Backwardness. Refers to children whose basic reading and arithmetic skills fall below levels of achievement of those of a similar age *irrespective* of intelligence. It differs from educational retardation which is seen as due to low intelligence.

Brainstorming. Enhances **creativity** through imaginative problem solving. First all possible solutions to some **divergent** problem are sought. Any ideas, however apparently improbable, are acceptable. After 5–10 minutes start editing the ideas, discarding any which are clearly impractical. Those remaining are now considered to see how they might be improved upon.

CAL (computer assisted learning). Also called Computer Aided Instruction. The computer may be used as tool, tutor or tutee. As a tool it allows real world events to be modelled as a means of aiding understanding of complex topics. As tutors computers are patient and untiring. They provide graded instruction, test understanding, offer instant feedback and pinpoint causes of error. In their 'tutee' role the computer is 'taught' as the student learns to program it. Writing programs helps enhance logical, analytical and problem solving skills.

Career choice/guidance. Provided by Local Education Authority. Careers Service officers work in liaison with schools' careers programmes that normally start in the third year of secondary education. Group and individual advice, guidance and counselling is offered, also encourage your child to contact companies, professional organizations etc directly.

Child centred learning. The movement started early this century as a reaction against unimaginative teaching methods and harsh discipline in 19th-century education. Present day supporters favour replacing the traditional subject-based timetable, with a more integrated curriculum. They also advocate significant changes in the exam system.

Child guidance clinics. Multidisciplinary centres for diagnosing and treating children with behaviour or developmental problems. Staffed by psychiatrists, **educational psychologists** and psychiatric social workers. Many work with the whole family rather than treating a child individually. Address of nearest clinic can be obtained from local education office.

Computers (*see also CAL*). Helpful but by no means essential to your child's education. Most schools use BASIC (Beginners All Purpose Symbolic Instruction Code) for teaching computer programming. An easier and more logically structured language, especially suitable for younger children, is LOGO developed by Seymour Papert. An O or A level computer pass is not necessary for entry into a university or polytechnic computing course.

Concentration. With intellectually demanding tasks, such as learning or revising, the average period of attention for older children is around 20 minutes. Sessions should be not much longer with a break of 5 – 10 minutes between them.

Convergent thinking. Refers to a way of approaching problems which have a single, correct answer. All problems comprise: (i) Information GIVEN, or assumed to be known (ii) OPERATIONS for manipulating it (iii) a GOAL, or answer, required. Failure to find a solution arises from mistakes made over one or more of these three factors. GIVEN errors usually stem from a careless reading of the problem or insufficient background knowledge. OPERATION mistakes occur when inappropriate procedures are used or the correct procedure incorrectly followed. Finally, mistakes arise when the correct GOAL is not identified.

Creativity.   Early experiences play a big part in fostering or frustrating creativity. Provide plenty of raw materials. Avoid the temptation to 'improve' early efforts. Use **brain storming** to encourage uninhibited thinking.

Curiosity.   Babies have boundless curiosity but early eagerness too often disappears as children lose confidence and become conformist. Avoid inhibiting curiosity by keeping discipline and family rules to the minimum necessary. Many questions provide wonderful 'teaching moments' during which your child's mind is very receptive to new ideas.

Depression.   Different from the short-lived sadness caused by death of a pet or return to school. Symptoms include tearfulness, disturbed sleep, loss of appetite and lethargy. Occurs when a child feels helpless in the face of some devastating change in their life. Use **diagnostic listening** to help pinpoint the cause. Remain physically and emotionally supportive throughout. (*See also* **stress.**)

Desensitization.   Helps a child cope with **anxiety** through gradual exposure to feared activity. First teach relaxation then, where applicable, prepare hierarchy starting with least feared and ending with most feared condition.

Diagnostic listening   A technique for identifying the underlying cause of problems. The keys to success are (a) never be judgemental while listening, it inhibits further disclosures, (b) say very little, encourage with smiles and nods, and (c) don't be afraid of silences and rush to fill them with words. Only offer explanations, advice, guidance or comment after obtaining all the information you can.

Discussions.   Around 75 per cent of all a child learns comes from talking and listening. Use active listening and reflect back on comments to show you have been paying attention.

Divergent thinking.   A way of approaching problems which have many possible answers but no absolutely correct answer. **Brainstorming** and **creativity** building activities help enhance this way of thinking.

Dyslexia.   Defined by the World Federation of Neurology as, 'A disorder in children who, despite conventional classroom experience, fail to attain the language skills in reading, writing and spelling commensurate with their intellectual abilities.' Recent research suggests dyslexics lack an inner ear for language, preventing them hearing words as they are read. Dyscalculia is the term applied to children who have similar problems with maths.

Early school entry.   Many schools will now take children into reception classes from the age of four or younger. The *minimum* legal requirement is for one teacher and one nursery assistant for every 26 children.

Educational psychologist.   Works mainly with children who have learning or behaviour difficulties and maladjustment in ordinary schools. Some trained in family therapy or behaviour modification. May act in consultative and advisory roles. Closely involved with remedial services and **child guidance clinics**.

ESN (educationally subnormal).   Applied to children moderately (M) or severely (S) educationally impaired. About a third of moderately retarded children also have significant behavioural disorders and many lack physical co-ordination. Severely mentally retarded children may need special nursing or social care. Today there is a move towards educating these children in ordinary, rather than special, schools.

Failure.   Children motivated by a fear of failure will either attempt only tasks where success is certain or, paradoxically, challenges so daunting they are virtually bound to fail. This is because lack of success can then be blamed on the difficulty of the task rather than personal inadequacy. Often arises when parents are overly critical, punishing mistakes but ignoring attainments.

Flash cards.   A technique used to teach reading and, less frequently maths. Words or dots represent numbers and are briefly flashed up on cards for the child to identify.

Foreign languages.   Exam marks awarded equally for speaking, understanding, reading and writing. Fluency more important than absolute accuracy. Holidays abroad and exchange visits make studies easier and far more enjoyable.

Games.   Provide an excellent way of teaching, especially with young children. With a young child devise games involving counting or word skills.

Gifted children.   Can involve superior artistic, writing, musical or dramatic talent, mechanical, physical or movement skills, scientific or intellectual abilities. For further information write to the National Association for Gifted Children (*see Useful Addresses*).

Homework.   Effective home study is essential to school success. Allows you to assess your child's progress and resolve any confusions. Fully understand procedures involved before attempting to help. Avoid temptation to speed the process by simply providing the right answers. Suggest ways problems should be approached or provide access to suitable **references**. Ensure your child has a quiet place to work without interruption. Develop good study disciplines from the start.

Intelligence.   Intelligence Quotients (IQ) calculated by dividing mental age (assessed by test) by chronological age and multiplying by 100. Average is 100, with superior IQ indicated by number above 100 and inferior IQ below 100. IQ tests helpful in identifying reasoning problems, but poor guide to mental ability.

Late developer. A term applied to children who realize their potential in all, or some, school subjects later than their fellows. It must be remembered there are considerable variations in the rate at which children develop, intellectually, emotionally, and physically. Encouragement at home, for instance, by reading with the child is often of considerable assistance in closing the gap.

Laziness. Be very cautious about employing this label as a child who has failed despite working hard will have confidence and self-esteem undermined. Check that time and effort are not being wasted due to inefficient study habits.

Life skills. Range from getting along with others to understanding how society functions. Some skills may be taught by direct instruction, for instance how to complete official forms. Others are best acquired through experience, ie dealing with money, making purchases, applying for a job. Children should practise dealing with real life challenges as early as possible.

Loneliness. Often due to lack of **social skills** or **shyness**. Especially likely after a move to a new school or neighbourhood. At such times provide reassurance and support, but don't insist they go out with others in the hope this will banish loneliness.

Marks – exams. As a general guide 70 + per cent gives A grade; 60 – 69 per cent B; 55 – 59 per cent D; 40 – 49 per cent E; 30 – 39 per cent; 29 per cent and below F. In some exams, however, only 5 points can separate A and C grades. In exams where mark allocation is shown, little time should be wasted seeking out answers to low value questions. When equal marks are allocated for longer answers, be sure to attempt ALL of them.

Maths anxiety. Children who grow up feeling comfortable with figures are much less likely to fear them later. Familiarity can be improved by playing games which require some kind of calculation well within the child's ability.

Memory training. The more memory is used and trusted the greater will be its efficiency. The brain has different memory stores, for sights, sounds, taste, touch and movement. Work actively with material. Ask and answer questions, create vivid mental images, write notes, make sketches. Tape record and replay information.

Montessori nursery schools. Based on the pioneering work of Maria Montessori, an Italian physician. The job of the teacher, in her view, was to facilitate the pupil to teacher relationship. Children are able to play with any materials in which they are spontaneously interested. They work independently or in groups, the class is ungraded and rules are intended to encourage co-operation rather than competition. Advice can be obtained from the Montessori Society and the Montessori Centre (*see Useful Addresses*).

Nursery education. (*See also **Montessori**.*) There is no legal obligation on Local Education Authorities (LEAs) to provide education until the term after your child's fifth birthday. When available free from a Local Education Authority, nursery education is more likely to be part than full-time. Every class is headed by a qualified teacher, often supported by trained assistants. Where no nursery education exists, parents can campaign to try and persuade their LEA to provide one. For advice and guidance contact The National Campaign for Nursery Education, or the British Association for Early Childhood Education (*see Useful Addresses*). Private nursery schools have to register with their social services department, although staff and premises are supervised by social services, there is no check on educational provision, nor is there any requirement for staff to be professionally qualified.

Options.   Secondary schools usually have a core course for the first three years of study, with more choice coming during years four and five. Before selecting O and A level subjects, check requirements of desired university or polytechnic course. English O level is always needed, while many ask for maths, or a science subject. Six out of eight Scottish universities, plus Oxford and Cambridge, require a foreign language at O level. Medical schools demand chemistry A level plus two from physics, maths or biology, while missing subjects must be taken at O level.

Pre-school playgroups.   Can be organized within the community or run as a private, profit-making, enterprise. If community-run, be prepared to help out on a rota basis. .

The child adult ratio averages eight to one with attendance for two or three half-days per week. There is no requirement for playgroup leaders to be qualified, although many are former teachers or have taken a part-time course of instruction. The Pre-School Playgroups Association publish a booklet about starting a playgroup which includes advice on finding suitable premises, keeping records and general organization, (*see Useful Addresses*).

Puberty.   Physical and psychological stresses arising at this time can adversely affect intellectual performance, and may produce **apathetic** or rebellious behaviour. Allow increasing independence and be patient with moods. Starts later in boys than girls. Average ages are – *Boys:* pubic hair appears 13.5; voice breaks 14.4; growth spurt starts 14.5 ends 17.8; first ejaculation 13.9. Production of sperm marks the end of puberty. *Girls:* pubic hair 12.3; breasts 12.4; growth spurt starts 12.8 ends 15.8; first menstrual period 13.0. Indicates end of puberty.

Punishment.   When used to excess produces a strong **fear of failure**. Physical punishment does far more harm than good. A better approach is to withdraw privileges, such as watching TV, for persistent misconduct.

Reference books.   Encourage your child to look facts up rather than waiting to be given them. A basic library should include: English dictionary, dictionary of quotations, world atlas, and a guide to English usage.

Encyclopedias must be recent to be reliable. Suggest your child starts their own archive, using newspaper and magazines cuttings, on subjects of personal or school concern.

Religious education.   Under the 1944 Education Act, RE is the only subject all UK primary and secondary schools are legally obliged to teach. Every State school must also start each day with a non-denominational act of worship. Parents have a legal right to withdraw their child from RE after discussions with the head teacher.

Rules.   Have three purposes, to safeguard a child, protect your sanity and teach socially acceptable behaviour. Keep to the minimum necessary for achieving these goals. Employ DO rather than DON'T rules whenever possible. Apply all rules consistently to ensure clear understanding of what is required.

School phobia.   School refusal and **trauncy** may be due to an intense fear either of school itself, some activity – such as games – other children, or teachers. Can also arise from a dread that something bad will happen at home while the child is away. School phobia occurs more frequently in sensitive children who shows other anxiety symptoms. Never punish a phobic child for staying off school.

Self-esteem.   Children with positive self-esteem are 'Can doer's'. Self-esteem stems from parental attitudes. Critical, over perfectionist parents have children who, however successful, have a low opinion of their abilities. Always notice and praise any positive features.

Shyness.   Occurs equally in boys and girls. Around 40 per cent of school children describe themselves as 'shy'. **Social skills**, especially assertiveness training, helps. Teaching play skills, such as inventing games, sharing toys, etc to a preschool child gets them into the habit of mixing with others. Adolescents often go through a shyness phase caused by uncertainty over sexual feelings and doubts about personal attractiveness. Firm but gentle encouragement to go out and meet others should assist in reducing these anxieties.

Sleep.   School-age children require some eight hours per night. Develop good sleep habits early by setting, and sticking to, a set bedtime. Uncharacteristic wakefulness or disturbed sleep are often symptoms of excessive **anxiety**.

Social skills.   Making friends, being assertive, co-operating with others and getting on with adults are important in ensuring happiness and success. Provide practical training by role playing social situations in which your child needs help. Co-operation with others, for instance, may be enhanced by taking part in non-competitive team activities.

Stress. Especially stressful events include a bereavement, moving house, changing schools, falling behind in class or worrying over exams. Risk of stress problems also increase at **puberty** when bodily changes lower physical resistance. Try identifying source of stress, using **diagnostic listening**. Be supportive, patient, practical and understanding.

Truancy. Differs from **school phobia**. Children dislike but do not fear school. Legally children must be in school for registration and remain all day. Legitimate reasons for absence are: (i) with permission of school (ii) illness, no medical certificate is necessary but the school should be informed, (iii) infectious disease, (iv) cleanliness ie infestation, (v) unavoidable cause ie rail strike, (vi) family holiday – two weeks per year allowable, (vii) religious observance, (viii) failure of authority to provide agreed transport and (ix) when child has local authority licence as professional stage or film performer. Where truancy is persistent parents may be prosecuted and fined a maximum of £200.

Under-achievers. Children whose performance is significantly below known ability and past results. May result from **anxiety** or **stress** related problems. Sometimes a child deliberately fails so as not to be different from a low achieving peer group.

Verbal reasoning tests. Verbal reasoning, the ability to make sense of word problems, is the aspect of general intelligence most strongly influenced by environmental factors. Not regarded as such an accurate indicator of academic success.

USEFUL ADDRESSES

British Association for Early Childhood Education
Montgomery Hall
Kennington Oval
London SE11 5SW
(Tel 071 582 8744)

Education Otherwise
25 Common Lane
Hemingford Abbots
Huntingdon PE18 9AN

Montessori Centre
18 Balderston Street
London W1Y 1TG
(Tel 071 493 0165)

Montessori Society
26 Lyndhurst Gardens
London NW3 5NW
(Tel 071 435 7874)

National Association for Gifted Children
1 South Audley Street
London W1

National Campaign for Nursery Education
33 High Street
London SW1V 1QJ

Pre-School Playgroups Association
Alford House
Aveline Street
London SE11 5DH
(Tel 071 582 8871)

INDEX